THE ADVAITA OF ART

The Advaita of Art

HARSHA V. DEHEJIA

Foreword by
KAPILA VATSYAYAN

MOTILAL BANARSIDASS PUBLISHERS
PRIVATE LIMITED • DELHI

First Edition: Delhi, 1996
Reprint: Delhi, 1997, 2000

ISBN: 81-208-1387-1 (Cloth)
ISBN: 81-208-1389-8 (Paper)

Also available at:

MOTILAL BANARSIDASS

236, 9th Main III Block, Jayanagar, Bangalore 560 011
41 U.A. Bungalow Road, Jawahar Nagar, Delhi 110 007
8 Mahalaxmi Chamber, Warden Road, Mumbai 400 026
120 Royapettah High Road, Mylapore, Chennai 600 004
Sanas Plaza, 1302 Baji Rao Road, Pune 411 002
8 Camac Street, Calcutta 700 017
Ashok Rajpath, Patna 800 004
Chowk, Varanasi 221 001

Printed in India

BY JAINENDRA PRAKASH JAIN AT SHRI JAINENDRA PRESS,
A-45 NARAINA, PHASE-I, NEW DELHI 110 028
AND PUBLISHED BY NARENDRA PRAKASH JAIN FOR
MOTILAL BANARSIDASS PUBLISHERS PRIVATE LIMITED,
BUNGALOW ROAD, DELHI 110 007

Dedicated to the
spirit of India,
where the deeds of man
may speak of his quests,
but the spirit of man
is revealed through his music.

Foreword

It is with much pleasure and some trepidation that I respond to Dr. Harsha V. Dehejia's request to write a foreword to a book which encompasses a stagerring variety of primary and secondary sources and sets out to investigate the aesthetic experience principally from the point of view of the aesthete, the receiver, rather than, the creator or artist. This is, by any account a daunting task which could be undertaken only by one courageous and unconventional.

Dr. Dehejia begins by distinguishing between art and religion, making it clear that he does not propose to look at all that may be understood as ritual, indeed that path he bypasses by volition. Instead, his quest is to identify the process of realising transcendence through art, which he considers by and large secular. He adopts *advaita* as an epistemic concept for this exploration, and clearly uses the term in an unconventional way to investigate the oneness of art and aesthetic experience as also the progressive and sequential bond of the *kavi* (creator, artist), *kāvya* (the art object) and *rasika* (the connoisseur, receiver). As almost a logical consequence he is obliged to probe deeply into the more fundamental concept of creativity and aesthetic experience as transcendency, as also the dynamics of the cognition and experience of art. For Dr. Dehejia there is an unbroken chain he calls *advaitic,* from creation to cognition and from cognition to realisation. Examination of the terms *pratibhā-kriyā* was natural, as also identification of the 'acausal' nature of the creative action. Although Dr. Dehejia's principal or ultimate concern is with the *rasika* (aesthete, the receiver) he covers the entire gamut of the artistic process from the point of view of meaning, form, function and communication. The discourse on content, form and technique, word and meaning is perennial and worldwide. From Plato to Longinus and Plotinus and from Aristotle to Horace, from Greek to Romans, from the Romantics to the Modernists, there has been a sustained discourse. Fundamental to the discourse are ontological questions on what constitutes 'reality' and what and how does the artist create a new universe. In India there has been a most refined and sopihisticated discourse, not only in texts of aesthetics, but also in those of speculative thought, be it the *Vedas* or the *Upaniṣads* or the six schools of philosophy and most of all Kāśmīr Śaivism. Dr. Dehejia traverses this vast canvas of primary sources and also embraces the writings of Aurobindo, Rabindranath Tagore, Stella Kramrisch, Alice Boner and Niharranjan Ray and others. In short, his method is to investigate each concept through the principal primary texts, with a marked preference for texts of Kāśmīr Śaivism and to juxtapose these with the intrepreters of the twentieth century. This interplay of the ancient and contemporary, the primary and secondary and tertiary sources, makes a fascinating puzzling journey which keeps the reader engaged.

The enquiry begins with the concept of *artha* (meaning) in the Indian tradition. The multiple levels and layers of meaning, the relationship of 'word' and 'meaníng', 'word', 'sound' and reverberation is investigated anew with a refreshing ease of moving from one philosophic school to another, to texts of aesthetics and grammar. All this demands an equal acquaintance of these sources from his readers. As is to be expected the key notion of *śabda, artha, sṛṣṭi* , *sphoṭa* are discussed. Bhartṛhari understandably is centre stage of the discussion. Also for the author, Bharata's *rasavāda*, although of fundamental importance, cannot provide the complete framework of aesthetics, as does Bhartṛhari' s *sphoṭavāda*. This is *śabdabrahman*, the meaning of meaning, the first of his concerns.

From the concern with 'word' and 'meaning' and meaning of meaning, he moves on to explore what he terms the encounter (*sākṣātartha*) with *rasabrahman*. The emphasis shifts from knowledge to emotion, the explicit and implicit levels of meaning, the literal and metaphorical, the connotative and denotative, the *pratyakṣa* and the *parokṣa*. The spectrum of inbuilt ambiguity is vast. The most sophisticated hair splitting debates on the subject are found in the works of the commentators of the ***Nāṭyaśāstra*** particularly Śaṅkuka and Bhaṭṭa Nāyaka, whom Abhinava quotes and refutes in both ***Abhinava Bhāratī*** and ***Locana***. Although Dr. Dehejia does not peruse or re-narrate the discourse, he focuses attention on the concept of *rasa* as experience and response. The concepts of *sādhāraṇīkṛta* (universalisation) and the nature of aesthetic experience as *alaukika*, the process of artistic creation as sudden flash of illumination, *camatkāra*, and the ultimate goal of quietitude, *viśrānti*, are examined. Through this argument Dr. Dehejia succeeds thorough many a minor detour, that there is a gradual but sure transformation of the mundane to the sacred, from the gross to the subtle and the movement is one of expanding consciousness in one unbroken chain and therefore oneness, totality and non-duality (*advaita*).

The encounter (*śākṣātartha*) with the art obejct is at the level of essence '*rasa*' emotive response, but the instrumentality of this is 'form', *rūpa*. We may add significant form. Dr. Dehejia's next concern is with *rūpa* (form) which he calls *rūpabrahman*. Here too, he draws upon the primary sources but leans heavily on the insights of Rabindranath Tagore, Kramrisch, Boner and Ray. He makes an important difference between a *rasika* and a *bhakta* and states that the experience of transcendence is not the exclusive privilege of the devotee, it can be, and is also of the cultivated and initiated *sahṛdaya* or *rasika*. This distinction is implied in Bharata and made explicit in the commentaries of Abhinavagupta. The texts of Indian aesthetics from Bharata to Viśvanātha, do not bring in either devotion or diety worship, as a criterion for attaining or experiencing the ecstasy of *rasa* or *ānanda*. It was the commentators of the ***Gītagovinda***, principally Rūpa and Jīva Goswāmī who evolved a category of *bhaktirasa*. Perhaps on account of the misplaced over-emphasis on religiosity in Indian art in the nineteenth century discourse, it was important to once again point at the distinction.

Dr. Dehejia culls out his material from multiple sources, ranging from the ***Vāstūsūtra Upaniṣad*** to the writing of Rabindranath Tagore, to once again prove that the Indian artist's quest was to give form and shape to the unmanifest. The movement is from the unmanifest (*avyakta*) to the manifest (*vyakta*) and from *arūpa* (no form or un-form) to *rūpa* and multiple forms (*rūpa* and *pratirūpa*) with the self avowed purpose of evoking through form, the experience of beyond form (*parārūpa*). Thus, although the form, abstract or concrete, is indispensable and critical, its most important function is to be the bridge and vehicle of that which is beyond form. Such a perception has far reaching implications for the study of Indian art, so far largely categorised as aniconic, iconic, representational, figurative or abstract, in recent critical works. Indeed, like the layers and levels of meaning, the form also is multi-layered with the incipient capacity of being comprehended singly and together at many concurrent levels of myth, iconography, geometrical motifs and perennial symbols.

Having delineated the three worlds of *artha* (meaning), *rasa* (experience) and *rūpa* (form), Dr. Dehejia goes on to explicate his chief concern on the dynamics of communications and response in an initiated aesthete. In the chapter on Epistemology of Aesthetics he examines the cognitive process from perception to emanation (*ābhāsa*) and reflection and release (*svātantrya*). The basis of his argument is the well-known position of Kāśmīr Śaivism, of the twin conjugal symbiosis of *bhoga* (determinate cognition) and *viśrānti* (rest, quietitude), of the joyous meeting of *prakāśa* (dominant self-luminosity) and *vimarśa*. Kāśmīr Śaivism has repeatedly drawn attention to the process of *viśrānti* as not only the culmination of cognitive experience in *ānanda* (bliss, ecstasy), but that stage "where the duality between subject and object ceases, and the subject looks upon the object as identical with oneself." Dr. Dehejia makes a penetrating observation in this context. He draws attention to the significance of Pārvatī holding a mirror in the Umā-Maheśvara images. Pārvatī is indeed holding up the mirror to Śiva. It illustrates the basic *pratyabhijña* principle that self-luminosity of cognition consists in making itself so manifest as to make others manifest, such that "knower and known in their distinctive nature shine in the subject". The motifs of mirror, light and reflection feature prominently not only in Kāśmīr Śaivism but in other systems, where non-duality, and the merging of the distinctions of subject, object, knower and known, are emphasised, as in some forms of Shintoism and Zen Buddhism.

The chapter on the Epistemology of Aesthetics is an appropriate prelude to the most rewarding and illuminating chapter on aesthetic implications of Divine consortship. Dr. Dehejia has some brilliant and refreshingly new insights into the meaning and implications of the conception of Divine consortship. He intreprets Rādhā and Kṛṣṇa, Śiva and Śakti and offers interpretations which are as new as are plausible. The ***Gītagovinda*** and the final meeting of Rādhā and Kṛṣṇa has been interpreted in many ways and at many places. Dr. Dehejia discerns yer another inbuilt layer. Jayadeva, Dr. Dehejia says "unleashes the power of aesthetic rapture to lead Kṛṣṇa and Rādhā to a final aesthetic bliss as Kṛṣṇa finds his deep locked emotions breaking and Rādhā sees her passion reach the soul of Hari...". This is the ciimax of the *rasa* experience when both Rādhā and Kṛṣṇa, *kavi* and *sahṛdaya, āśraya* and *ālambana*, lose their duality and yet maintain their identity, as they are joined together in aesthetic embrace, tasting the same *rasa* "like a dark lotus root wrapped in veils of yellow pollen". Dr. Dehejia asserts that "the right question then to ask is not who is Rādhā, but what is Rādhā. And the right answer is Rādhā *raseśvarī*." This one insight and identification of another deep layer of the ***Gītagovinda***, as a statement of the aesthetic experience, and Divine consortship as being another way of stating the essence of the theory of *rasa*, will I am sure, stimulate and provoke others to re-examine Indian iconography in these terms. The conception and image of the *ardhanārīśvara* has been much commented upon. Dr. Dehejia cites this as another example of identity in difference, *bheda-abheda*. There is in that Divine consortship of Umā-Maheśvara a double movement from subject to its mirror image and from the image back to the subject. The image gives credence not only to art objects but equally to aesthetic experience and ultimately the experiencer himself. Art historians have spoken of these images in several contexts but few have underpinned so clearly the implications of these to the theory of Indian aesthetics.

Dr. Dehejia concludes his study with a discussion on aesthetics and Idealism and reminds his reader in the Epilogue that his concern has been to investigate the total dynamics of the artistic process. Dr. Dehejia no doubt succeeds in keeping his readers engaged in sharing this journey of exploration through meandering paths of texts of aesthetics and philosophy.

While many readers may find it exacting and demanding and others may question the acceptance of categories, *mārgī* and folk, sacred and secular, there is nevertheless a wealth of material, introspection and insight, a rare combination of the diagnostic skills of a physician and the artistic insights of an aesthete, to survey a vast and continuously flowing stream of Indian aesthetics.

New Delhi
May 25, 1995

KAPILA VATSYAYAN

Prologue

Art and religion, which are so basic to the Indian way of life, and particularly to the Hindu tradition, defy simple definitions. The two terms remain without their exact Sanskrit equivalents. And in the understanding of this apparent difficulty perhaps lies the answer. For pithy definitions may sometimes foster complacency and discourage a serious inquiry, an ardent quest.

In its broadest sense, religion in the Indian tradition is understood to be realisation of ultimate Reality. However in its more limited and prevalent sense, religion implies ritual, creates sects, incorporates the occult and the magical, and has room for ritual acts. Religious practice cannot divorce itself from the concept of divinity, it must also insist on a moral outlook, allow considerations such as merit (*puṇya*) and grace (*prasāda*), and presuppose the twin concepts of *śraddhā* understood as faith and commitment, and *śaraṇāgati* or surrender and the taking of refuge in the Lord. This latter understanding of religion is closely intertwined with the concept of *bhakti* or devotion. In view of this, many Hindus may perhaps consider it to be almost a sacrilege that one could bypass religion as narrowly defined, in our quest for transcendent realisation through art. The Hindu tradition, in its vastness and catholicity, has room for all types of transcendent experience. In presenting the *advaita* of art it is exactly this other path, which bypasses the ritualistic, commonly understood, variety of religion, that we are treading. In removing art from the framework of narrowly defined religion, we are not pitting art against religion, but merely ensuring that art will be appreciated and understood on its own merit and for its own sake, sensually and not ritually, that the aesthete will be recognised in his own right and that aesthetics will be given its rightful, autonomous and non-sectarian place as a means of higher knowledge and higher awareness.

If religion in the Indian tradition defies definition, the definition of art remains equally elusive. For Tagore, the question of providing a definition of art is not important.[1] Some Western art critics have defined art as an object that provides "a satisfactory aesthetic experience".[2] This definition, in laying stress on the subjective aspect of the aesthetic experience, is partially acceptable to us, for ultimately, as we shall show, the aesthetic exprience must come to a 'rest' (*viśrānti*) in the cognising subject. However in not precisely defining the art object the definition suffers from the problems of modern art and art criticism in being too abstract and open and shying away from objectivity. Another Western art critic has defined aesthetic experience "as one which the subject is undergoing while sustaining an aesthetic attitude".[3] The reluctance on the part of Western critics to refer to the specifics of an art object is not shared by us in the classical Indian tradition; for us the aesthetic experience must stem from a definite art object; objectivity in the Indian artistic tradition is not a hindrance but a help. Furthermore, the central thrust of Indian philosophy is the bringing together of the objective with the subjective, and Indian aesthetics shares this concern and seeks an understanding not only of the art object but equally the cognising subject. The classical Indian tradition lays down strict criteria for an art object, and in this sense an art object may be defined as *saṃskṛta* or an object of beauty, not utility, that has been perfectly made and which is in conformity with the artistic tradition. As will be shown, classical Indian art achieves perfection through the skill of the artist and inspires a similar quest for perfection in the aesthete. In opting for this definition, we wish to underscore not only artistic perfection, which is a hallmark of classical Indian art, but also the embodiment of an idea, an emotion, a universality, and above all, a vision that is also a ***sine qua non*** of classical Indian art.

This inquiry is undertaken on behalf of the aesthete who is persuing a serious and deliberate aesthetic experience, not for mere sensual titillation but as a *sādhanā*, and for this type of aesthete the art object has be to specified and cannot be left open. As long as the aesthete remains with the *mārgī* tradition, this is hardly a problem, as the tradition provides the aesthete with bonafide art objects, objects that have survived the test of time and have proved meaningful to the tradition. However the problem arises with the aesthete who wishes to undertake an experience from objects not within the tradition such as those belonging to modern art. Although such an aesthete is not under our consideration, it is important to point out that for art to be *advaitic* both the aesthete and the art object must meet certain criteria. In other words, the objectivity of the art object cannot be left undefined and open. Aesthetic experience stemming from an unspecified art object cannot be sustained under the *advaita* of art. In defining the art object, the tradition and the art critic alike have a role to play, but this process of art criticism, is not under our purview.

Yoga, etymologically defined as 'union' refers to the union of the individual with ultimate Reality and is a pan-Indian concept, and stays outside sectarian distinctions. In electing to keep art out of the narrow concept of religion, it is but natural that this inquiry seeks the inclusion of art as a yoga within the larger context of *advaita*.

Literally *advaita* merely means non-dual, the negative emphasising the oneness, but even more importantly *advaita* is essentially an epistemic concept. Abhinavagupta rightly says that "ignorance is the sense of duality".[4] However in the Indian tradition the term *advaita* always refers to matters transcendent and not merely mundane. When it came to the *darśanas* the term *advaita* came to be used to identify a certain school and in particular the Advaita Vedānta of Śaṅkara, which is our *pūrvapakṣa*. Our usage of the term *advaita* in this inquiry stays away from these conventional usages but instead investigates the oneness of art and aesthetic experience, the bond of the *kavi*, *kāvya* and *rasika*, the unbroken unity of *kāvya*, *artha* and *ānanda*, the biune unity of the cognising subject and the object of cognition in an artistic epistemic experience, the *advaita* that retains the material and the vital of a *puruṣa* but pushes to the spiritual of the *Puruṣa*, an *advaita* that sustains itself not by negation but by assertion, an *advaita* of joyous celebration of the creative spirit of man, an *advaita* of artistic creation and aesthetic recreation, an *advaita* of freedom, an *advaita* that stirs the aesthete to experience the art object and exclaim *Śivo'ham*.

NOTES

1. Tagore, Rabindranath. ***Personality***. (London: Macmillan and Co., 1959) p. 5.
2. Munro, Thomas. ***Form and Style in the Arts***. An Introduction to Aesthetic Morphology. (Cleveland. Case Western Reserve University. 1970) p. 11.
3. Schlesinger, George. Aesthetic Experience and the Definition of Art. ***British Journal of Aesthetics***. Volume 19. 1979. p. 170.
4. *dvaitapratha tadajñānam tucchatvād bandha ucyate*
   Abhinavagupta, ***Tantrāloka*** 1.30.
   from K. Mishra, ***Significance of the Tantric Tradition***. (Varanasi, Ardhanarisvara Publications, 1981) p. 136.

Acknowledgements

Any attempt to acknowledge the large number of individuals who have played a part in this undertaking is somewhat akin to tracing the roots of a tree and, and like the roots, I am sure, many of them would not like to be publicly recognised. Yet it is my pleasure to take this opportunity to acknowledge gratefully at least some of them. To my mentor Prof. V.K. Chari of Carleton University, Ottawa, Ontario, Canada I owe a debt of deep gratitude; it was he who not only planted the seed by introducing me to the treasures of Aesthetics but painstakingly read a number of texts with me. Dr. Nalini Devdas guided my Masters work at Carleton University and it she who showed me the giant trees of the Indian tradition and thereby ensured that I set my standards high. Dr. Vishwanath V. Gangal, formerly of the Ananthacharya Indological Research Institute of Bombay has been a source of strength and inspiration throughout, and in so doing has ensured that what started as a seed has blossomed. Dr. K. Venkatachari, former Director of the Ananthacharya Indological Research Institute, has been most generous with his time and were it not for the many fruitful discussions I have had with him this thesis would have lacked any erudition it might have. Dr. Walimbe's insightful comments particularly for the chapter on *rasa* were most valubale and ensured that a certain fragrance is maintained in my writing. And finally without the help and kindness of everyone at the Ananthacharya Indological Research Institute in Bombay and the Department of Religion of Carleton University in Ottawa, Canada, I would have been like a gardener without sunshine. My wife Sudha has been constantly by my side, supporting, helping, and encouraging me at all times in countless ways and who has ensured that while I till the soil I do not forget to look at the sky above. My two sons, Vivek and Rajeev, have defined and thereby instilled into me the basics of intellectuality and as I went on the many winding paths in the garden of aesthetic flowers, it were they who ensured that I stay on the straight and narrow path of rational discourse. It fell to the efficient and gentle hands of Shri N.P. Jain of Motilal Banarsidass Publishers Private Limited to ensure that a bouquet of flowers was prepared from my garden to take to the market so that *rasikas* like you can get it; to him my grateful thanks. Dr. Kapila Vatsyayan of the Indira Gandhi National Centre for the Arts, who wrote the Foreword, and to whom I am deeply indebted, lends grace and dignity by her mere presence. Finally, in the spirit of the *ūrdhvamūlam adhahsakham asvattham* of the *Bhagavadgītā*, I acknowledge the ultimate source of all roots.

Contents

Foreword vii

Prologue xiii

Acknowledgements xvii

Chapter 1. Introduction 1

Chapter 2. The Meaning of Meaning 19

Chapter 3. *Śākṣātartha: Rasabrahman* 45

Chapter 4. *Śākṣātartha: Rūpabrahman* 65

Chapter 5. *Parokṣārtha* 83

Chapter 6. Epistemology of Aesthetics 121

Chapter 7. Aesthetic Implications of Divine Consortship 153

Chapter 8. Aesthetics and Idealism 169

Epilogue 183

Bibliography 185

Index 191

Chapter 1

Introduction

"Men must find and feel and represent in all their creative works Man the Eternal, the creator."

Rabindranath Tagore, ***The Religion of Man***

In an unbroken tradition, from times pre-historic to the present, art has remained an integral part of Indian life, and has not only cut through social, religious and cultural barriers within the country, but has accompanied Indian trade and thought in their movement across the frontiers. The Indian tradition accords an exalted position to art and, significantly, holds both the artist and the aesthete in equal esteem. Historically speaking, art and aesthetics in India have interacted with social, political and cultural factors, and in every age have produced their own artists and astheticians, who while carrying the tradition within them, have reacted to situations that prevailed in their age. The turn of this century was an axial period in the history of art and aesthetics in modern India. It was a period when Indian artists and aestheticians were reacting to Western ideas and counter-reacting to Western interpretations of Indian art; it was a time of a modern Indian artistic renaissance when, after long years of colonialisation, Indians were rediscovering themselves; it was an era of self-discovery and self-affirmation. Ananda Kentish Coomaraswamy was one such modern aesthetician and it was he who brought into focus, "... the important part once played in Indian thought by the concept of Art as Yoga, a subject sufficient in itself for a whole volume."[1]

Coomaraswamy was one of the first modern aestheticians, of the Indian sub-continent, to have used the phrase "yoga of art", and the present inquiry owes its inspiration in a large measure to that statement. The concept of art as yoga not only exalts art, suggests its autonomous and non-sectarian position but at the same time points out the possibility of ensuring aesthetic experience a transcendency and that too within the framework of *advaita*. Coomaraswamy was a pioneer who drew attention to certain deeper, and more fundamental epistemic aspects of art and aesthetic experience, features that have been present all along in the ancient Indian tradition but which were probably being forgotten by early twentieth century art critics in India. Art involves equally the artist and the aesthete, and an examination of art must include both the creation and the appreciation of art. However, the focus of this inquiry is the aesthete rather than the artist. While the artist occupies an exalted position in the Indian tradition, the aesthete is charged with an equally heavy responsibility. Art in the Indian tradition is not merely ornamental or decorative, not just an idle pastime or sport, not an outpouring of a superficial state of mind; and the aesthete in turn was not a mere spectator or voyeur but one who was expected to apply himself seriously and deliberately in the enjoyment and understanding of art.

The purpose of this inquiry is to explore, on behalf of the aesthete, how art leads to transcendent knowledge which, in the spirit of Vedānta, is nothing other than self-knowledge. The thrust of the arguments are mainly epistemic, the direction of our endeavour largely to uncover the dynamics of the initial cognition and subsequent experience of art, our purpose is to seek the *artha* in art, and further to show that the entire artistic process from the artist to the aesthete, from creation to cognition, and from cognition to realisation, is an unbroken *advaitic* chain.

It is important at this stage to lay out the scope and parameters of this inquiry and highlight the background upon which this inquiry is being undertaken. Any philosophic, as opposed to historic inquiry, about art cannot rest with merely psychological, historical, social and anthropological considerations. Art is a statement of the philosophy of the age that produced it and remains an inspiration for the ages that followed. In this matter, Indian art is no exception. However, it is to be noted that neither Indian philosophy nor Indian art emphasise novelty. On the contrary, there is a constant return to certain foundational concepts that were thought out early in the tradition and given voice in the *nigamas* and the *āgamas*. It has been rightly said that "that which assumes novelty every moment (even though the same) is the form of beauty".[2] For this reason, in interpreting the intention of the Indian artist, one has to suspend archaeological presuppositions and art criticism and art history as commonly understood, and penetrate the form to experience the spirit of art. Havell reminds us that, "if we apply Western analytical methods to the exegesis of Asiatic aesthesis we shall never form any just or complete conception of them, until we have learnt to discard all our Western academic prejudices and realised the paramount importance of Indian philosophy and religion among the great creative forces which moulded Asiatic art."[3] Accordingly, in this inquiry, Indian aesthetics will be approached within the context of the Indian philosophic tradition, and Indian art will be interpreted from this perspective.

The idea of poetic vision presented in the ***Ṛg Veda*** has deeply influenced the manner in which Indian aestheticians approach art creation. Following Śrī Aurobindo, Jeannine Miller, in her studies of the Vedas, speaks of the difficulties of modern scholars in interpreting the creative inspiration of the Vedic poets, which is expressed in a flow of inter-connected symbols. She states that, "the highly civilised mind is incapable of probing beyond the physical and the rational...and can take in only two dimensions of existence."[4] The ***Ṛg Veda*** itself has said of the sage-poets, "Their lowest abodes are visible, they dwell in realms concealed beyond."[5] In keeping with this idea, the Indian artists have, "used their visionary gifts, their own method of observation to determine what lies beyond physical appearances."[6] Indian art, along with aesthetics, is an attempt to reach that "*guhyeśū vrateśū*", "those hidden realms".[7] Śrī Aurobindo writes that, "the whole basis of Indian artistic creation...is directly spiritual and intuitive...and its highest business is to disclose something of the Self, the Infinite, the Divine."[8]

Reminding us of the suprarational origin of art, Śrī Aurobindo says "The intellect is not the poet, the artist, the creator within us; creation comes by a suprarational influx of light and power which must work always...by vision and inspiration."[9]

An artist in India has been called *prajāpati* or creator, and the Indian aesthetic tradition has maintained with unwavering consistency, that at a philosophic level of understanding, creation in general and art creation in particular remains sacrosanct. While the Advaita Vedāntin considers creation a mystery the Kāśmīr Śaivite calls it *spanda*, but both prefer not to probe into the creative process. Such an activity would be unaesthetic. Accordingly, the Indian aesthetic tradition has focused on aesthetic appreciation, which is considered to be explicable to a large extent, rather than on the mystery of the artist's inspiration. The essence of creativity or artistic inspiration is termed *pratibhā*. Etymologically related to the root 'light', the word *pratibhā* signifies a burst of enlightenment. Abhinavagupta describes it as "an intuitive capacity to produce novel objects".[10] A text of Kāśmīr Śaivism, the ***Īśvara Pratyabhijña Vimarśinī***, equates *pratibhā* with Maheśvara Himself. According to the Kāśmīr Śaivites, Śiva's primal act of creation is considered to be neither the fulfilment of a lack nor the outcome of a self-imposed purpose, but an utterly spontaneous act of unbroken delight, symbolised by his dance, not a *māyā*, but a *līlā*. The Kāśmīr Śaivite literature speaks of human creativity as a *spanda*, a spontaneous act born of bliss, re-enacting and representing "that essential nature of the Universal Consciousness which is responsible for its apparent change from the state of absolute unity."[11] According to the tradition, it is a *kriyā*, a free and spontaneous act, not a *karma* or a volitional act. According to this tradition, both Śiva's primal act of creation and the human artist's creative expression are *kriyā*, spontaneous activity that does not lead to bondage, and not *karma* or volitional activity with consequences in the process of rebirth. This line of thought is first expressed in the creation hymn of the ***Ṛg Veda***, which states that perhaps even "the Lord in Heaven" cannot explain the essence of creative *kriyā*, and ends with the cryptic line, "He, truly, knows it, or maybe He does not know!"[12]

The Vedas do offer some hints at the process of artistic creation.

The one sustained symbol of artistic creation in the Vedas is the *ratha* or the chariot, since the chariot for the Vedic *ṛṣis* was a symbol of the means of communication, implying that the function of art was primarily to communicate a vision. Another symbol of artistic creativity in the Vedas was the "*suparṇa*"[13] or the golden bird, emphasising once again the flight of vision. Despite these and other hints about artistic creation, there is no doubt that the creative process is sacrosanct and no amount of probing will yield any useful or rationally meaningful answers. This reminds one about the passage in the ***Chāndogya Upaniṣad,*** "Verily, my dear, that finest essence which you do not perceive verily, my dear, from that finest essence this great *nyagrodha* tree arises."[14] *Pratibhā* is not only *nirguṇa* but *nirvikalpa*. Dasgupta points out that the "aesthetic state is...in itself a wholly new state which no fruitful analysis of its causes and conditions can manifest to us."[15] He goes on to say that, "how the conscious mind helps to create a definite picture of the shadowy subconscious image or emotion is very difficult to ascertain." Rabindranath said in one of his poems that he could not describe "the nature of his mysterious working which was there all the time."[16]

There is yet another problem that one encounters in dealing with artists and the creative process. This problem especially pertains to the Indian tradition, where succeeding generations of artists, most of whom remain entirely unknown, tended to amplify and reinterpret earlier artistic forms rather than to create entirely novel forms. Artists can be divided broadly into three groups. The first generation artists, the *ādiśilpīs* or the sage-artists, were the pristine artists, especially in the *śilpa* tradition, about whom we know nothing, for they are not only anonymous, but the *śāstras* are silent about their *pratibhā*. The second and subsequent generations of master artists worked within the tradition, recreating art forms from the prescriptions laid down in the *śāstras.* Thirdly, the craftsmen, who often were artists in their own right, worked in *śreṇī* or guilds under the guidance of the master artist, functioning more as artisans than as artists, in creating the art object. All these three types of artists worked under different states of art creation, and very little of what can be said about the one would apply to the other. In the light of these constraints, in interpreting artistic inspiration and art creation, this inquiry will follow the approach of the traditional Indian aestheticians and will focus its attention exclusively on art appreciation, as conducted by an adept and prepared aesthete, and not on art creation, realising of course that the artist is very often also an aesthete. Although the *advaita* of art, for the purpose of this inquiry, does not investigate the process of art creation in any detail, it is important to examine the creative process as this throws light on the aesthetic process.

Aesthetics, unlike other diciplines has been a great social unifier in the Indian context. The Hindu tradition sets up the *nāgarika* or the urban elite as the aesthete ***par excellence***, so that art appreciation has been able to cross religious, social, racial, sectarian and caste barriers. While upholding the concept of the *nāgarika* as the prototype of our aesthete, it is important that this *nāgarika*, if he is to undertake art as *advaita*, is also a *brahmajijñāsu* and therefore Śaṅkara's qualifications for *brahmajijñāsu* apply to the aesthete as well. Śaṅkara says: "Therefore something should be stated after which alone an inquiry into *brahman* can be undertaken. It is stated: (that the essential requirements are) discrimination between the eternal and the non-eternal objects, detachment to the enjoyments of objects of this and that world, equipment such as control of senses and mind and desire for *mokṣa*."[17]

The Indian artistic tradition has not only accorded an exalted place to the aesthete but has given him an independent standing, keeping apart the *rasika* from the *bhakta*. The question of sacred versus secular in Indian art is an engaging one and has occupied the attention of scholars. Our interest lies in establishing the validity of a purely secular, autonomous, non-sectarian approach to art objects and their appreciation, in other words upholding the bonafides of a *rasika*. Early in the Indian tradition the distinction between the sacred and the secular was not sharp. The *kavi*, as exemplified by the Vedic poet who wrote visionary poetry, and the Tamil Saṅgam poet who wrote erotic poetry, was not only a supreme artist but considered a *prajāpati* and a seer, and had a standing equal to that of a priest, a tradition that was to continue in an unbroken stream at least till the medieval period. Chattopadhyaya notes that "the acceptance of all creative force as an integrated power emerging from a single source became deified as Viśvakarma—the maker of the universe. The making of things was therefore a noble act, the object, a manifestation of Viśvakarman".[18] This meant that not only arts such as *kāvya* but *śilpa* or crafts as well enjoyed this exalted status.

The evolution of the sacred and the secular can best be understood in a socio-historic context. Although autochthonous terracotta images were probably made in the pre-Vedic period, the Vedic poet functioned largely in an aniconic ambience. The age of Bharata was also similarly aniconic, marked as it was by the predominance of *nāṭya*, and the theatre going *rasika* was the prototype of the aesthete. Aesthetic pleasure was Bharata's chief concern, for the ***Nāṭyaśāstra*** was composed by him for the gods "who wanted an object of diversion".[19] The concept of sacredness in visual art seems to have started around the first century BC with the search for and the development of the Buddha's image. As Coomaraswamy says "The Buddha image came into being because a need had been felt for it, and not because a need had been felt for art".[20] It is only an anthropomorphic image that can generate the question: is it beautiful or is it God? For, if the image is beautiful the onlooker can be a *rasika* and undertake an aesthetic inquiry but if the image is that of God, he wonders whether he must become a *bhakta* and involve himself in a religious appreciation of that image; he cannot be both at the same time. What started with the Buddha image then, continued in the tradition with the development of a plethora of mythic religious images. Subramanian[21] refers to the sixth century AD as a turning point in the performing arts and advances political reasons for this transformation from an essentially secular to a sacred oulook of these arts. He also refers to the presence of Islam in India, a presence which was to concretise the sacred when it came to the plastic arts, and notes that "the marriage of religion and art through *bhakti* had a damaging effect"[22] as it set-up a hierarchy between the two forms.

However, it is well to remind ourselves that even as the mythic images were being developed and plastic art began to take an increasingly sacred nature, *kāvya* as a secular art form and the poetic tradition flourished. The concept of a *rasika* as an urban, pleasure seeking elite, surrounded by courtesans, in quest of sensuous beauty, was never given up, and the tension between the sacred and the secular continued. Mammaṭa speaks of *kāvya* as that "which leads to fame, procurement of wealth, knowledge of the ways of the world, cessation of inauspicious, immediate bliss and one that imparts advice in the manner of the beloved."[23] Hiriyanna is right in pointing out that "the experience of art, like that of the ideal condition, is an ultimate value, in the sense that it is sought for its own sake and not as a means to anything else."[24] The aesthete was a person of refined and cultivated taste, heightened sensitivity, a *sahṛdaya* and it was important for the *kavi* to seek his approval. Kālidāsa in ***Mālavikāgnimitra*** recognises the *rasika* when he says "I long to carry out the order of the spectators which I have already received with my head bowed."[25] The distinction between the sacred and the secular may be both at the objective and the subjective level with the possibility that there may be an overlap in some cases. At times the difference between the sacred and the secular may not be a difference in content but of attitude on the part of both the artist and the aesthete. A good example is that of the status of Kṛṣṇa in the ***Bhāgavata Purāṇa*** and the ***Gītagovinda***; in the former, he is a deity, in the latter a *nāyaka*. Another example, cited by Subramanian is that of the king-god where the "deity in the temple was equated with a king and the temple with a palace, so that secular elements with sensuous pleasure could be included in the guise of *rājopacāra.*"[26] There was thus both a "symbiosis and a synthesis"[27] between the sacred and the secular in the Indian arts and the sacred was in many ways a transformation of the secular, a position suited to Tāntric epistemology. This inquiry investigates the secular approach to art and questions whether or not this secular aesthetic experience can be elevated to the status of a yoga and that too within an *advaitic* framework.

In art, as in other diciplines like linguistics, a distinction has been made very early in India between the classical and the folk, or the *mārgī* and the *deśī*, with the implication that the classical is higher and *svargya* or heavenward leading, and that the folk is plebian and meant merely for *lokānurañjana* or worldly entertainment. The exalted position given to Sanskrit is a good example of this division, while other languages like Prākṛt have enjoyed a secondary position. It is important to note that while we give a secondary status to Prākṛt when it comes to aesthetic discourse, it was the language of common discourse and in that latter sense a primary language. Although there has been a cross-fertilisation between the two traditions over the centuries, the dichotomy and the hierarchical attitude between the two has remained, and it is only recently, in the spirit of post-modernism, that an attempt is being made to understand folk art and to restore to it its lost glory. It has rightly been said that the classical and the folk are like two banks of the river of Indian civilisation. There are interesting and important anthropological questions that remain to be settled regarding the origin and development of folk art, questions beyond the scope of this purview. Most forms of folk art have no formal aesthetics as yet, and there are no *śāstras* of folk art; this type of art does not lend itself to a critical analysis and therefore cannot be featured in this inquiry.

Mārgī has both a chronological and stylistic connotation. Chronologically, *mārgī* refers to the classical period of Indian art which "begins with the official adoption of Buddhism by the emperor Aśoka in the third century BC and ends with the invasion and occupation by Muslim powers."[28] Other scholars would regard the Gupta period (320 AD to 650 AD) as the classical period of Indian art. Stylistically *mārgī* art refers to the type of art that is prescribed in the *śāstras*. Occupying an intermediary position between the *mārgī* and the *deśī*, and not forming part of our inquiry, is Tāntric or ritual art. It is significant that although we shall be applying Tāntric methods to our analysis of *mārgī* art, Tāntric art ***per se*** as exemplified by *yantras* will be excluded. This is so because as, Devangana Desai puts it, "The art of Tantra is religious in function and is not primarily meant for aesthetic appreciation."[29] At no time, it must be remembered, has the division of art into these three categories remained in watertight compartments.

The thrust of this inquiry is essentially epistemic and *artha* becomes the cornerstone of the investigation. A two step *artha*, namely *sākṣātartha* or the primary meaning and *parokṣārtha* or a secondary or hidden meaning are envisaged. Two art processes, rather than specific art forms, have been chosen for this study, namely *rasa* or aesthetic emotion and *rūpa* or aesthetic form, for we are interested in studying aesthetic principles rather than art objects, in understanding the vocabulary and grammar of art rather than a particular artistic composition, in uncovering the epistemic dynamics rather than studying a superficial art encounter. *Artha* is essentially objective and is a property of the art object, but a proper, deep and penetrating subjective aesthetic experience cannot take place without a realisation of the *artha*. It is *artha* that bridges the gap betwen the art object and the aesthete. Our efforts must be largely directed in uncovering the dynamics of the *artha*, for if we were to bypass this we could not talk of a meaningful art experience. In presenting the dynamics of these two art processes, it will be demonstrated that the Indian artist uses artistic forms and techniques to embody an idea, a vision, and it is the task of the aesthete to partake of this vision. As the ***Dasarūpa*** states, "The work of art can only nourish the spectator, he can only have delight in it, when he is not cut off from its meaning."[30] An art object, for an aesthetician, is not only a source of beauty, but also, at the same time, an invitation to explore the reason or *artha* for that beauty. Aesthetics should not only involve studying artistic forms, but more importantly present a method of arriving at the artistic meaning. Coomaraswamy has suggested that "we ought to abandon the term aesthetic in its present application and return to rhetoric", the latter understood as "the art of giving effectiveness to truth".[31] Underlying this statement of Coomaraswamy is a clear warning that unless the aesthete makes *artha* the focus of the inquiry the ultimate aesthetic experience is bound to be trivial, truncated and superficial.

Rasa has remained the cornerstone of Indian art and provides not only a chronological continuity to art in the *mārgī* tradition, but more importantly, establishes the link between different art forms. The term *rasa* has many nuances of meaning which can be summed up as "aesthetic emotion" or "aesthetic flavour". *Rasa* is essentially a dynamic process, which is initiated by the contact between the prepared aesthete and the emotive situation presented by the art object, and which is brought to fulfilment in the mind of the aesthete. An understanding of *rasa* is pivotal to Indian aesthetics and there is general acceptance of *rasa* as the most important component of traditional Indian art. Niharranjan Ray points out that "when *rasa* came to be regarded as the most important determinant of the artistic ultimate...a higher conception of art seems to have emerged and art expression appears to have come to be invested with a deeper meaning."[32] The dominance of *rasa* or aesthetic emotion pertaining to the art object over *vāstu* or the external form of the art object, and over *alaṃkāra* or creative imagination in the embellishment of the art object, points to a recognition by the Indian aestheticians of the inward and personal aspect of art. This dominance of *rasa* made sure that art had to be inwardly experienced and not merely appreciated at a sensory level, for "the aesthetic mode is an experience of the whole man and not a part of him".[33] The exalted status of *rasa* also ensured and underlined the importance of transcending superficial mental states in an aesthetic experience, a point that will be explored in the following chapters. Pandit states that *rasa* "became in Indian aesthetics and art-theory the most comprehensive principle signifying the art-process in all its phases, the creative, the created and the appreciative", and she goes on to say that "*rasa* as a quality of the art object and of aesthetic consciousness could synthesise both aspects [namely emotional and intellectual, sensual and spiritual, practical and contemplative] and offer a point of reconciliation."[34]

The value of *kāma* or the search for emotional fulfilment in the Indian arrangement of *puruṣārthas* or the goals of life is well acknowledged. Pandit reminds us that "emotions alone provide the material for a subjective re-living which transcends the objective order."[35] "When *rasa* is taken to be the essence of the art work, it is perceived like a quality, as preciousness is in diamonds...but it is that totality of effect which arises from the object as a whole."[36] *Rasa*, from very early in the Indian tradition, has been able to provide the bridge between the objective and the subjective aspects of aesthetic experience, that is between knowledge and the experience of that knowledge. This is so because *rasa* as "aesthetic flavour" comprehends both the arousal and development of an aesthetic emotion in the mind of the aesthete, as well as the objective components of the art object, which arouse and sustain that emotion. Following the central importance given to *rasa* in Indian aesthetics, in this inquiry, the question of art as *advaita* is approached from within the dynamics of aesthetic emotion.

Rasa can be studied from many different perspectives, not all of which are important to us in this inquiry. In particular, the question of the number of *rasas* has been strenuously argued by aestheticians for centuries. The question whether *śānta rasa* or *bhakti rasa* is the ultimate *rasa* has engaged the minds of aestheticians as well. Our interest lies essentially in the dynamics of *rasa* and our purpose is to determine whether or not *rasa* can lead the *rasika*, the one who experiences the *rasa*, to a higher realisation, independently, and without becoming related to the traditional practices of *jñāna yoga* and *bhakti yoga*. Accordingly, the argument regarding the number of *rasas*, although of passing interest, will not occupy our primary attention.

If *rasa* or aesthetic emotion has provided the cornerstone of Indian art and art theories, *rūpa* or aesthetic form is the very idiom of Indian plastic art. For this inquiry, it is of cardinal importance to note that, in the *mārgī* tradition, only an art form that conforms to the prescriptions laid down in the *śāstras* and which is a visual symbol of the cosmic *Puruṣa* can be called a *rūpa*. The term *rūpa*, in this inquiry, has been used in its wider sense of form as understood in the *mārgī* tradition. A certain bias, within the tradition, in favour of *śilpa* or sculpture in bas relief, as opposed to *citra* or painting, must be admitted. It should be pointed out that *nāṭya* or dance and *śilpa* have a close connection and what can be said about *śilpa* applies in general to *nāṭya*. However, as Barrett and Gray point out the "history of Indian ... painting is too fragmentary".[37] Ancient Indian painting was predominantly of the form of wall painting, and most of it was in caves and cave temples and was meant mainly for the monks. Although art historians have spoken of its antiquity in India, and illustration of sacred texts was an ancient Buddhist and later Jain practice, painting in the *mārgī* Indian visual art tradition has not enjoyed an exalted status. Traditional plastic art in India was mainly public art, and *śilpa* rather than *citra* was the perfect artistic expression for this purpose. It was not until the Mughals patronised painting as a court art, that painting became part of a more popular movement, a movement that was later to be embraced by the artists of the Punjab hills and Rajasthan who developed miniature paintings in the Hindu tradition.

Śilpa or sculpture in the Indian context is synonymous with sacred imagery and this provides an interesting contrast with *rasa*. While *rasa* as an aesthetic principle stands above the division of art into sacred and secular and thereby pertains to both, *rūpa* parts company with the secular and stays exclusively within the sacred. However, the approach taken in this inquiry is, that though *rūpa* is defined as a symbol of the cosmic *Puruṣa* and therefore by definition sacred, it can be viewed as an art object, which is to be enjoyed solely for its aesthetic qualities, and not as a focus of ritual practices. It will be shown that *rūpa* can lead to a higher experience on the basis of its sensual aesthetic qualities alone. The case for the *advaita* of art is even stronger if it can be shown that *rūpa*, purely on aesthetic grounds, outside of religious ritual, can lead the prepared aesthete to a higher experience. For, in the ultimate analysis, while *rūpa* is a plastic form of deep aesthetic value, what is more important to aestheticians is the idea or the vision that the *rūpa* embodies and the way in which it does it. As Kramrisch points out the cardinal feature of the Indian *rūpa* which is essentially architectonic, is "transubstantiation ... made visible by the transformation of the plastic means".[38] According to Rabindranath Tagore, *rūpa*, as a symbol of the Infinite, moves from the formless to form and carries the mind of the aesthete to the formless again:

> Incense craves to dissolve itself into fragrance and fragrance wants to remain enveloped in incense. Melody seems to find itself articulated in rhythm and rhythm wants to get back to melody. Idea craves to be embodied in form and form seems to release itself in idea. The limitless seeks its intimate association with the limited, and the limited craves to lose itself in the limitless. I know not whose logic it is in creation and destruction, that there is an unceasing intercourse after freedom and freedom is always looking for a nest in bondage.[39]

A complete inquiry into Indian aesthetics should ideally include *nāda* or the aesthetics of sound, *tāla* or the aesthetics of rhythm, and *vāstu* or aesthetics of architecture, which are artistic expressions of great importance in the total gamut of the Indian art experience. Within the scope of this inquiry it will not be possible to examine this total spectrum of classical Indian art. However, an important feature of Indian art is that there is a thread of continuity, not only in a chronological sense, but from one art form to another. And therefore, the principles of *rasa* and *rūpa* could be extended to the other art forms. The following dialogue between a *ṛṣi* and a king brings out this interconnection between the various art forms rather vividly:

> King: O Sinless One! Be good enough to teach me the methods of image-making.
>
> Sage: One who does not know the laws of painting can never understand the laws of image-making.
>
> King: Be then good enough, O Sage, to teach me the laws of painting.
>
> Sage: But it is difficult to understand the laws of painting without any knowledge of the technique of dancing.
>
> King: Kindly instruct me then in the art of dancing.
>
> Sage: This is difficult to understand without a thorough knowledge of the laws of instrumental music.
>
> King: Pray teach me the laws of instrumental music.
>
> Sage: But the laws of instrumental music cannot be learnt without a deep knowledge of the art of vocal music.
>
> King: If vocal music be the source of all the arts, reveal then to me, O Sage, the laws of vocal music.[40]

The relationship between art and religion in the Indian tradition is an intricate one, particularly when it comes to sacred imagery. *Bhakti* has been a prime moving force in the development not only of the temple but of the various arts that the temple fostered. The

Indian viewpoint generally is very often a holistic one, and to sequestrate one activity or principle and study it in isolation, is to truncate and distort the Indian view of life. The thrust of our argument will be that, in its widest sense, Indian art directs the aesthete towards ultimate Reality and therefore qualifies to be considered under the aegis of *advaita*. However, from the standpoint of *bhakti yoga*, it is difficult to isolate art from religious ritual and everything it signifies, and therein lies the fundamental problem for us. "Ritual and prayer are the two expressions in art and word of man's sense of dependence on divine or supernatural powers".[41] Aesthetics stays outside the realm of ritual and prayer which are a fundamental part of *bhakti yoga*. Stated differently, *bhakti yoga* requires that ultimately all other considerations be subordinated to it. We find support for this position with Śrī Aurobindo as well when he says:

> Religion in attempting to satisfy the thinking mind (has) more often succeeded in oppressing or fettering it with a mass of theological dogmas ... Religion was driven to cut existence into two by a division of knowledge, works, art, life itself into two opposite categories, the spiritual and the worldly, religious and mundane, sacred and profane ... the theory that sees an intimate connection between religious aspiration and the truest and greatest Art is in essence right; but we must substitute for the mixed and doubtful religious motive a spiritual aspiration, vision, interpreting experience.[42]

Śrī Aurobindo's statement is in keeping with our position that *bhakti* aesthetics, although of considerable significance in the Indian tradition, cannot be sustained as an *advaitic* experience. Another example that has already been cited above that supports our position, is the difference between the Kṛṣṇa of the ***Bhāgavata Purāṇa*** and the Kṛṣṇa of Jayadeva's ***Gītagovinda***; in the former Kṛṣṇa is the object of *bhakti* and in the latter of *śṛṅgāra rasa*. The ***Bhāgvata Purāṇa*** became the source of Vaiṣṇava theology whereas the ***Gītagovinda*** can remain a secular *kāvya*.

Our concern is to justify aesthetics as an independent and

bonafide discipline, not to be subordinated by any other, and capable of leading the prepared aesthete to a higher experience, a transcendent vision, outside of *jñāna yoga* or *bhakti yoga*; in other words, to demonstrate that art experience is an *advaitic* process and a yoga on its own. Justification for art as a yoga in this inquiry will be sought not in the *jñāna* or the *bhakti* traditions but in the epistemology of the *advaita* of Kāśmīr Śaivism. It will be shown that this system of thought can give ultimate validity to aesthetic experience and yet retain it within the strict confines of *advaita*. It is more than of passing interest to point out that Abhinavagupta, who championed the *rasa* theory, was also the high priest of the Kāśmīr Śaivite school.

And finally, a few words about the methodology and the approach of this inquiry: the method is essentially an epistemic analysis of the concepts of *rasa* and *rūpa* from the texts, and of the epistemology of aesthetics from texts of Kāśmīr Śaivism. No field surveys, of artists or aesthetes, were undertaken.

The main *rasa* texts consulted were those by Bharata, Ānandavardhana and Abhinavagupta. It is interesting that while *rasa* as an aesthetic principle has been exhaustively written and commented upon by Indian aestheticians, when it comes to *rūpa* there has been an influx of Western aestheticians in the field, aestheticians who were totally immersed in the Indian tradition, wrote from within the tradition. From amongst these, mention is specially made of Kramrisch and Boner, whose writings have brought to light some important aesthetic principles especially in *śilpa*, and whose findings therefore are important to us. The *śilpa* texts in general give elaborate information about the construction of sculpture and the religious rituals that go with it, and do not seem to deal with aesthetic theories in any depth. For this reason, the ***Vāstusūtra Upaniṣad*** is a text of great importance for our purpose, as it is perhaps the only text that sets out in clear terms the aesthetic principles that underpin the concept of *rūpa*. And finally, equally important are modern Indian aestheticians, who influenced as they were by Western aesthetic ideas, dug into their own roots, to present their own aesthetic views. In this group are mainly Rabindranath Tagore, Śrī Aurobindo and Ānanda Kentish Coomaraswamy, along with M. Hiriyanna and Niharranjan Ray. It is important to include these modern aestheticians in this inquiry, both of Western and Indian backgrounds, to show that Indian aesthetics is a very vibrant, modern and ongoing concern, and that art and aesthetics in all its aspects has enjoyed an unbroken tradition in India.

NOTES

1. A.K.Coomaraswamy, ***The Dance of Shiva***. (New Delhi: Sagar Publications, 1976) p. 26.
2. *kṣaṇe kṣaṇe yannavatāmupaiti tadeva rūpam ramanīyatayaḥ.* Magha, ***Śiśupālavadha***. (Bombay: Nirnaya Sagar Press, 1940) 4.17.
3. E.B.Havell, ***The Art Heritage of India***. (Bombay: D.B.Taraporevala Sons & Co. Ltd., 1964) p. 125.
4. J.Miller, ***The Vedas.*** (London: Rider & Company, 1974) p. 5.
5. *Ibid.*, p. 14. ***Ṛg Veda*** III.54.5.
6. *Ibid.*
7. *Ibid.*
8. Śrī Aurobindo, ***The Hour of God***. Centenary Edition Vol 17. (Pondicherry: Śrī Aurobindo Birth Centenary Library, 1971) p. 198.
9. Śrī Aurobindo, ***The Human Cycle***. (Pondicherry: Śrī Aurobindo Ashram, 1971) p. 128.
10. ***Locana*** 1.6 (*pratibhā*).
11. K.C.Pandey, ***Abhinavagupta: An Historical & Philosophical Study***. (Varanasi: Chowkhamba Sanskrit Series Office, 1963) p. 329.
12. J.Miller, p. 53.
13. *Ibid.*
14. *Chāndogya Upaniṣad*, 6.12.2 from R.E.Hume, ***The Thirteen Principal Upanishads***. (London: Oxford University Press, 1975) p. 248.
15. S.N.Dasgupta, ***Fundamentals of Indian Art***. (Bombay: Bhartiya Vidya Bhavan, 1960) p. 60.
16. *Ibid.*, p. 5.
17. *tasmāt kimapi vaktavyam, yadanantaram brahmajijñāsatrā upadis'yate vadati. ucyate nityānityavastuvivekaḥ ihāmumarthabhogaviragaḥ samadamādisādhanasampat mumukuṣtvam ca iti.* Śaṅkara Adi, ***Śāṅkarabhāṣya.*** 1.1.1.
18. K. Chattopadhaya, ***India's Craft Tradition***. (New Delhi: Publications Division, Government of India, 1980) p. 6.
19. Bharata, ***Nāṭyaśāstra***. 1. 7-12.
20. R. Lipsey, (ed.), ***Coomaraswamy***. Selected Papers, Volume 1. (Princeton: Princeton University Press, 1977) p. 164.
21. V.Subramanian (ed) ***The Sacred and the Secular in India's Performing***

Arts—Ananda K. Coomaraswamy Centenary Essays. (New Delhi: Ashish Publishing House, 1980) Chapter 1. pp. 110.
22. *Ibid.*, p. 11.
23. Mammaṭa, ***Kāvyaprakāśa.*** (Delhi: Motilal Banarsidass, 1967) 1.2.
24. M. Hiriyanna. ***Art Experience***. (Mysore: Kavyalaya Publishers, 1954) p. 27.
25. Kālidāsa, ***Mālavikāgnimitra***. 1.2.
26. V. Subramanian, *op.cit.,* p. 9.
27. *Ibid.*, p. 9.
28. D.Barrett & B. Gray, ***Indian Painting***. (New York: Rizzoli International Publication Inc., 1978) p. 11.
29. Smt. Devangana Desai, personal communication.
30. R.Lipsey (ed.), ***Coomaraswamy***. p. 85.
31. *Ibid.*, pp. 14-15.
32. N.Ray, ***An Approach to Indian Art***. (Chandigarh: Panjab University, 1974) p. 131.
33. S.Pandit, ***An Approach to the Indian Theory of Art and Aesthetics.*** (New Delhi: Sterling Publishers Pvt. Ltd., 1980) p. 19.
34. *Ibid.*, p. 32.
35. *Ibid.*, p. 40.
36. *Ibid.*, p. 43.
37. Barrett & Gray, preface. ***Indian Painting***. New York.
38. S.Kramrisch, ***The Indian Sculpture.*** (Delhi: Motilal Banarsidass, 1981) p. 59.
39. Original by Dadu translated by Rabindranath Tagore, quoted in N.Ray, ***Idea and Image in Indian Art.*** (Delhi: Munshiram Manoharlal Publishers Pvt. Ltd., 1973) p. 5.
40. Original from ***Viṣṇudarmottaram*** quoted in M.R.Anand, ***The Hindu View of Art.*** (Bombay: Asia Publishing House, 1957) p. 61.
41. V.S.Apte, ***The Cultural Heritage of India.*** ed. S. Radhakrishnan. Vol 1. (Calcutta: Ramakrishna Mission Institute of Culture, 1937) p. 234.
42. Śrī Aurobindo, ***The Synthesis of Yoga***. (Pondicherry: Śrī Aurobindo Ashram, 1955) pp. 131-33.

Chapter 2

The Meaning of Meaning

vāgarthaviva sampṛktau vāgartha pratipattaye
jagataḥ pitarau vande pārvatiparamesvarau
Raghuvaṃsa, 1.1

Central to an epistemic inquiry into art in the Indian tradition is the concept of *artha*. It is important to examine the various *pramāṇas*, and the Indian logicians have devoted themselves strenuously to this task; but of greater concern to aestheticians is the nature of the objective knowledge gleaned from those *pramāṇas* and its relationship to the subjective experience arising from that knowledge. The epistemic entity of *artha*, for it to qualify as *advaitic* on the one hand and be of value to aestheticians on the other, should not only illuminate the nature of knowledge and provide different levels of meaning, but ideally provide a bridge across the gulf between objective and the subjective, uniting understanding with realisation. It is against this backdrop that this inquiry is undertaken.

It has been said, and quite rightly too, that "Indian philosophy is repeated twice over, once in the accredited metaphysical systems as we know them and, once again, in their standpoint with regard to language."[1] Any discussion about *śabda* inevitably brings us face to face with the different schools of Indian philosophy. Most Indian schools accept three *pramāṇas* or sources of knowledge. They are *pratyakṣa* or perception, *anumāna* or inference and *śabda* or verbal testimony. From three the number of *pramāṇas* increased as each school included yet another source of knowledge. The others that were added include *upamāna* or comparison, *arthāpatti* or presumption, *anupalabdhi* or non-apprehension, *aitihya* or tradition, *sambhava* or inclusion, *ceṣṭā* or gesture and *pariśesa* or elimination. It is important to point out that *pratyakṣa* is the central *pramāṇa* and one that is acceptable to all schools. It also needs to be stressed that most schools accepted the interrelation of one *pramāṇa* to another. Of all the *pramāṇas*, *śabda* more than any other, has a wider scope and range, for it can accommodate not only an epistemic function but can include *anubhava* or experience as well. It, more than any other *pramāṇa*, incorporates a world of living experience, a cosmology, a world-view and is therefore important to us as aestheticians. *Śabda* remains not only an epistemic tool but readily leads to ontological implications as well. *Artha* understood in its wider sense as experience is what bridges the two functions, epistemic and ontologic, of *śabda*. Our attention in this inquiry will focus mainly on the *artha* of *śabda*, but our wider aim is to extend the concept of *śabda* from the Vedic word to *kāvya* and then to all art forms. The concept of *śabda* is a dynamic one, and one that has evolved even with the Indian tradition, and it would not be wrong to say that in the expansion and extension of the concept of *śabda* is to be found the history of Indian culture. This evolution was not without its opponents and critics, debates and arguments. For each school was vehemently committed to its own interpretation of *śabda*. The scholarly debates between different schools of the Indian tradition are indeed of some interest to us but cannot occupy our central attention.

In the Vedas, which are accepted as the starting point of the classical Indian tradition, *śabda* stood for the exalted vision of the *ṛṣis*. In the Vedic tradition *śabda* had a sacred implication and stood for a "valid source of knowledge and the means by which such knowledge may be communicated to others as verbal testimony."[2] The ***Ṛg Veda*** hints at the mystic nature of speech in more than one place. In a candid admission of the limitation of speech as a faculty, the Vedic *ṛṣis* have said "What shall I speak? What really shall I think?"[3] They further talk of four types of speech of which "three are hidden in the cave".[4] The Vedic word was also a source of *artha* understood variously as experience or meaning and it could not be separated from the Vedic experience of *yajña* as ritual invocation or incantation. Along with the sacred implication was the connotation of the Vedic *śabda* being a function of the oral tradition and therefore of sound. More importantly in the Vedic rites *śabda*, as exemplified by *mantra*, was the bearer of power, almost in a magical sense. The Upaniṣadic *ṛṣis*, although internalising many of the Vedic concepts, continued to give *śabda* an exalted but mystical status when they decalred, "*yato vāco nivartante aprāpya manasa sahā*".[5] The Indian tradition begins with this type of reverential and exalted attitude towards speech, an attitude that limits the scope of speech on the one hand and the enjoyment and appreciation of speech for its own sake on the other. Stated differently, the Vedic-Upaniṣadic tradition did not permit a liberal interpretation of *śabda* and did not overtly accept the transcendence of *śabda*. Questions concerning the aesthetic worth of language were not raised during this period, and aesthetic experience did not feature in their ideas. One hastens to add that aesthetic ideas in a seminal form however did exist with the Vedic Indians. The Vedas are full of exquisite poetry and there are strong hints of the exalted nature of Vāk in lines such as:

> And it is I, who like the wind, breathe forth
> and set all existing worlds in motion.
> Beyond heaven and beyond the earth am I
> and all this I have become in splendour.[6]

This attitude was to last several centuries and it was not until the beginning of the first millennium AD that questions were being raised about the inherent worth of *śabda* or speech. In other words, the question that now was being asked was whether *śabda* was merely a *pramāṇa* or did it have any intrinsic aesthetic worth and from then did it have any value in providing a transcendent experience. Patañjali offers this widened definition of *śabda* in his ***Mahābhāṣya*** as "that on the utterance of which there is common understanding regarding objects",[7] a definition that seems arid and without any hint of aesthetic implications. It were the *śramaṇas* who were mainly responsible for initiating the process of enlarging the concept of *śabda*, a process that was completed by the *alaṃkārikas* for whom *śabda* was *kāvya*. Stemming as it did from their challenge of the supremacy of the Vedas, the Buddhists and the Jains not only widened the concept of *śabda* to include scriptures other than the Vedas, but also insisted that *śabda* be not only oral but written, events of considerable importance in the Indian tradition and especially in the field of aesthetics. The credit for the written word must go to the Buddhists. Aśvaghoṣa's ***Buddhacarita*** is regarded as the first *kāvya* in classical, as opposed to Vedic *sanskrit*. Already the stage was set for accepting *kāvya* and *itihāsa* in the same hierarchy as *śruti* and *smṛti*, a development of seminal importance to aestheticians. The idea that valid and bonadife experience was possible outside and beyond the Vedic word and ritual was clearly taking hold in the Indian tradition, a position that was to make room for not only aesthetic experience but religious experience as well. Thus, it is quite clear that even within the Indian tradition, the concept of *śabda* evolved from its connotation as *yajña* to its interpretation as *kāvya*, from the strictly sacred to include secular language as well, and that the study of language for its own sake was a later Indian concern. One must take note that while the analysis of language was an ongoing concern from Yāska through Jaimini to Pāṇinī, it was universally accepted that language took its authority from wordly usage and therefore from people at large; this was never in dispute. The central issue for us is to find the missing link in the evolution of *śabda* as subservient to *yajña* to a position of *śabda* representing *kāvya*, for in that link may be found some aesthetic ideas in a seminal form.

Any semantic discussion on the concept of *artha*, or the meaning of meaning, as it is sometimes called, must begin with an examination of the position on this subject of the Realists. For, they, more than any other group, investigated the subject extensively and wrote about it with vigour and enthusiasm. It is pertinent that the early discourse on *artha* centred on *śabda* or language as a tool of verbal cognition. It has been claimed by Śabara that, "speech (or *śabda*) has the unique power of generating cognitions which present objects of the past, present and future, gross and subtle, remote and near. Other *pramāṇas*, such as perception, do not enjoy this unique power which *śabda* possesses."[8] It is because of this uniqueness of *śabda*, which is *saṃskṛta* or man-made, that the usual arguments pertaining to the external world do not apply. *Śabda* has to be taken as given for the purpose of this inquiry and its ontological status not questioned at this initial stage, which is devoted to the question of how *śabda* releases and propels itself to its meaning. We are not concerned with the origin of *śabda*, and the issue of the origin of language, for interesting as it is, the problem will not occupy our attention. Inherent in this statement is the assertion that *śabda* by itself is not the *artha*. *Śabda*, however, is not to be entirely exempt from the strict questioning of ontological validity of the Indian tradition, as the problem will be taken up later on in the inquiry under the auspices of Kāśmīr Śaivism.

The Indian tradition was essentially an oral tradition, and although the antiquity of visual or performing art is undisputed, language became the prototype of formal inquiry into *artha*, and this was undertaken through Vedic exegesis. It will be the endeavour in this inquiry to extend the connotation of the term *śabda* not only to language but to all expressed concepts, namely art, but our inquiry must begin with an examination of the position of the Indian tradition into language. It is important to stress at the outset that our interest is not merely epistemological, although that is indeed the starting point, but equally importantly ontological. To put it differently, we are interested not only in cognitive knowledge but equally in subjective realisation. With this in mind one can draw one's parameters of the present inquiry to include in it only those philosophical schools which have a contribution to make in the field of aesthetics. The scholarly disputes between different schools of the Indian grammatical-etymological tradition are indeed of some interest, but not helpful to us in arriving at our position regarding the meaning of *śabda*. A case in point is the "dispute between the Buddhists and the Nyāya schools of thought over the nature of perception, the critique and the criteria of knowledge, and the status of the external world (which) lasted a little over twelve centuries",[9] a dispute though erudite but which need not occupy our attention. Our interest lies in a close examination of Bhartṛhari's analysis of language to see if it can provide that missing link in the evolution of *śabda* understood as *kāvya*.

The Realists include the Mīmāṁsakas as well as the Nyāya-Vaiśeṣikas for both of which schools language was real. Between the two groups we will closely examine the Mīmāṁsaka position. From amongst the Mīmāṁsakas four names stand out, namely those of Jaimini, Śabara, Prabhākara and Kumārila, whose writings contain a spirited discussion of *artha* as derived from language. The initial connotation of *śabda* or verbal cognition was essentially hermeneutic and implied exclusively the Vedic word, but went further to deny other *pramāṇas* such as sense-perception the same status.[10]

Śabda as verbal cognition epistemically functions through *artha* or meaning. The word *artha* is capable of several definitions, but even from the dictionary definitions of this word two main streams of ideas emerge. One definition of *artha* is "use, utility, value, aim, interpretation, explanation or purpose", ideas that focus on the outer or imperative aspects of *artha*. In this sense, *artha* becomes synonymous with *puruṣārtha* or the ultimate aim of human endeavour. The other definition of *artha* is "substance, inherent nature, experience, understanding or essence", ideas that direct our attention to the inner aspect of *artha*. It is the former that became the main concern of Mīmāṁsakas, who were a school of exegetes and for whom no inquiry was more important, more valuable, more urgent than "*dharmajijñāsā*"[11] derived from "*codanalakṣaṇo*"[12] or Vedic injunctions and exemplified by the Vedic *yajña*. The Vedic *yajña* became for the Mīmāṁsakas the originary experience, and *prītiḥ* (the word *prītiḥ* has been variously translated as "happiness, meaningful, pleasure or ultimate significance") its ultimate significance. It is interesting to note that the word *mimāṁsā* in its generic sense means investigation or inquiry and can be applied to any inquiry, and can include the present inquiry into the meaning in art.

Before we proceed to examine the Mīmāṁsā position on *artha*, it is important to place it in the context of Indian aesthetics. As Chari notes, "The Mīmāṁsā principles of interpretation were derived from a long tradition of Vedic exegesis ... (and) this exegetical tradition produced what may be called a science of interpretation with a body of rules that could be applied to any linguistic text, scriptural or non-scriptural."[13] Thus, while we will reject the Mīmāṁsā position eventually, much of what it has to say about *śabda* and *artha* is universally accepted and useful to us. Chronologically the Mīmāṁsakas thrived at a time when classical Indian art, especially plastic art, was almost non-existent, and performing art was not yet concretised. More importantly, the *śramaṇas* as exemplified by the Buddhists and the Jains had openly attacked the supremacy of the Vedas, and the whole concept of *dharma* as enunciated in the Veda had been shaken. It was a time when heterodox ideas were gaining acceptance and the Vedas needed to be defended. For the Mīmāṁsakas the supremacy and infallibility of the Vedas were their main concerns and it is against this background that their position on *artha* must be examined.

Eternality of *śabda* was the basis of the Mīmāṁsā doctrine, and Jaimini's declaration "*autpattikastu śabdasyārthena sambandaḥ*"[14] becomes the foundation of the Mīmāṁsā position on language. Eternality for the Mīmāṁsakas was a two-fold concept. Not only is language eternal or *nitya*, and uncreated or *apauruṣeya*, according to the Mīmāṁsakas, but within language itself the relation between *śabda* and *artha* is also timeless and unchangeable, "not the product of human convention...something inborn...(and) free from all possibility of error...(and the means) par excellence of knowing of *dharma*."[15] Stated differently, the Mīmāṁsā position meant that the word-meaning relation was invariable and constant. The concept of *nityatva* or eternality of *śabda* developed by the Mīmāṁsakas and universally accepted by all schools, has several important implications for the Indian aesthetic tradition. In its broadest sense, it emphasises that the creative process is sacrosanct and to be taken as given and one that is not to be probed. Applied to *śabda*, it means that etymology or the origin of words and how words acquire their meaning, and further the problem of how these meanings are learned, are not fit subjects of inquiry for an aesthetician. The Mīmāṁsakas refer to *vyavahāradarśanam* or the ability to learn by observation of elders which places *śabda* securely within the confines of the tradition. *Artha*, though ultimately individual, is to a large extent the treasure of the tradition. This point will become clearer when we discuss visual and performing art under the rubric of *parokṣārtha*.

It becomes clear that the Mīmāṁsā position on *śabda* as verbal cognition was limited and developed largely to preserve the sanctity and authority of the Vedas from the onslaught of the heterodox schools. Jaimini energetically defends opponents of the *śabdanityatva* doctrine and reminds us that "the word must be regarded as eternal because the utterance is for an altogether different purpose".[16] Kumārila leaves no doubt about the eternality of words when he says "*yadā hi kṣaṇikah śabdo na śakto arthāvadharaṇe*".[17] Besides, the eternality or autonomy of verbal meaning, impersonality of verbal meaning was a second major canon of the Mīmāṁsā position; *nityatva* and *apauruṣeyatva* are the twin pillars of Mīmāṁsakas. By impersonality is meant "independence of any external authority or of corroboration by another source of knowledge."[18]

The Mīmāṁsā position on *śabda* and *artha* was avowedly for the establishment and fulfilment of *dharma* and protection of the Vedas, but unwittingly it helped the cause of aesthetics. The Mīmāṁsā position established for the Indian tradition that "words are an independent source of knowledge and self-revealing (and) that they do not require for their meaningfulness any person or any other means of knowledge."[19] In a certain sense, it was a precursor of the *sphoṭa* doctrine, for it implied that the "word-meaning relation must be assumed to have existed prior to the uttering of the word."[20] Eternality, understood both as *nityatva* and *apauruṣeyatva* of words, is a concept that runs right through the Indian artistic tradition. *Śabda* in the Indian tradition, after the Mīmāṁsakas, meant not only just the word but the concept underlying it, not merely a command but an expression of an idea, not just an audible sound but knowledge, not just a collection of letters but the first formulation of an experience.

While Mīmāṁsā laid some fundamental ideas in the field of language, there remained major problems with the Mīmāṁsā position on *śabda* and *artha* for the aestheticians. Interested as he is in the interpretation of *śabda* as *kāvya*, there was nothing in the Mīmāṁsā tradition that would help him do this. In positing reality in *śabda* the Mīmāṁsakas limited the scope of *artha*. The eternality of both words and language was important to the Mīmāṁsakas and they argued, "(In a sentence) all words denoting things are in close textual juxtaposition with the word expressive of an action, specially because the meaning of the sentence is dependent upon the meaning of the words composing it."[21] The unit of meaning, in the Mīmāṁsā scheme of things, was the word and the meaning of the sentence was therefore tied firmly to the words forming the sentence, and the ultimate meaning of the sentence, according to them, arose from the sum of the component words. The Mīmāṁsakas paid great attention to the constituent words forming a sentence and Kumārilabhaṭṭa makes it quite clear that these words are held together in a sentence by *ākāṅkṣā* or mutual expectancy, *yogyatā* or appropriateness and *sannidhi* or the contiguity of words.[22] The Mīmāṁsakas sought to infuse unity and integrity in language with these three concepts out of which *ākāṅkṣā* was of prime importance. While the significance of these three fundamental concepts as responsible for the integrity and viability of a sentence can be universally accepted, it is important to note, that for the Realists such as the Mīmāṁsakas, they were vital and indispensable, for to them the source and seat of *artha* was the *pada*, a position that was not acceptable to Bhartṛhari.

Ideally there can be no question of any duality between *artha* and *śabda* whatever system one follows; however the position of the Realists in general and the Mīmāṁsakas in particular, sets up a duality between *śabda* and *artha* on the one hand and consciousness of the speaker and the listener on the other. For the listener, in the Mīmāṁsā scheme of language, are divested of any role either in the creation or interpretation of *śabda.* In this sense, the Mīmāṁsā position can be considered pluralistic in nature. It fragments the sentence into its component words which are the meaning bearers, held together inorganically and loosely, alienating language from consciousness, and not permitting the formation of any aesthetic concepts within their framework.

As can be clearly seen, there was no room in the Mīmāṁsā experience of language for *pratibhā* or the creative imagination or interpretation in the experience of language either on the part of the *kavi* or the aesthete. Thus, there can hardly be any doubt that with their emphasis on *kriyārtha* the Mīmāṁsakas though not anti-aesthetic were surely unaesthetic. It has been rightly said that, "The Mīmāṁsā view of language was founded not so much on the information that it provided as on the transformation it worked; and transformation is caused not so much by the meaning part of language as by its meaningfulness."[23] In its quest for meaningfulness the Mīmāṁsakas preserved piety but lost poetry. As Śabara points out "*Śabda*...is meant to reveal not so much itself as its meaning."[24] Beauty of language was not an issue with the Mīmāṁsakas as long as it fulfilled the ritualistic imperative and it was this imperative that propelled a sentence to its meaning. In order to underscore the imperative to act ritualistically, the Mīmāṁsakas brought in the doctrine of *bhāvanā*. It was *bhāvanā* of the sentence that provided the efficient-force, that compelled the individual to bring into being the meaning of the sentence. *Vākyārtha* for the Mīmāṁsakas became synonymous with *bhāvārtha*.[25] The Mīmāṁsakas further made language a "thematization of the innermost needs of man",[26] thereby making it a reality in itself. In securing for language the status of reality, the Realists neglected the innate beauty of language and refused to move the ultimate seat and source of *artha* beyond the *pada*, an issue that was taken up by Bhartṛhari and later fully exposed by the *alaṃkārikas*. For the Mīmāṁsakas the concept of *artha* could never contain aesthetics.

Language as an expression and an epistemological tool of ultimate Reality was a concern of the Indian Idealists as well. The Advaita Vedāntins preferred to take an entirely hermeneutic approach to language. An important document ***Pañcaprakriyā*** attributed to Sarvajñātman in the ninth-tenth century AD states unequivocally that, "the knowledge of words is the prime cause of final release and the joys of heaven for a person in the world".[27] However, a closer examination of their position makes it abundantly clear that the concept of *śabdajñānam* cannot have any room for aesthetics. The Advaita Vedāntins part company, quite quickly and significantly, from the Realists when they assert that "*mukhyāvṛtti*"[28] or words in their primary sense are unfit for an examination of the nature of ultimate Reality, "on account of the fact that (in the case of the *pratyagātman*) mundane things such as relation, quality, activity, universal or convention which are the basis of *mukhyāvṛtti* do not exist."[29] Sarvajñātman goes on to point out that *lakṣaṇa* and that too only of the *jahādajahāllakṣaṇa* type is adequate to undertake an examination of the nature of ultimate Reality. While *lakṣaṇa* can function as an aesthetic tool of some merit, it cannot in itself contain the totality of aesthetic experience. And what is more, the Advaita Vedāntins did not undertake an inquiry into the nature of aesthetic experience. Whatever be the type of *lakṣaṇa*, it will be shown, in the discussion on Ānandavardhana's *dhvani*, that it cannot qualify as an aesthetic tool, and it remains the primary ***modus operandi*** for the Advaita Vedāntins.

The Viśiṣṭa Advaitins did develop aesthetic concepts, but an examination of this tradition is out of place at this stage for a variety of reasons. Firstly, the Viśiṣṭa Advaitins came much later historically and to bring them in at this stage would be an anachronism. Secondly, and more importantly, for the Viśiṣṭa Advaitins every idea had to be subsumed under *bhakti*, and therefore aesthetics could not have an independent standing. *Artha* for the Viśiṣṭa Advaitins cannot be divorced from *bhakti*, a position that cannot foster the *advaita* of art.

Although Bhartṛhari is classified as a Vedāntin by some he stands out in a class by himself. He parts company from others with his concept of *śabdabrahman*. For Bhartṛhari "language is the basis of all knowledge including art",[30] and he goes on to assert that "consciousness can exist in all creatures only after it is preceded by speech."[31] Bhartṛhari begins the ***Vākyapadīya*** with the powerful declaration, "*anādinidhanam brahma śabdatattvam yad akṣaram*" "That eternal one, the imperishable *brahman* of which the essential nature is the Word."[32] *Brahman* for Bhartṛhari is inextricably bound with *śabda*, or to put it in other words, *brahman* is conceptual and not concept-free. For Bhartṛhari "the power which is based on words controls this universe."[33] Bhartṛhari leaves no doubt when he says "In this world no comprehension is possible except as accompanied by speech."[34] It is this that sets Bhartṛhari apart from other philosophers. Whereas for both Śaṅkara and the Buddhists *śabda* or concepts are an impediment in ultimate realisation, for Bhartṛhari there can be no realisation except through *śabda*, for he strives for, not a concept-free, but concept-loaded cognition and realisation. This is an important departure, for it established the epistemic bonafides of a *saguṇa brahman* and one that was crucial to the ultimate development of aesthetic theories. *Śabda* was for Bhartṛhari a "*vṛṣabha*"[35] or a great bull. The *śabdabrahman* of Bhartṛhari was a dynamic rather than a passive principle, an *advaitic* rather than a pluralistic concept, and which within the framework of *advaita* could provide for levels of *artha*, a position of significant importance to aestheticians. It was this concept of *śabdabrahman* that was responsible for making *śabda* the "bridge between the visible and the invisible, between life and liturgy, between the temporal and the tempiternal",[36] which within the framework of *advaita* could provide for levels of *artha*, a position of some importance to aestheticians.

Bhartṛhari in his day made several significant contributions to the grammar and philosophy of language, but it was his doctrine of *sphoṭa* that laid the foundation of Indian aesthetics in a germinal form, and helped move the tradition from the Realism of the Mīmāṁsakas to the Idealism of the grammarian-philosophers, from the perspective of language as a mere imperative to action to the realisation of language as an expression and experience of transcendent beauty, from a pluralistic position of the Realists to the *advaitic* position of the *sphoṭavādins*, from the concept of *śabda* as a *yajña* to that of *śabda* as *kāvya*. Within Bhartṛhari's framework of the experience of language there was no room for any sense or aspect of duality, but language in his view was still able to contain levels of meaning, a concept of cardinal importance to aestheticians. It is important to note that the historical time of Bhartṛhari was one of active linguistic speculation, and that he was preceded by grammarian-philosophers, and Patañjali in particular who undoubtedly influenced him and paved the way for his doctrine of *sphoṭa*. As Raja puts it, "The *sphoṭa* theory of Bhartṛhari is the culmination of many such attempts in the solution of the linguistic problems that were worrying scholars in the various philosophical schools."[37] The underlying tension was obviously this: should *śabda* be regarded as a mere pragmatic tool of ritual as the Mīmāṁsakas would have us believe, or is there any intrinsic or innate beauty in *śabda* which can be enjoyed for its own sake and which in turn leads to cognition and higher realisation? Stated differently the question was: is *śabda* merely useful for *yajña* or can *śabda* be understood as *kāvya*? This was an axial time in India's cultural history when *kavis* and *śilpīs* were giving expression to their sense of beauty and the question was indeed relevant.

The minutia of the debate between the different philosophic schools need not detain us here as our interest lies principally in the problem of *artha* as it relates to aesthetics. However, it is important to note, that the grammarian-philosophers were going against the tide of the day. For, if the Mīmāṁsakas were staunch Realists and did not subscribe to the *sphoṭa* doctrine, the Buddhists were linguistically nihilists and felt that concepts were only impediments in ultimate realisation. For Buddhists like Diññāga "percepts are pure data free from any *vikalpa* or conception."[38] The *apoha* doctrine of the Buddhists could not lead to an aesthetic theory.

At this juncture it would not be out of place to probe the question of the relationship between art and aesthetics. More importantly, it can be asked whether a school of philosophy that is negative to language can influence the development of art. There is hardly any doubt that when it came to the three main cultural traditions in ancient India, namely the Hindu, Buddhist and the Jain, the Buddhist were the least prolific when it came to art, at least in the initial stages. It is interesting to compare for a moment the Buddhist and the Jain positions; for while on the one hand they had quite a few features in common, they parted company when it came to the role of concept or *śabda* in ultimate realisation.

Translated wrongly as "explosion" *sphoṭa* should ideally be understood as "blossoming". It is synonymous with the Western conception of 'logos' or 'innate idea'. Coward explains it, from the point of view of the listener, as "the transcendent ground in which the spoken sylablles and conveyed meaning find themselves united."[39] Radhakrishnan calls it the 'indivisible idea'.[40] S.K.Dey looks upon *sphoṭa* as a "somewhat mystical conception" and explains it as the "sound of a word as a whole".[41] Some others have called *sphoṭa* the "real word" or the "universal word", emphasising that reality resides in the marriage of *śabda* and *artha*.

Bhartṛhari's *sphoṭa* develops from his position that it is the *vākya* and not the *pada* that is the unit of meaning. A *vākya* according to Bhartṛhari is "an utterance which is one and devoid of parts".[42] for "it is the ignorant who split it into parts and hence get a different meaning",[43] for the "ultimate meaning resides in the unity of the collection of words and not in individual words singly or together",[44] and "the nature of all word meaning is dependent on the meaning of the sentence".[45] Bhartṛhari gives the example of *narasiṃha* for neither the "concept of a man nor of a lion is present in the connotation of man-lion."[46] To illustrate further, the sentences " 'Bring a cuckoo from the forest' and 'Bring a creeper from the forest' have nothing in common between them."[47] This position of Bhartṛhari is therefore sometimes referred to as the *akhaṇḍavāda*. As Subramania Iyer says, "what Bhartṛhari tries to establish is that the sentence and the sentence-meaning are indivisible units and that they alone are *satya*. Individual words and their meanings have neither definiteness nor reality."[48]

Briefly stated, the *sphoṭa* doctrine postulates that *śabdabrahman* or the *śabdatattva* is the undifferentiated speech, resting "egg-like" in the consciousness. This level of linguistic experience is also called *paśyanti* or *pratibhā*. At the next stage, *śabdatattva* explodes into the *vācaka* and *vācya* or *śabda* and *artha*, also called the *mādhyama* phase of speech. Bhartṛhari emphasises that "speech and meaning being the two halves of one fact are not distinct and separable",[49] reminding us of Kālidāsa's lines: "*vagārthaviva samprṛktau vagārtha pratiprattaye*".[50] The unity of *śabda* and *artha* in the *sphoṭa* is a concept with far reaching implications. Aesthetically it means that no *śabda* is without its *artha*, no art without meaning, at the level of the *sphoṭa*. So far the *śabda* is entirely within the consciousness of the speaker and inaudible. In the third stage, the *sphoṭa* is audibly or visibly expressed. This audible part of *śabda* is called *dhvani*, *śruti*, *vaikhari* or *nāda*. To distinguish it from the *dhvani* of Ānandavardhana, which came later and which has a different connotation, the term *nāda* will be used throughout to denote the *dhvani* of Bhartṛhari, which stands for the audible sound.

It is important to note that *śabda* at the level of the *sphoṭa* is functionally quite distinct from *nāda*. Bhartṛhari leaves no doubt when he asserts that "*śabda* and *nāda* are different entities",[51] emphasising that *nāda* is impotent without its component of *artha*. The marriage of *śabda* and *artha* is temporarily divorced at the level of the *nāda*. For, at this stage, as Matilal puts it "meaning is divorced from the word, the real word (*sphoṭa*) through our verbal behaviour and 'remarried' to the thing..."[52] At this level *nāda* stands bereft and without *artha* like an unmarried daughter as it were, reminding us of Kālidāsa's lines "*artho hi kanya parakīya eva, tamadya sampreśya parigrahituh. jato mamayam viśadah prakamam pratyapitanyasa evantaratma.*"[53] According to Bhartṛhari *nāda* is *asat*, incomplete, erroneous or illusion. Coward is right in pointing out that the *nāda* is "an universal error which ultimately leads to the perception of the truth",[54] once *artha* is attached to it. The metaphysical implications in this are obvious and the aesthetic implications are of considerable value. Metaphysically it is in keeping with the common Indian Idealist position that what is apparent is not ultimately real. It becomes quite apparent that the *nāda* by itself is meaningless. However, "whereas the Advaitin usually describes the error as being transcended via negation, the grammarian holds that the error is positively overcome by increasingly clear cognition",[55] once the *artha* is attached, a position that was later to be championed by the Kāśmīr Śaivites. Aesthetically, the Tāntric overtones in this concept of *asat* are hard to miss and they reaffirm that the grammarian-philosophers, who were Advaitins in their own right, took a stand quite different from the Advaita Vedāntins.

The listener who starts at the stage of the *nāda* is then charged with the responsibility of reuniting the *nāda* with the *artha*, without which no linguistic experience can take place; for the avid listener is like the father of the daughter, who cannot find peace in his heart till he has given the daughter to her husband, which is where she belongs. This underscores the fact that *artha* is the eventual responsibility of the consciousness and not the *śabda* and that it is equally a function of the *svarūpa* of the *nāda* which must propel itself to its meaning because of its inherent qualities. Stated differently, quintessentially *nāda* by its very nature, however simple or elaborate, either a word, a sentence or an epic, is esentially a metaphor or a symbol which has to be decoded, understood, experienced and realised, and which only then bridges the gap between the speaker and the listener, the *kavi* and the *rasika*. This also makes it clear that *artha*, which is neither the *nāda* nor the object meant, is a function of the consciousness of the artist on the one hand and the aesthete on the other. As Pandeya puts it, "Meaning being a relation is neither the word nor the object, it depends upon them and is yet beyond them. This proves the existence of meaning as a metaphysical entity."[56] The transcendence of *śabda* therefore cannot take place without *artha*.

To investigate what propels *nāda* to its reunion with *artha* and the dynamics of how *nāda* and *artha* are reunited, is the heart of the problem for aestheticians; this is the problem of meaning in art. Although *nāda* has epistemic potential and devoid of *artha*, yet its form has a vital function. It is "only through the *nāda* that the immutable *sphoṭa* will eventually arise."[57] It is a necessary intermediary in language, for "one strives for Reality remaining on the path of unreality."[58] The *nāda* is merely a spring board and not a final destination. For Bhartṛhari, language had not only an "*artharūpa*" but also a "*svarūpa*",[59] not only "*grāhyatva*" (conveying its own form) but also "*grāhakatva*" (conveying an object)[60] it is not only "*prakāśaka*" but also the "*prakāśyatvam*",[61] not only, as it were, light but a source of illumination at the same time. It is the *svarūpam* of the *nāda* that is a repository of an innate meaning and one that plays a pivotal role in propelling it to its ultimate *artha*.

In the listener or the aesthete, engaged in experiencing *nāda*, the process has to be reversed and the *nāda* is to be realised through its *artha*. It becomes obvious that although *artha* resides in a germinal form in the *nāda*, the cognition of that *artha* results from his own cognitive effort or interpretation and therefore rightly belongs to him and not to the *nāda*. Stated differently, words according to Bhartṛhari, move in the realm of secondary being or "*upacārasatta*";[62] in the realm of primary being, that is without its meaning, it has no standing.

For Bhartṛhari the *sphoṭa* in the listener emerges as flash of intuitive understanding, which is quite different from the logical meaning of the individual words added together. It is quite apparent that when the whole sentence is understood, the meaning appears to be quite different, or stated differently, the ultimate meaning of the sentence is greater than the sum of the individual meaning of words. Bhartṛhari's *sphoṭa* as the ultimate repository of *artha* moves meaning from intellect to intuition, from *manas* to *pratibhā*, from arid logic to a supra-logical realisation, from a fixed and limited mental activity to a limitless function of consciousness, from a fragmented intellectual function to an *advaitic* and creative process. At this stage, it is important to point out that the concept of *pratibhā* understood as a flash of intuitive knowledge, a concept which is central to Bhartṛhari's *sphoṭa* doctrine, implies a previous existence. The psychological and metaphysical implications of previous existence, such as *karma* and rebirth need not detain us, for as Coward rightly points out, it is a presupposition that is accepted by virtually all schools of Indian thought.[63] This aspect of *pratibhā* will be further brought out in the chapter on the epistemology of aesthetic experience.

The implications of the *sphoṭa* doctrine of Bhartṛhari are quite significant. In the first place with the doctrine of *sphoṭa*, the onus of the meaning of the sentence, shifts from the outer result or effect of the sentence, as in the Mīmāṁsaka system, to the consciousness of the listener.

The *nāda*, as exemplified by the sentence becomes merely the messenger of the meaning, the actual meaning being the function of the *pratibhā*, or super-sensuous perception, which has the ultimate responsibility for formulating and experiencing the meaning. In Bhartṛhari's doctrine "*pratibhā*"[64] is given the pride of place, and meaning consists in the transformation of the *śabdatattva* into the *nāda* and back into the *śabdatattva* again, a movement of consciousness from the formless into form and back into the formless again. It is important to point out that for Bhartṛhari *nāda* is the product of the *śabdatattva*. Arising from the highest reaches of the mind, or *pratibhā* of the speaker, it impregnates itself with *artha* during the *sphoṭa* formation, and through the *nāda* it reaches a similar state of the mind of the listener.

Bhartṛhari is a staunch *advaitin* and at no point in his doctrine of *sphoṭa* is there any duality, *śabda* and *artha* remaining differentiation of the one and the same self, and not really different from each other. Bhartṛhari's *sphoṭa* gives us the differentiation of *śabda* into *śabda* and *artha* without introducing any trace of duality, reminding us of the common motif of the Indian artist of the woman looking at herself in a mirror, as if *śabda* realises itself when it encounters its *artha*. As Sastri puts it:

> The grammarian posits word as consciousness. The two words are, to all intents and purposes, synonymous. And consciousness is an indivisible entity. It is matter that is divisible, and it is the indivisibility of consciousness which distinguishes it as a spiritual fact from matter.[65]

This is the uniqueness and strength of Bhartṛhari's position, for it elevates *śabda* from matter to spirit, from mere *prayojana* to *artha* and it thus becomes the cornerstone of aesthetics in the Indian tradition. Bhartṛhari's *sphoṭa* leaves an indelible imprint of spirituality on language. Left to the Mīmāṁsakas *śabda*, both as *pada* and *vākya*, would remain material entities, performing a piece-meal function, capable of expressing a limited meaning and ceasing to be when the meaning is expressed. This piece-meal approach of the Realists, stemming from their dry and relentless logic, separates *śabda* on the one hand and *brahman* on the other, with no attempt to bridge the two. Their position stultifies and truncates language and verbal cognition, and makes it incapable of exercising an aesthetic function.[66]

Although Bhartṛhari was a grammarian-philosopher and not an *alaṃkārika*, he should be considered the true father of Indian aesthetics for his doctrine of *sphoṭa* permitted *śabda* to be understood as *kāvya* and further linked *śabda* with *brahman* thereby ontologically giving verbal cognition a legitimacy. Bhartṛhari's *sphoṭavāda* did this by providing the framework for the exaltation of *śabda* to *śabda-brahman*. It was his doctrine that allowed a purely sensory *nāda* to achieve a cognitive status by rediscovering its *artha*, thereby giving epistemic bonafides to a *saguṇa brahman*. This it did by two main processes. In the first place, by making *artha* a function of the artist's and the aesthete's *pratibhā* and *cittavṛtti*, Bhartṛhari allowed for the growth of *artha* through *parokṣārtha*, a concept of fundamental epistemic importance to the aesthetician. As Matilal points out "mediate perception can be arguably shown to be an inference."[67] It will be shown later that Ānandavardhana's *dhvani* which is the cornerstone of Indian aesthetics is a function purely of inference. Aesthetic inference delimits the art experience and gives room for infinite expansion of the original *śabda* or artistic concept, and calls into play the *saṃskāras* and the *śikṣā* of the aesthete. It is this growth in meaning from the *sākṣātartha* to the *parokṣārtha*, as envisaged by the *sphoṭa*, that is the forerunner of the basic Tāntric idea that the infinite is to be realised through the finite, thereby giving credibility to the finite *nāda*. For it is the process of *sphoṭa* that limits the formless into form and then lets the form expand into the limitless formeless once again. No other concept of *artha* has room for this vast and catholic interpretation, no other school of philosophy gives this exalted role to the concept of *artha* in the Indian tradition. It is only Bhartṛhari's *sphoṭa* that encourages a deep and deliberate epistemic experience of *śabda* instead of a superficial epistemic encounter brought on by the logical concept of *artha* as proposed by the Realists such as the Mīmāṁsakas and the mataphorical concept of *artha* of the Idealists as expemlified by the Advaita Vedāntins.

Secondly, the concept of *shpoṭa* also allowed *śabda* to separate into its formal element on the one hand and the meaning element on the other, permitting an enjoyment of its formal, sensual or structural aspects in tandem with a super-sensual expansion and realisation of its ultimate meaning. Stated differently, *sphoṭa* ensures that *śabda* is not only instrumental but inherent in cognition through verbal testimony, that *artha* stems from but does not dispense with the outer sensual aspect of the *śabda*. Bhartṛhari's doctrine showed the way towards a higher realisation through verbal cognition without insisting on any form of renunciation, in pushing towards *artha* one did not have to give up the *śabda*. This as will be shown later is a fundamental Tāntric concept and it was this holistic approach that can be made the cornerstone of the *advaita* of art, it was this that paved the way for the interpretation of *śabda* as *kāvya* and *artha* as aesthetics. After Bhartṛhari *artha* remained not just "a relation between a word and an object",[68] as it was with the Mīmāṁsakas, the Nyāyikas and the Buddhists and the Vedāntins, but it became the vehicle of the two-fold process of the enjoyment of language and sensual experience on the one hand, leading to cognition and a higher realisation on the other. Bhartṛhari's *sphoṭa* ensured that language was meant not only for commercial or ritual use and in that sense experience was not relegated to the realm of *mithyā*, but that it had its own credibility, its own *svarūpa* capable of leading the prepared aesthete to a higher cognitive experience. It is the *svarūpa* of the *śabda* that propells it to its ultimate meaning, which gives *svarūpa* not just an ornamental but an epistemic function. It recognised the essential role played by the apparently superficial qualities and attributes of the *śabda*.

Yet another fruit of Bhartṛhari's *sphoṭavāda* was to establish the aesthetics of symbols and make the understanding of symbolism an epistemic activity. Symbolism is the very essence of Indian art and the ***sine qua non*** of Indian visual and performing art in particular. All *nāda* according to Bhartṛhari is essentially a symbol, a *saṅketa*, and all that it can do is to offer hints, hints that a trained aesthete picks up and couples with its *artha*, so that the *nāda* can move on to the highest reaches of consciousness and to its ultimate resting place as the *śabdabrahman*. Without the *sphoṭa* doctrine symbols would be left meaningless and incomplete for it is the *sphoṭa* that makes the implicit meaning explicit, gives life to symbols, as it were.

And finally, Bhartṛhari's *sphoṭa*, in its *advaitic* approach, does not make a distinction between the sacred and the secular. All *śabda* according to Bhartṛhari, irrespective of whether it is sacred or secular, is capable of being transformed back into *śabdabrahman*. This was an important step as a prelude in the development of Indian aesthetics where ideas of the sacred or holy or religious did not matter, what mattered was the intrinsic quality of the *śabda* and its capacity of evoking a transformation in the consciousness of the listener. *Śabda* and its consequent *sphoṭa* was an agent of transformation, and not just communication.

Bhartṛhari's *sphoṭa* is more than a theory of language. The strong hints of aesthetics, albeit in a seminal form, are hard to miss. It has provided aesthetics in the Indian tradition not only with a definition but given it a validity and structure. Aesthetics has sometimes been referred to as *alaṃkāra śāstra* or the science of ornamentation. While *alaṃkāra* remains an integral part of *śabda*, Bhartṛhari's *sphoṭavāda* has clearly shown that *śabda* is the *saṅketa* of *saccidānanda*, waiting to be driven to its ultimate end point through *artha*. In other words it was Bhartṛhari who showed that *śabda*, understood as verbal testimony, is a valid means of cognition, not just at the level of *yajña* but even as *kāvya*. Traditionally, Indian philosophers had given credence to *pratyakṣa* or perception and *anumāna* or inference as means of knowledge or *pramāṇa*. Although *śabda* could be considered as a form of auditory perception, for some have argued that "all *pramāṇas* are preceded by (sensory) perception".[69] Bhartṛhari's *sphoṭa* elevates *śabda* to *śabdabodha* and lets us interpret *śabda* in a wider perspective and apply the term *śabda* to *kāvya* and from there to all forms of art. *Sphoṭa* provided the mechanism for the understanding of what gives meaning to *śabda*, not denying *śabda* its own bonafides. This quintessentially is the essence of aesthetics in the Indian tradition. The concept of *artha* as enunciated by the Realists, the Vedāntins or the Buddhists could never serve as the fountainhead of aesthetics as Bhartṛhari's *sphoṭa* has done in the Indian tradition. Further, Bhartṛhari's *sphoṭa* provides the bridge between aesthetics and Tantra, and specially Kāśmīr Śaivism. It forershadows and anticipates the concept of *ābhāsa* and *bhoga* so central to the Kāśmīr Śaivites. Bharata's *rasavāda* although of fundamental importance to Indian aesthetics cannot provide the complete framework of aesthetics as does Bhartṛhari's *sphoṭavāda*. It cannot be denied that Bharata did not explicate the entire gamut of aesthetic concepts from his doctrine of *rasa*. The reasons for this are not readily available and may have to be searched in socio-historical factors prevalent during Bharata's times. In particular, it can be argued that Bharata based his aesthetic concepts on performing art such as *nāṭya* and Bhartṛhari on *sāhitya*, and that this was responsible for the change in emphasis.[70] There is evidence to show that *vācika abhinaya* or the spoken word in Bharata's days was of lesser importance, and that it gained in importance over the centuries till the time of Bhartṛhari. Although such theories must remain at best speculative, there is hardly any doubt that Bhartṛhari's *sphoṭavāda* put an indelible and distinct imprint of *kāvya* on Indian aesthetics, an impression that was to spill into the plastic and visual arts that followed. Art in India was to become visual poetry, the *kavi* the prototype of the artist, and art encounter not different from poetic experience. Bhartṛhari's *sphoṭa* clearly was a harbinger of Ānandavardhana's *dhvani*, an aesthetic concept of prime importance as will be shown later, and then on to Abhinavagupta's *rasadhvani*, providing yet another reason for reserving the pride of place in Indian aesthetics to Bhartṛhari. *Sphoṭa* is an essential intermediate step from the Vedic *ṛṣi* and Bharata on the one hand to the *alaṃkārikas* on the other. One can safely assert that Bhartṛhari rather than Bharata should rightly be considered the father of Indian aesthetics.

Vāk evolved and progressed in the Indian tradition from its connotation as Vedic *śabda* to *kāvya* and then on to *śilpa* understood not just as sculpture but as all forms of visual art. An understanding of this progression is largely possible because of Bhartṛhari's *sphoṭavāda*, a doctrine that made sure that *śabda* is understood not merely as a sound but an outer expression of the spirit that lies within that imperishable *śabda*, the *akṣara*. It is not mere coincidence that the term *akṣara* is applied not only to letters but also to *brahman*, and the tradition of Indian grammarians exemplified by Bhartṛhari made sure that a word is more than just a sound symbol but an outer expression of *caitanya*. One can readily affirm with Ramakantha that "he who realises the word-reality realises the reality of consciousness".[71] It is this *akṣara*, the real form of Vāk, as opposed to the external sound that lies far beyond the range of perception. Vāk is said to reveal her divine self only to those who are able to understand her real nature, "as a loving wife, finely robed, reveal hers to her husband."[72] This progression and "realisation of the beauty that lies hidden in the Word"[73] has been possible because of the underlying thread of *artha* that connects Vāk, *kāvya* and *śilpa*.

NOTES

1. Harold G. Coward, ***The Sphota Theory of Language***. (Delhi: Motilal Banarsidass, 1986) p. viii.
2. *Ibid.*, p. 63.
3. *kim svid vakṣyāmi kimu nū maniṣye.*
   Ṛg Veda 6.9-6 taken from A.C.Bose, ***The Call of the Vedas.*** (Bombay: Bhartiya Vidya Bhavan, 1970) p. 160.
4. *catvāri vāk parimitā padāni.*
   Speech of four types have been measured.
   Ṛg Veda 1. 164.45 quoted by A.C.Bose, p. 161.
5. *yato vāco nivartante aprāpya manasā saha.*
   Where the words turn back baffled
   Taittirīya Upaniṣad. Brahmānandavallī.4
6. *ahameva vātaiva pra vāmyārabhamāṇa, bhuvanāni viśva, paro divā para enā, pṛthivyaitāvatī mahinā sambabhūva.*
   And it is I, who like the wind, breathe forth and set all existing worlds in motion. Beyond heaven and beyond the earth am I and all this I have become in my splendour.
   Ṛg Veda X.125.8 taken from A.C.Bose, ***The Call of the Vedas.*** p. 306.
7. Harold G. Coward, p. 63.
8. Bimal K. Matilal, ***Logic,Language & Reality.*** (Delhi: Motilal Banarsidass, 1985) p. 204.
9. Bimal K. Matilal, ***Perception***. (Oxford: Clarendon Press, 1986) fly-leaf.
10. Bimal K. Matilal, ***Logic, Language & Reality***. p. 204.
11. Ganganath Jha, ***Pūrva Mīmāṁsā Sūtras of Jaimini***. (Varanasi: Bhartiya Publishing House, 1979) 1.1.1.
12. Jaimini, 1.2.
13. V.K.Chari, ***Sanskrit Criticism.*** (Honolulu: Univesity of Hawaii Press,1990) p. 350.
14. Jaimini, 1.5.
15. Ganganath Jha, pp. 8-9.
16. *nityastu syāt darśanasya parārthavat.*
    The word must be regarded as eternal because the utterance is for an altogether different purpose. Jaimini, 1.18.
17. *yadā hi kṣaṇikah śabdo na śakto arthāvadharane.*
    Ślokavārtika Śabdanityatādhikaraṇam, 3-7 quoted by Francis X. D'Sa, ***Śabdapramāṇyam in Śabara and Kumārila***. (Vienna: The De Nobili Research Library, 1980) p. 114.
18. Chari, p. 356.
19. *Ibid.*
20. *Ibid.*, p. 357.
21. *tadbhūtānām kriyāthena samanāyaḥ athasya tannimittatvāt.*
    (In a sentence) all words denoting things are in close juxtaposition with the

word expressive of an action, specially because the meaning of the sentence is dependent upon the meaning of the words composing it. Jaimini 1.25.

22. *ākāṅkṣā sannidhinam ca yogyatā ceti ca trayam.*
Words are held together (in a sentence) by *ākāṅkṣā yogyatā* and *sannidhi.* K. Kunjunni Raja, ***Indian Theories of Meaning***. (Madras: The Adyar Library Series, Vol 91 1963) p. 156.
23. Francis X. D'Sa, *op. cit.*, p. 31.
24. *Ibid.*, p. 38.
25. *bhāvārthah karmaśabdas tebhyah kriyā pratīyeta, yajetatyevamadibhyah. kutah bhāvārthavad eva.*
Ibid., p. 102.
26. *Ibid.*
27. *śabdajñānam nīdanam bhavati hi jagataḥ śreyasaḥ preyasaśca.*
Ivan Kocmarek, ***Language and Release***. Sarvajñātman's Pancaprakriyā. (Delhi: Motilal Banarsidass, 1985) p. 50.
28. *pratyagātmani mukhyavṛttiḥ pratiśidhyate.*
Ibid., p. 48.
29. *Ibid.*
30. *sā sarvavidyā śilpānam kalanām copabandhinī.*
It is speech which binds all branches of knowledge of arts and crafts. ***Vākyapadīya***. 1.125 taken from ***The Vākyapadīya***, by K. Raghavan Pillai, (Delhi: Motilal Banarsidass, 1950).
31. *tan mātramupyeti krāntam caitanyam sarva jatiṣu.*
Consciousness can exist in all creatures only after it is preceded by speech. ***Vākyapadīya***. 1.126.
32. *anādinidhanam brahma śabdatattvam yadakṣaram, vivartate arthabhavena prak iya jagato yataḥ.*
That beginningless and endless One, the imperishable Brahman of which the essential nature is Word, which manifests itself into objects and from which is the creation of the Universe. ***Vākyapadīya***. 1.1.
33. *śabdeśvevāśritā śaktiḥ viśvasyāsya nibandhanī.*
That power which is based on words controls this universe. ***Vākyapadīya***. 1.118.
34. *na so sti pratyayo loke yah śabdanugamādṛte.*
In this world no comprehension is possible except as accompanied by speech. ***Vākyapadīya***. 1.123.
35. *prāhur mahāntam vṛṣabham yena sāyujyamiṣyate.*
Vākyapadīya. 1.131.
36. D'Sa, p. 9.
37. K. Raja, p. 109.
38. B. Matilal, ***Perception***. p. 398.
39. Harold G. Coward, ***Bhartṛhari.*** (Boston: Twayne Publishers, 1976) p. 82.
40. K. Raja, p. 145.
41. *Ibid.*, p. 141.
42. *eko nāvayavah śabdah.*

(A sentence) is an utterance which is one and devoid of parts.
Vākyapadīya. 2.1.

43. *vibhāgaiḥ prakriyābhedam avidvān pratipadyate.*
The word has no parts; how then can its meaning have any parts?
Vākyapadīya. 2.13.
44. *arthaḥ sahabhūteṣu vartate.*
The meaning of the sentence which is completed in the individual words (thus) resides in the collection.
Vākyapadīya. 2.115.
45. *rūpam sarvapadārthānam vākyārtha upa nibandhanam.*
The nature of all word meaning is dependent on the meaning of the sentence.
Vākyapadīya. 2.324a.
46. Gaurinath Sastri, ***The Philosophy of Word and Meaning.*** (Calcutta: Sanskrit College, Calcutta Sanskrit College Research Series No. V) p. 99.
47. *Ibid.*, p. 99.
48. K.A.Subramania Iyer, ***Bhartṛhari.*** (Poona: Deccan College Postgraduate and Research Institute, 1969) p. 182.
49. *ekasyaivātmano bhedau śabdarthāvapṛthak sthitau.*
Speech and meaning being the two halves of one fact, are not distinct and separable. ***Vākyapadīya.*** 2.31b.
50. Kālidāsa, Raghuvasa 1.1.
51. *dvāv upādanaśabdeṣu śabdau śabdavido viduḥ, eko nimittam śabdānām paror'the prayujyate.*
Grammarians consider that there are two word-entities in functional words; one is the cause of the words and the other is used in connection with meanings. ***Vākyapadīya***. 1.44.
52. B. Matilal, ***Perception***. p. 397.
53. Kālidāsa, ***Śākuntala***. 4.22.
54. H. Coward, ***Sphoṭa Theory of Language***. p. 112.
55. *Ibid.*, p. 113.
56. R. Pandeya, ***The Problem of Meaning***. (Delhi: Motilal Banarsidass, 1963) p. 40.
57. *vikārasya śabdasya nimmitairvikṛto dhvaniḥ, upalabdhau nimmitatvam upayāti prakāsavat.*
Just as light (reveals objects), the speech sounds produced by (their) causes become the cause of the immutable word.
Vākyapadīya. 1.94.
58. *asatye vartmani stithvā tataḥ satyam samīhate.*
Remaining on the path of unreality one strives after Reality.
Vākyapadīya. 2.238.
59. *ātmarūpam yathā jñāne jñeyarūpam ca dṛśyate, artharūpam tathā śabde svarūpam ca prakāśate.*
Just as in (perceptual) knowledge there can be seen both itself and the object of knowledge so in the word there appears the meaning element and the formal element. ***Vākyapadīya.*** 1.50.

60. *grāhyatvam grāhyakatvam ca dve śaktī tejaso yathā, tathaiva sarvaśabdānāmete pṛthagavasthite.*
Just as light has two powers, namely the power of being perceived and the power of causing the perception of objects, similarly all words have these two distinct powers. ***Vākyapadīya.*** 1.55.
61. *prakāśakaprakāśyatvam kāryakāraṇarūpatā, antamātrātmanastasya śabdatattvasya sarvadā.*
The power of being the revealer and the revealed, the cause and the effect, eternally belongs to the word principle which is essentially internal. ***Vākyapadīya.*** 2.32.
62. *vyapadeśe padārthānām anya sattāupacarikī, sarvāvasthāsu sarveṣāmanyarūpasya darśikā.*
Vakyapadiya. III, 1.9.
quoted by Iyer, ***Bhartṛhari.*** p. 477.
63. H. Coward, ***Sphoṭa Theory of Language***. p. 124.
64. *viccheda grahane arthānām pratibhānyaiva jāyate, vākyārtha iti tamahuḥ padārthairūpapāditam.*
When the word-meanings in a sentence are detached and understood a different flash of insight is produced. That presented by the word-meanings is described as the meaning of the sentence.
Vākyapadīya. 2.143.
65. G. Sastri, *op. cit.*, p. 251.
66. *sakṛtpr uyuktaśabdsya viramya vyāpārānupapattiḥ.*
from *Nayanaprasadini* commentary on *Tattvapradipika*
quoted by G. Sastri, p. 175.
67. B. Matilal, ***Perception***. p. 257.
68. R. Pandeya, p. 244.
69. B. Matilal, ***Perception***. p. 22.
70. Personal communication from Prof. V. Subramanian of Carleton University, Ottawa, Ontario, Canada. Prof. Subramanian is a noted sociologist of the arts.
71. *vāgbrahmaṇi niṣṇataḥ cidbrahmapnoti yena kathayanti, siddhir'muktis ca parā nādajñānakriyā ca saphaleti.*
Ramakantha, ***Nada Karika.*** 20.
Ramakantha was a twelfth-century Kāśmīr Śaivite. His entire *kārikā* has been quoted by K. Sivaraman in "The Word as a Category of Revelation", in ***Revelation in Indian Tho***
ught. Harold Coward and Krishna Sivaraman (editors) (Calfornia: Dharma Publishing, 1977) pp. 54-59.
72. *jāyeva patyā uśatī suvāsāḥ.*
Ṛg Veda X.71.4.
from Bose, ***The Call of the Vedas***. p. 163.
73. *bhadraisām lakṣmīrnihitādhivāci.*
Ṛg Veda X.71.2
Ibid., p. 162.

Chapter 3

Sākṣātartha: Rasabrahman

raso vai saḥ. rasam hyevāyam labdhvā ānandi bhavati
Taittirīya Upaniṣad, 2.7

The initial epistemic encounter with the art object leads to the first of the two levels of meaning, the *sākṣātartha*. The aesthete having availed himself of the appropriate *pramāṇas* undertakes the sensual appreciation and understanding of the object. It is important to note that for us, in the Indian tradition, *manas* or the emotive mind is considered the sixth sense-organ; therefore, this initial assessment includes not only a response to the art object's sensuous data but its emotive qualitites as well. *Sākṣātartha* is therefore the epistemic response to *rasa* and *rūpa* or aesthetic emotion and aesthetic form. A feature of the *sākṣātartha* is that, in the prepared aesthete, it is spontaneous and direct, and not reasoned and indirect, as it is in the case of the *parokṣārtha*. At the state of *sākṣātartha* we are letting the senses be flooded by the objective artistic data and formulating not only our artistic judgement but letting our entire being respond to it, emphasising that its directness and spontaniety will not admit any superficiality. It is important to make the distinction between *artha* which is objective epistemic artistic judgement from *ānanda* which is the subjective aesthetic response which comes later. *Artha* is a necessary and important intermediary between the art object and the aesthete's subjective response, for without *artha* the entire art experience will become a superficial and trivial art encounter. It is *artha* that ensures that art will lead to transcendent knowledge and an ultimately blissful experience. In positing two levels of meaning it is important to point out that the two levels of meanings are intrinsically and organically related, with the *parokṣārtha,* or deeper meaning, stemming from the *sākṣātartha*, or initial meaning. This is in keeping with the Indian epistemic tradition which regards *pratyakṣa* as the ultimate *pramāṇa*. This chapter and the next will discuss the *sākṣātartha* that stems from aesthetic emotion and aesthetic form. It will mainly present the epistemic dynamics, and not engage in an historical evaluation, of the art object.

In the Indian scheme of the goals of life or *puruṣārtha*, emotional fulfilment has an important place, and in keeping with that schema, which dominates every aspect of Indian thought, it is postulated that each activity of man fulfills itself only when it leads to *mokṣa* or spiritual freedom. *Kāma* or emotional fulfilment is one of the four ends of life. The *rasa* theory of Indian art is an example of how emotions can be utilised and transformed through the medium of art for a higher end.

The Indian tradition deals at length with the origin and function of emotion as a part of the human consciousness. Early in the tradition it is made clear that emotional processes are an integral part of a larger and more exalted state of being and not merely the flickerings of a superficial mental state. There is no better place to start an examination of emotion as a human faculty than the Vedas. We are told that the *dhīyas* or thought-visions of the Ṛg Vedic *ṛṣis* arise from a coming together of the *hṛd* or heart, *manas* or mind and *maniṣa* or intuitive reflection, "*indraya hṛd manasa maniṣa...dhīyo marjāyanta*".[1] The Vedic scholar Gonda explains at length the function of the 'heart' and the association of the 'heart' with the *rasa* of *soma* in the vision of the Vedic poets: "the process which the visions undergo in the heart is in the ***Ṛg Veda*** explicitly described as purification or clarification".[2] He reminds us that the "*soma* juices which are drunk by the officiants are believed to be in their hearts"[3] and "by finding with, or in the heart the light of higher insight ... one becomes an all seeing-*ṛṣi*."[4] Gonda points out that terms such as "ocean in the heart" and "sieve of the heart" are commonly used in the Ṛg Vedic hymns. It is clear, he writes, that the term 'heart' does not denote a physiological or anatomical organ but the "centre of the integral individual".[5] According to Caraka, the ancient Indian physician, "the heart is the only seat of consciousness".[6]

Modern aestheticians have drawn on the Vedic concept of 'heart' in their interpretations of the dynamics of *rasa*. Coomaraswamy draws our attention to the Upaniṣadic term *antar-hṛdaya-ākāśa* or the "immanent space in the heart...at which place the only possible experience of reality takes place"; "it is the totality of this ideal space at the innermost core of our being where only the full content of life can be experienced."[7] Rabindranath Tagore refers to the "cave of the heart...where the song is heard".[8]

All this leaves hardly any doubt that in the Indian tradition emotional consciousness, designated 'heart' is not the seat of raw or gross emotions, not a mere psychological entity, but rather a focal point of emotional, intellectual and intuitive integration, a point of refined emotional realisation and one that can lead the individual to a transcendent state. It is important to keep this in mind when one discusses *rasa* or aesthetic emotion, for aesthetic emotion is not just a heightened state or another type of emotion, but emotion purified, refined and transformed into an altogether new state. An understanding of this constitutes the essence of the epistemic dynamics of *rasa*.

The concept of *rasa* is fundamental to Indian art and has provided the continuity in its long and unbroken tradition. It is the thread which has held all its various and diverse art forms together. The meaning and implication of the term *rasa* has evolved over the millennia. In the ***Ṛg Veda***, *rasa* seems to mean juice or sap or essence, and in keeping with the general tenor of the ***Ṛg Veda*** it perhaps was meant in a botanical sense. In the *Upaniṣads* however, *rasa* came to acquire a more exalted meaning, signifying *brahman* as the bliss immanent in the universe, and it was this that led the Upaniṣadic *ṛṣis* to declare "*raso vai saḥ*"[9]. It would be appropriate to state that the term *rasa* in the *Upaniṣads* did not mean aesthetic emotion as it came to called later on, but rather referred to the core or essence of one's being. It was Bharata writing in the first century BC, (Bharata's dates vary from the third century BC to the third century AD) who made *rasa* the cornerstone of aesthetic experience.

From Bharata to Ānandavardhana and then to Abhinavagupta, with many commentators in between and beyond, the concept of *rasa* grew integrally and evovled within the tradition. The contribution of Kāśmir Śaivism to the development of the *rasa* theory is a very significant one, although, *rasa* has not remained the sole possession of any one school. In this chapter, our concern is not with the historical evolution of the concept of *rasa* but with the dynamics of *rasa* as a process of transformation, which occurs in the hearts of the artist as well as the aesthete, through the medium of the art object. In the Indian tradition the term 'art object' is used in its widest sense and includes not only performing and visual art but in particular *kāvya* or poetry.

It has already been mentioned in the first chapter that Indian aestheticians hesitate to probe the heart of the artist, preferring to view artistic creativity as an unfathomable mystery. The emphasis in our exploration of the *advaita* of art from the *rasa* standpoint is on the experience of the aesthete and not on art creation. The following discussion leads to the understanding of the transformation of raw emotion to aesthetic emotion, which takes place in the heart of the artist and is re-enacted in the heart of the aesthete.

Bharata is considered by some to be the father of the *rasa* school and this has important implications for Hindu aesthetics. In the first place *nāṭya* or dramatic expression, for that was what Bharata wrote mainly about, becomes the artistic form ***par excellence*** and a model for all other art forms. *Nāṭya* is a performing art, which integrates several different major art forms such as *nāṭya*, *nṛtya*, *saṅgīta* and *kāvya* or dance-drama, pure dance, music and poetry, along with other minor arts such as stage decorating and the making of costumes. The dialogue between King Mārkaṇḍeya and a *ṛṣi* quoted in the ***Viṣṇudharmottara Purāṇa*** further brings out the interrelation of one art form with another in the classical Indian tradition.[10] In dance-drama, *rasa* or aesthetic emotion is aroused on the basis of specific dramatic situations, and this principle is extended to all other art forms. This explains, for example, the intense dramatic quality of Indian sculpture. Another feature of *nāṭya* as an art form is that it highlights the important role the spectator or the art beholder plays in the dynamics of art. And finally, Bharata points out the mythical origin of *nāṭya* as an activity mainly for "*krīḍā*"[11] or sport, which subsequent aestheticians uphold, asserting that the main purpose of art is *prīti* or delight, understood in its association with *rasa* as pleasure that transcends the senses. By making *krīḍā*, the spontaneous play of delight, the basis of art creation and appreciation, Indian aestheticians seek to free art from primarily utilitarian or didactic concerns. The implications of the idea of spontaneous play as creativity for the *advaita* of art will be explored in the concluding chapter. Here, it suffices to emphasise that both for the artist and for the aesthete, the well-spring of *rasa* is a spontaneous heart.

Bharata's *Nāṭyaśāstra* exalts the position of the *kavi* or the poet and sets him up as the prototype of all other artists. This distinguishes aestheticians from art historians, for the latter take their cue from visual art, with a preference for monumental art, whereas Indian aestheticians give pride of place to the *kavi* and *kāvya*. While not ignoring the contributions of the folk artist, in classical Indian art, ideologically, if not chronologically, the *kavi* came first and should be regarded as the first artist. It is the *kavi* that provides the link between the Vedas and aesthetic tradition. In the ***Ṛg Veda***, the term *ṛṣi* is used interchangeably with *kavi*, emphasising that the poet is not only an artist but a seer, that he has not only imagination but vision. When Rabindranath Tagore says "ami kavi", he is, in no uncertain terms, tracing his lineage to the Vedic *ṛṣis*.

The Indian tradition places a heavy responsibility on the poet and in turn requires that he be "well versed not only in poetic composition but learned in the ways of the world",[12] emphasising the *śikṣā* or the training that is required of him. However, the *kavitābīja* or the 'seed of poetry', it is said quite clearly, is the *pratibhā* or the poetic genius. The 'seed of poetry' is nurtured by training, but is not produced by it. In fact, what the later aestheticians term *pratibhā* is not different from the *dhī* or the 'thought-vision' of the Vedic poets. Gnoli, a modern aesthetician, says in his interpretation that *pratibhā* arises for a moment from the contact of the poets's mind with the essential nature of the *ātman*.[13]

It is important to note that the tradition does not excessively probe into the poet's genius beyond maintaining that it is a *saṃskāra*[14] or a "latent (psychic) impression" brought forward from past births. The term *saṃskāra* carries with it undertones of *karma* and rebirth, concepts deep in the Indian consciousness, giving rise to popular statements such as, 'poets are born, not made'. Not resting with these attributes the *kavi* has been further called a "*prajāpati*"[15] a term usually reserved for the Lord of the Universe, which not only puts the poet on a pedestal, but more importantly gives a secure place to his creation, namely, *kāvya*. We are told that so skilled is the poet that protean are his themes and equally endless his creations.

Bharata defines *rasa* as "*tatra vibhāva anubhāva vyabhicārī saṁyogāt rasa niṣpattiḥ*",[16] "*rasa* is produced by a combination of determinants, consequents and complementary psychological states." Interpreted differently, it means that *rasa* is created by the artistic coming together of the primary emotion, the secondary emotional manifestations of that primary emotion and the landscape in which the emotion is played out. Several important ideas stem from this rather cryptic definition of Bharata, ideas that have been commented on exhaustively by later aestheticians, but the most important concept in this definition is that the cardinal process underlying *rasa* is one of transformation, from *sthūla* to *sūkṣma* or gross to the subtle, from *laukika* to *alaukika* or mundane to supramundane, from *sāṃsārik* or worldly realism to artistic reality, from individual to universal and from the particular to the general. In interpreting the transformation that takes place in the heart of the artist, later aestheticians have implied such processes as 'distancing' or 'detachment' and 'quietening'. The classical example given in the texts is that of the poet Vālmiki, who when he was grieved with the poignant death of the *krauñca* couple, did not write of his personal sorrow, but converted this deeply emotional experience into the epic of ***Rāmāyaṇa***.[17] The implications of the link between *rasa* and these psychological attitudes of detachment and quietening, for the *advaita* of art, will be explored in the concluding chapter. Here it is sufficient to note that, whereas detachment and quietening are hard-won fruits in the traditional diciplines of *yoga*, they arise spontaneously in the heart of the artist, as antecedents of his creative inspiration.

The word '*niṣpatti*' in Bharata's definition, the dictionary definition of which is 'to bring about', is open to at least two interpretations. It can be argued that *rasa* is a totally new creation, a new state, from the basic emotive situation. It can equally be argued that it is not a new creation, but merely an uncovering or revelation, not cognition but recognition. *Rasa* will then become an uncovering of that which is already present in the depths of consciousness, and *rasa niṣpatti* would then be a revelation to oneself of one's own depths. Bhaṭṭa Nāyaka championed this latter theory. He is quoted as saying, "that the real meaning of birth (*niṣpatti*) as used by Bharata cannot be perception or production or manifestation, rather it lies in something entirely different...namely in revelation (*bhāvanā*)." *Rasa* is realised when, "the thick layer of mental stupor occupying our consciousness is lifted."[18] The Upaniṣadic implication in this concept of *rasa*, namely that *vidyā* or knowledge is none other than the removal of *avidyā* or ignorance, is clearly evident. According to this interpretation, *rasa* is ultimately a form of self-knowledge, and this has profound implications for our inquiry into the *advaita* of art. We shall return to this idea of *rasa* as self-knowledge in our discussion of the *rasa* experience of the aesthete. Before concluding this section it is important to make one further point and that is this: *rasa* is best suggested and never overtly expressed and therefore strictly speaking it should be called *rasadhvani*. The dynamics of *dhvani* will be discussed in the section on *parokṣārtha* but since the cognition of *rasa*, even though it is suggested, is essentially a process of *mānasika pratyakṣa*, and therefore falls under the heading of *sākṣātartha*. In being suggested rather than directly expressed, the enjoyment of *rasa* requires that the aesthete dip into his creative faculties for the enjoyment of that *rasa*.

A special quality of *rasa* is said to be its ability to be transmitted or to flow in the same state and without change from the artist to a *sahṛdaya* or a prepared aesthete, a quality unique to *rasa* as opposed to *bhāva* or raw emotion. The tradition affords equal status to the art beholder as to the artist, but in turn expects the same training or *śikṣā* and assumes the same inherent capacity or *saṃskāra* in the beholder who is undertaking an art experience. Thus the capacity to experience art, is itself an art, and the aesthete should be given the same standing as the artist. Abhinavagupta says, "the poet's experience is the same as the spectator's".[19] Commenting on this statement of Abhinavagupta, Hiriyanna remarks that the "appreciation of poetry is essentially the same as the creation of it."[20] This movement of *rasa*, which aestheticians have compared to the movement of the seed through the tree to the fruit,[21] takes place not only because of the capacity of *rasa* to flow from the artist to the aesthete through the art object, but also, and equally importantly, because of the capacity or readiness with which the aesthete accepts the art experience, as readily as, "dry wood accepts fire".[22]

Abhinavagupta defines a *sahṛdaya* as "those people who are capable of identifying with the subject-matter since the mirror of their heart has been polished, through constant recitation and study of poetry and who sympathetically respond in their own hearts; he is one whose heart melts and whose heart is not hardened by the readings of dry texts on metaphysics."[23] The link of the term '*sahṛdaya*' with the Vedic *hṛd* is obvious, emphasising that the aesthete, like the poet, analyses poetry not at a superficial mental level but brings to bear all his higher faculties on the art experience. The term 'polishing' in Abhinavagupta's definition also has the Upaniṣadic implication of 'removal of ignorance'.

It is only the 'polished heart' of the aesthete that is capable of total identification with the art object, a process called *tanmayībhāva*. *Tanmayībhāva* signifies that the heart of the *sahṛdaya* engages itself with the art object seriously, deliberately and completely, leaving no room for feelings such as, "it is happening to me, no it is not happening to me",[24] removing the duality of the subject-object consciousness and assuring a total and advaitic art experience. *Tanmayībhāva* implies the concepts of 'distancing' and 'detachment'. Identification with the art object or situation is not possible if the aesthete becomes personally involved with it, clings to it or craves to possess it. Thus the height of aesthetic ecstasy takes place when the self, released from the burden of its egoistic afflictions, finds complete identity with the aesthetic situation, a process called *sādhāraṇīkṛta*. Gnoli notes that "the task of generalisation carried out by the poetic expression breaks the barrier of the limited "I" and eliminates in this way the interests, demands and aims associated with it."[25] The *rasa* theory regards the process of identification as a distinct and positive phase of the art experience, consisting mainly of an expansion and enlargement of the self on a new plane of existence. Identification implies "an urge for a 'withness' with the object, for becoming one with it; this urge is in the form of a drive which seeks constantly to transcend the self to a plane of existence, where the unhampered consciousness can dilate on and enjoy an uninterrupted delight."[26]

Tanmayībhāva cannot take place unless the fetters of the superficial mind have been released. Understood in this sense, *tanmayībhāva*, where the *rasika* melts his personality in the art experience, cannot be totally different from a *yogic dhyāna* in which the mind of the *yogī* achieves oneness with the object of concentration.

The term *sahṛdaya* for a prepared aesthete, focuses attention once again on the seat of art experience namely *hṛd*, which as explained earlier, is not merely a centre of raw emotions but a focus of emotional, intellectual and volitional forces that are capable of lifting the entire personality to a higher state of being. Śrī Aurobindo uses the term "supra-rational aesthetic soul"[27] as synonym for *hṛd*. The parallels between a *kavi* and a *sahṛdaya* are too obvious to be missed. Also the link of the term *sahṛdaya* with the Vedic *hṛd* is very clear, emphasising that the aesthete, like the poet, experiences art, not at a superficial mental level, but by bringing to bear all his higher faculties on the art object. Between the two there is a dynamic relationship, artist and aesthete, bound together by *rasa*, reminding us of Tagore's words: "Idea craves to be embodied in form and form seems to release itself in idea."[28]

Our exploration of the *advaita* of art leads us to questions about the specific nature of the expansion of consciousness that is indicated as *rasa*. Traditional aestheticians seem to hesitate to answer this question, and they point to the indescribable sense of wonder or *adbhuta* aroused in the aesthete who experiences oneness with the art object. Aestheticians speak of how *rasa* arises and how it affects the aesthete, but a valid question that can be asked is: what exactly is *rasa*? Much can be asked and a lot has been written about the *rasa* experience. Etymologically, it can be said, *rasyate iti rasaḥ*, what is relished is *rasa*. Equally cryptically, it has been said, "*pratītireva viśiṣṭa rasana*",[29] *rasa* experience is a special kind of knowing. Yet these statements are not altogether satisfactory and it would be not unreasonable to seek in the *śāstras* a description of this unique aesthetic state called *rasa*. Abhinavagupta calls it, "a form of self-contemplation",[30] a "magic flower",[31] a "life emotion freed of its limiting factors".[32] Coomaraswamy suggests *saṃvega*, which he translates as 'aesthetic shock', as the essence of *rasa* experience, and goes on to explain that *saṃvega* is "by no means merely an interested aesthetic response but much rather ... disinterested aesthetic contemplation."[33] He goes on to say that "in the deeper experience that can be induced by a work of art our very being is shaken."[34] Viśvanātha summarises the *rasa* experience as, "*camatkāra*"[35] or a sense of wonder, characterised by *cittavistara* or expansion of the heart.

However, after one has exhausted all similes and adjectives to describe the *rasa* experience, one is forced into a Upaniṣadic *neti neti* situation to describe the *rasa* state, as does Abhinavagupta, when he says that "*rasa* is altogether different from *saṃyagjñāna* (correct knowledge), *bhrānti* (erroneous cognition), *anadhyāvasāya* (uncertainty), *vijñāna* (ordinary knowledge); it is distinct from worldly objects and also different from such things as their imitation, reflection and pictorial presentation, determination, fancy, magic and so on."[36] This statement of Abhinavagupta again reminds us that *rasa* is hard to define in concrete terms and remains a "magic flower", rooted in ordinary emotional and sensory states, it blooms into an ineffable rapture and sense of wonder.

Related to the question, "what is *rasa*?", is the question, "is *rasa* one or many?" If there are many *rasas*, we would have to raise the question whether some *rasas* or some types of *rasas* are more conducive than others in fostering an *advaita* of art. There is considerable discussion about the exact number of *rasas*. Bharata postulated eight basic *rasas*. Later a ninth, the *śānta rasa* was added. From nine the number kept on growing and several subtypes were added. Ramachandra and Gunachandra divide the eight aesthetic sentiments into two classes viz. pleasant and painful; the erotic, comic, heroic, marvellous and quiet are classified as being pleasant, whereas the pathetic, furious, odious and terrible are categorised as painful.[37] However, there is agreement that, even though the *rasa* experience may begin with specific emotions, it culminates in a sense of wonder, which transcends all classifications and divisions of emotion. The sense of wonder indicates a unique and unified *rasa* experience which goes beyond the pleasure and pain of specific emotions. Raghavan in concluding his discussion on the number of *rasas*, accepts that "all the *rasas* are but forms of some one of them...*rasa* is *rasa*. It is one. It is like the *brahman* or the *sphoṭa*. *Rasa* is fundamentally one and hence it is that Bharata refers to it in the singular number."[38] Mammaṭa supports the unified concept of *rasa* and declares that "the suggestion of *rasa* is counted as only one kind on the basis of general characterisation, namely non-perceptibility of the sequence."[39]

The idea of a unified *rasa* experience is suited particularly to our quest for an *advaita* of art, for ultimately we are concerned not so much with the preparatory dynamics of *rasa* and the specific emotions linked with it, as with its culmination and eventual fulfilment. The culmination of *rasa* will be the theme of the concluding section of this chapter, where we will focus on the telling statement that the tasting of *rasa* is the 'twin' of the tasting of *brahman*.

In our discussion of the origin and dynamics of *rasa* we have suggested a correspondence between the expansion of meaning reverberating from the art object and the expansion of *rasa* towards an exalted state of wonderment. We now explore what the texts say about the highest reaches of *rasa*. We shall focus on three ideas: *rasa* as a supramundane state, the experience of *rasa* as the 'twin' of the experience of *brahman* and the linking of outflowing dynamism (*vimarśa*) and inward rest (*viśrānti*) in the *rasa* experience.

The key to the understanding of the *rasa* experience lies in the concept of *bhuj* (to enjoy) or *bhoga* (fruition). *Bhuj* for Bhaṭṭa Nāyaka meant aesthetic pleasure arising because of release from individuality and specificity, a state described by him as *sādharaṇīkṛta* or universalisation. Gnoli notes that the task of generalisation carried out by the poetic expression breaks the barrier of the limited "I" and eliminates in this way the interests, demands and aims associated with it.[40] An *alaukika* state, it may be argued, can stem also from a religious experience. Indian aestheticians addressed themselves to this problem in no uncertain terms, and have said "the Vedas issue commands like masters and the *itihāsas* give us good counsel after the manner of friends; but poetry differs from them and is unique in its capacity to instruct one delightfully like one's sweetheart."[41] Abhinavagupta echoes the same feelings when he categorises *śāstras* as "*laukika*".[42] Bhaṭṭa Nāyaka notes that, "this *rasa* is poured forth spontaneously by the word which is like a cow, for love of her children; for this reason it is different from that which is (laboriously) milked by the *yogins*."[43] The almost pejorative reference to learning and the learned in this verse are too obvious to be missed, a position that is consistently taken by all *rasavādins*. It is significant that though *rasa* is not noetic in nature, it leads the *rasika* to a state of intuitive knowledge. Ray reminds us that "the language of art is not the language of intellectual but of intuitive knowledge, knowledge gained through feeling and experience and hence through actual living."[44] He goes on to say that, "art experience is an experience of being, not of knowing."[45]

Indian aestheticians maintain that the artist is not concerned with giving us a 'photographic' description of an emotional situation as it actually occurs in the everyday *laukika* world. The emotional situation is transformed by the poet's sensitive heart and his imaginative power. The art object expresses the poet's vision of an emotional situation, and not raw emotion. As a consequence art objects do not claim to satisfy egoistic or practical needs. Their appeal is not limited to specific persons and they can be enjoyed by all sensitive aesthetes. Since art objects do not bolster anyone's ego or become confined to anyone's specific needs, they can be enjoyed in and for themselves.

The essence of the ultimate *rasa* experience is found is this famous and often quoted verse of Viśvanātha:

> *Rasa* is tasted by qualified persons. It is tasted by virtue

> of the emergence of *sattva*. It is made up of full intelligence, beatitude and self-luminosity. It is void of contact with any other knowable thing, twin brother to the tasting of *brahman*.[46]

This leaves no doubt about the exalted state of *rasa*. The transformation that started with the raw emotional state completes itself in the *camatkāra* or the state of aesthetic wonder or rapture. The *rasika* in a state of *camatkāra* has left the ordinary world of nature and history, with its spatial and temporal limitations, a world of dualities of pleasure and pain, of subject-object consciousness, and has taken an aesthetic leap into a world of bliss. It is important to point out that Indian aestheticians do not discuss the psychology or the intermediate steps of this "aesthetic leap".[47] "The aesthetic experience though composed of the same material as the ordinary states, breaks away in the intuitive moment from its empirical base and becomes momentarily a new and different kind of experience."[48] The *camatkāra* of the *rasika* is a totally new state of consciousness, a state of "pure contemplation, characterised by a total absence of conceptual thought... According to Indian thought the whole realm of intuitive knowledge wherein the aesthetic also partakes, belongs to the highest order of human consciousness."[49]

It is significant that the *camatkāra* of *rasa* refers not only to a transformation of the emotional state with which the experience started, but a total transformation of the personality of the *rasika*. It becomes clear why the Ṛg Vedic *ṛṣis* considered *hṛd* as only one component of the larger *dhī*, which signifies intuitive understanding or wisdom, for one cannot alter the *hṛd* without affecting the *dhī*.

Aestheticians of the Indian tradition maintain that the exalted wonderment of *camatkāra* is brought about by a combination of *druti* or fluidity, *vistāra* or enlargement and *vikāsa* or expansion,[50] which are states of consciousness brought about by aesthetic contemplation, and which aid in breaking the limitations of the ego. It has rightly been said that, "Aesthetic experience is a modality of this unbounded consciousness, characterised by the immersion of the subject in the aesthetic object to the exclusion of everything else."[51]

The one single feature of the *camatkāra* of aesthetic experience, which truly makes it an *alukika* experience, is *viśrānti*. This is defined as resting on one's own state of consciousness, a state also described as *svaprakāśa* or self-luminous. *Sāṃsārika* or *laukika* experiences, and raw emotion in particular, lack the all important quality of *viśrānti*, for as Abhinavagupta would say, this type of consciousness is not free from "obstacles", "*vītavighnapratītigrāhyo bhāva eva rasaḥ*".[52] He goes on to enumarate numerous obstacles because of which "he (the aesthete) cannot immerse his consciousness in them (the art object), so that no rest...can take place."[53] The implications of the term *viśrānti* become evident only when it is recognised that Abhinavagupta and many other aestheticians espoused Kāśmīr Śaivism. The metaphysics of Kāśmīr Śaivism provides for two conceptually distinguishable, but existentially inseparable, modes of consciousness: *viśrānti* where consciousness is turned inward, abiding in its own luminosity, and *vimarśa* where consciousness moves outward to embrace objects. The outward movement of *vimarśa* is followed by a reversal, whereby consciousness 'returns' as it were, and rests in its own luminosity or self-awareness. This epistemic rest is technically called *viśrānti*. It is in the understanding of this *viśrānti* or consciousness resting on itself, that the essential feature of Kāśmir Śaivism, a school to which Abhinavagupta and many other aestheticians belonged, comes through. "The intimate essence of consciousness according to the Śaiva is beatitude, a resting in oneself to the exclusion of everything else."[54] And it is in the understanding of this concept of *vimarśa* followed by *viśrānti* that Kāśmīr Śaivism parts company from other philosophic schools, and in particular, from Advaita Vedānta. Pandey writes that "admission of *vimarśa* or self-consciousness in the Absolute by the Śaiva is the point of distinction between the Śaiva and the Vedāntic conception of ultimate Reality. The latter holds that the *brahman* is *santa*...it is self-shining and not self-conscious...The Śaiva maintains that the Absolute is not only self-shining but also self-conscious."[55] Pandey goes on to say that in ignorance of Abhinavagupta's system of Kāśmīr Śaivism, scholars tried to interpret his aesthetic theory in the light of systems such as Vedānta, but without success. To put it differently, one can say that although one need not follow any of the accepted schools of philosophy when discussing aesthetic experience, there is no doubt that it is best understood within the framework of Kāśmīr Śaivism. Abhinavagupta, who wrote from within the tradition of Kāśmir Śaivism, also wrote extensively on aspects of it, which makes it that much more important to choose Kāśmir Śaivism as a basic frame of reference in the understanding of the ultimate *rasa* experience.

Abhinavagupta postulates two steps in the total aesthetic experience. The first step, namely *tanmayībhāva* or total identification of the *rasika* with the artistic situation has already been touched upon. It is the stage at which the "universal mental state is apprehended...(having been) awakened from the subconscious (*saṃskāra*)"[56] by the aesthetic situation. This corresponds to the *parāsaṃvit* of Kāśmir Śaivism or the *nirvikalpa samādhi* of the Advatita Vedāntin. The Advaita Vedāntin would stop at this stage contending that this is the ultimate Reality and that one need go no further. The Śaivite, however, posits a single reality with two aspects, one transcendental and the other immanent, the Śiva *tattva* and the Śakti *tattva*, which operate inseparably at all levels of experience. Therefore the aesthetic experience cannot stop at the stage of *tanmayībhāva*, which is marked by an identity without a trace of difference. At best *tanmayībhāva* can provide the background upon which the next step should take place. The second stage of the aesthetic experience, according to Abhinavagupta, is when the universalised basic mental state sinks back as it were, to open up the Śiva and the Śakti aspects, as they operate in the aesthete, and hold these two in a tension free state of rest or dynamic harmony, which is nothing other than *ānanda*. It is only by understanding the Śiva and the Śakti *tattvas* that one comprehends fully why the Śaivites maintain that the Absolute is not only self-luminous but reflexively self-conscious of its luminosity. The *sāmarasya* of Śiva and Śakti is beautifully brought about in the androgyn image of *ardhanārīśvara*. The ultimate *rasa* experience, therefore is not just a contentless aesthetic ecstasy, but a *camatkāra* that holds the richness and splendour of *rasa* in perfect harmony with consciousness itself, a state of consciousness also called by the Śaivites '*vyatireka turīyatīta*'. The metaphysics of Kāśmir Śaivism provides for the interpretation of *rasa* as an experience in which consciousness rests within itself, holding together the subjective and the objective aspects in ecstatic harmony. Within the richness of the *rasa* experience there is both *viśrānti* and *vimarśa*. The implications of this 'two-in-oneness', a biune unity, of *viśrānti* and *vimarśa* will be discussed in chapter six. There is no negation of the world, no denial of objective experiences, for the Kāśmir Śaivite, but merely *bhoga* or pleasure, understood not in a hedonistic but in an artistic, epistemic sense. Although *rasa* was developed in the ambience of *nāṭya*, and later extended to *kāvya*, there is nothing in the dynamics of *rasa* which we have just explored, that prevents us from extending it to other art forms. *Rasa* is a state of aesthetic pleasure where an emotional experience, which began with the encounter of the artistic situation, has not been heightened but transformed into a totally new state, in which the Śiva and the Śakti *tattvas* are held in a state of dynamic equilibrium. At this stage of the aesthetic experience one can rightly acclaim "*raso vai saḥ. rasam hyevāyam labdhvā ānandi bhavati*".

NOTES

1. *indrāya hṛdā manasā maniṣā...dhiyo marjayanta.*
   Ṛg Veda, 1.61.2 quoted in J. Gonda, ***The Vision of the Vedic Poets.*** (The Hague: Mouton & Co., 1963) p. 278.
2. *samyak sravanti sarito na dhena antar hṛda manasā pūyamānaḥ.*
   Like streams, the words of religious inspiration flow, in the interior together clarified by heart and mind.
   Ṛg Veda, 1.62.2 in J. Gonda, p. 278.
3. *Ibid.*, p. 279.
4. *Ibid.*, p. 280.
5. *Ibid.*, p. 286.
6. *hṛdayam cetanādhiṣṭham ekam.*
   The heart is the only seat of consciousness.
   Ibid., p. 286.
7. *antar-hṛday-ākāśa.*

Immanent space in the heart.
Chāndogya Upaniṣad. 8.1.13 quoted in A.Coomaraswamy, ***The Transformation of Nature in Art.***(New York: Dover Publications, 1956) p. 174.

8. Ami chini go chini (from a poem in Bengali by Tagore)
A.Coomaraswamy, ***The Transformation of Nature in Art.*** p. 173.

9. *raso vai saḥ.*
rasam hyevāyam labdhvā ānandī bhavati.
For He is *rasa*, having obtained which, one attains bliss.
Taittirīya Upaniṣad. 2.7.

10. Original quotation from the ***Viṣṇudharmottara*** quoted in Mulk Raj Anand, ***The Hindu View of Art.*** (Bombay: Asia Publishing House, 1957) p. 61.

11. *krīḍanīyakam icchāma dṛśyam śrayam ca yad bhavet.*
We want something by way of diversion, something that engages both the eye and the ear.
Bharata, ***Nāṭyaśāstra.***(ed). M. Sastri, (Varanasi: Benaras Hindu University, 1972) 1.11.

12. *śaktirnipuṇatā lokaśāstra kavyādyavekṣnāt.*
kāvyājnaśikṣāyabhyāsa iti hetustadudbhave.
Poetic imagination, proficiency resulting from a study of the world, sciences, poetical compositions and the like, practice under the guidance of those who know poetry these constitute (conjointly) the cause of origin (of poetry).
Mammaṭa, ***Kāvyaprakāśa***. (ed) R.C.Dwivedi, Vol. 1 (Delhi: Motilal Banarsidass, 1977) 1.3, pp.6-7.

13. Masson and Patwardhan, ***Santarasa & Abhinavagupta's Philosophy of Aesthetics***. (Poona: Deccan College Postgraduate & Research Institute, 1970) p. 19.

14. *śakti kavitvābījarūpaḥ saṃskāraviśesaḥ.*
Poetic imagination is a peculiar latent impression which forms the seed of poetrty.
Mammaṭa, ***Kāvyaprakāśa***. 1. 3 gloss, p.6.

15. *apāre kāvyasaṃsāre kavirekaḥ prajāpatih,*
yathāsmai rocate viśvam tathedam parivartate,
śringari cetkaviḥ kavye jātam rasamayam jagat,
sa eva vītarāgaścet nīrasam sarvameva tat.
In the limitless world of poetry the poet is the sole creator. The world changes in the way he conceives it. If the poet is inspired by love then the whole world becomes filled with *rasa*. If he is devoid of *rāga* (passion) then everything becomes insipid and spiritless.
Ānandavardhana, *Dhvanyāloka*. (ed) K. Krishnamoorthy, (Delhi: Motilal Banarsidass, 1982) 3.42. p. 250.

16. *tatra vibhāva anubhāva vyabhicāri samyogād rasa niṣpattiḥ.*
Emotion in poetry comes to be expressed through the conjunction of their causes in symptoms and other (ancillary) feelings which accompany the emotions.

Bharata, ***Nāṭyaśāstra.*** 6.31, gloss

17. *kāvyasyātmā sa evārthas tathā cādikaveḥ purā, krauñcadvandvā viyogotthaḥ śokaḥ ślokatvamāgatah.*
That meaning (*rasa*) alone is the essence of poetry, so it was in the case of the first poet (Vālmīki), whose sorrow arising out of the *krauñca* couple took the form of poetry.
Ānandavardhana, ***Dhvanyāloka.*** 1.5.
18. R. Gnoli, ***The Aesthetic Experience According to Abhinavagupta.*** (Varanasi: Chowkhamba Sanskrit Series Office, 1968) p. 173-75.
19. *nāyakasya kaveḥ shrotuḥ samāno anubhuvas tataḥ.*
The experience derived from a drama by the actor, poet and listener are bound together in a common experience.
Abhinavagupta, ***Locana.*** 1.6, ***Dhvanyāloka.*** (Kāvyamālā rpt.) p. 34.
20. M.Hiriyanna, ***Indian Conception of Values.*** (Mysore: Kavyalaya Publishers, 1950) p. 343.
21. The *rasas* stand in the relation of the seed to the tree. The *rasa* present in the mind of the poet is like the seed in relation to the tree. The poem is in the position of the tree. The poetic ornaments and expressive actions are like the flowers blossoming forth from the tree. And the delectation of the spectator is the fruit. Therefore the whole world is filled with *rasa*. The poet's experience is the same as the spectator's.
Abhinavagupta, "Abhinavabhāratī." (***Nāṭyaśāstra***) 6.38.
22. *yo artho hṛdayasaṁvadī tasya bhāvo rasodbhavaḥ, śariraṃ vyāpyate tena suṣkam kāṣṭhámivāgnina.*
When a meaning, charged with emotion, strikes the heart of the symapthetic reader, it courses through his body, like fire through a dry log.
Bharata, ***Nāṭyaśāstra.*** 7.7.
23. *yeṣām kāvyānuśīlanābhyasavaśad viśadībhūte manomukure varṇanīyatanmayībhāvanāyogyatā te svahṛdayssaṃvādabhājah sahṛdayāḥ.*
Abhinavagupta, ***Locana.*** quoted in Masson and Patwardhan, *Aesthetic Rapture*. Vol 2. (Poona: Deccan College Postgraduate and Research Institute, 1970) p. 10.
24. *parasya na parasyeti mameti na mametiti ca, tadāsvāde vibhāvādeḥ paricchedo na vidyate.*
This is another's (experience) only; this is not another's—this is mine; no, this is not mine'. In the gustation of the emotive situation there is no consciousness of any such distinction.
Viśvanātha, ***Sāhityadarpaṇa.*** Hindi edition, (ed.) Satyavrat Singh (Varanasi: Chowkhamba Sanskrit Series, 1976) 3.43.
25. R. Gnoli, *op. cit.*, p. xxi.
26. S.Pandit, ***An Approach to the Indian Theory of Art and Aesthetics.*** (New Delhi: Sterling Publishers Pvt. Ltd.,1952) p.47.
27. Śrī Aurobindo, ***Hour of God.*** Volume 17. (Pondicherry: Sri Aurobindo Birth Centenary Library. Sri Aurobindo Ashram Trust, 1971) p. 224.
28. N.Ray, ***Idea and Image in Indian Art.*** (Delhi: Munshiram Manoharlal

Publishers Lvt. Ltd., 1973) p. 5.
See foot note 39 in Chapter 1.

29. *pratīreva viśiṣṭa rasanā.*
Rasa is a special type of knowing.
Abhinavagupta, ***Locana***. 2.4. p.84.

30. *svātmarūpamatiḥ svātmadvāreṇa viśvam tathā paśyan.*
His mind fixed on his own self and assuming the form of the self, he sees the world in that very form, through the contemplation of his own self.
Abhinavagupta, ***Abhinavabhāratī.*** 1.107, p. 114.

31. *vibhavādi carvaṇādhbhuta puṣpavat tatkāla sāraivoditā na pūrvapara kāla anubandhiniti laukikasvādād yogivisayac ca anya evayam rasasvadaḥ.*
The gustation of the presented emotive situation is like a magic flower, something that arises out of that presentation and lasts only for the duration of that gustation. It is not related to either the moment preceding or the moment following. Therefore this *rasa* experience is distinct from ordinary relishing as well as from the experience of *yogīs*.
Abhinavagupta, ***Locana***. 1.21, p.70.

32. *rasānatmakavīta vighnapratītigrāhyo bhāva eva rasaḥ.*
Rasa is the life emotion apprehended as being freed from its limiting factors.
Abhinavagupta, ***Abhinavabhāratī.*** 6, p. 657.

33. A.Coomoraswamy,(ed) R. Lipsey, ***Selected Papers***. Volume 1, Traditional Art and Symbolism. (Princeton: Princeton University Press, Bollingen Series, LXXXXIX, 1977) p. 182.

34. *Ibid.,* p. 184.

35. Viśvanātha, ***Sāhityadarpaṇa.*** 3.13. gloss p. 106.

36. *tatra nāṭyam nāma laukika padārtha tad anukāra vyatiriktam pratibiṁba alekhya sādraśya āropa adhyavasāya utprekṣā svapna māyendrajaladi vilakṣaṇam tad grāhakasya samyagjñāna bhrānti saṭsaya anavadhāraṇa anadhyavasāya vijñāna bhinna vṛttāntasvādarūpa saṃvedanā saṃvedyam vastu rasasvabhāvam iti.*
Rasa is altogether different from correct knowledge, erroneous cognition, uncertainty, ordinary knowledge. It is distinct from worldly objects and also different from such things as their imitation, reflection and pictorial presentation, determination, fancy, magic and so on.
Abhinavagupta, ***Abhinavabhāratī.*** 1.1, pp.15-16.

37. J. Sinha, ***Indian Psychology***. (Calcutta: Sinha Publishing House, 1961) p. 318.

38. V. Raghavan, ***The Number of Rasas***. (Adyar: The Adyar Library, 1940) p. 176.

39. *asaṃlakṣyakramatvam tu sāmānyam āśritya rasādi dhvanir ekabheda eva gaṇyate.*
But the suggestion of *rasa* etc. is counted as only one kind on the basis of general characteristic, namely, non-perceptibility of the sequence.
Mammaṭa, ***Kāvyaprakāśa***. 4.42ab gloss.

40. R.Gnoli, *op. cit.,* p.xxi.
41. Mammaṭa, ***Kāvyaprakāśa***. 1.2 gloss.
Also see Masson and Patwardhan, ***Aesthetic Rupture***. p.21.
42. *uttara karatavya aunukhyena laukikatvāt.*
A statement (such as the *śāstras* make) is said to be worldly (or mundane) because it is directed towards the performance of a duty.
Abhinavagupta, ***Locana.*** 1.18, p. 70.
43. R.Gnoli, *op. cit.,* p.48.
44. N. Ray, ***An Approach to Indian Art.*** (Chandigarh: Publication Bureau, Punjab University, 1974) p.142.
45. *Ibid.,* p. 149.
46. *sattvodrekād akhaṇḍasvaprakāśanandacinmayaḥ,*
vedyāntarasparśaśunyo brahmāsvādasahodarah.
lokottaracamatkārapräṇaḥ kaścit pramātṛbhiḥ,
svākāravad abhinnatvenāyam āsvādyate rasaḥ.
Rasa is tasted by qualified persons. It is tasted by virtue of the emergence of *sattva.* It is made up of full intelligence, beatitude and self-luminosity. It is void of contact with any other knowable thing, twin brother to the tasting of *brahman.* It is animated by a *camatkāra* of a non-ordinary nature. It is tasted as if it were our very being, in indivisibility.
Viśvanātha, ***Sāhityadarpaṇa.*** quoted in R. Gnoli,***The Aesthetic Experience according to Abhinavagupta***. p. 47.
47. S.Pandit, p. 22.
48. *Ibid.,* p. 28.
49. R. Gnoli, *op. cit.,* p. 47.
50. S.Pandit. p. 21.
51. R.Gnoli, *op. cit.,* p. 62.
also see K.C.Pandey, ***Indian Aesthetics.*** (Varanasi: Chowkhamba Sanskrit Series Office, 1959) p. 103.
52. *Ibid.,* p. 63.
53. S.Pandit, *op. cit.,* p. 23.
54. Original quotation by K.C.Pandey, in S.Pandit, *op. cit.,* p. 21.
55. K.C.Pandey, ***Indian Aesthetics***. p. 140.
56. *Ibid.,* p. 141. Pandit, p. 23.

Chapter 4

Śākṣātartha: Rūpabrahman

rūpam rūpam pratirūpam bhavati
Ṛg Veda, 6.47.18

Whatever be the medium, all art needs to express itself ultimately in plastic form. Every civilisation eventually gives visible expression to its concept of beauty; artistic vision if strong enough cannot remain mute and aniconic and must translate itself into form and acquire the immediacy of the visible and the palpable, and in so doing acquires a dimension of reality. Man, as Tagore says, is indeed a "maker of forms";[1] for he is not content to contemplate beauty, but he is impelled to give his vision a visible form. The ***Vāstūsūtra Upaniṣad*** (hereafter called *VSU*) says, "on account of having two aspects (*nirguṇa* and *saguṇa*) *brahman* acquires form."[2] It is important at the outset to recognise that the Indian visual tradition gave credence to timed rather than timeless plastic art. The *ādi śilpī* of India was a potter, in the *deśī* tradition, who made forms from terracotta, forms that were enjoyed and used but then discarded. Not only was there an inhibition of making images that would be permanent, such as the later stone images, but in the making and then unmaking of visual forms, the Indian artist saw a certain metaphysical principle. It is interesting that this seminal practice still survives in contemporary India. The immersion in water of Gaṇeśa and Durgā images, at the end of the annual festivals, is an example.

Kramrisch rightly states that "India thinks in images".[3] When it comes to visual form, there are a large, almost bewildering, number of visual images that one has to contend with even within the *mārgī* or the classical tradition, and perhaps even more in the folk or *deśī* tradition. At the outset a distinction must be drawn, for the purpose of this inquiry, between aesthetic and religious experiences associated with images within the *mārgī* tradition, emphasising that one experience need not negate the other. An aesthetic encounter stems from purely physical and sensory stimuli presented by the image, and in the prepared aesthete who is fully immersed in the tradition and who is willing to undertake a sustained epistemic inquiry, that will incorporate both a *sākṣātartha* and a *parokṣārtha*, and which can be converted to a higher experience, an experience which will be shown to be *ānanda* or spiritual bliss. A religious encounter with sacred images, on the other hand, is undertaken with a specific ritual or *sādhanā* which includes, "*abhigamana* or going to the temple or deity with the speech, the body and the mind centred on him, *upādāna* or collecing the materials of worship such as flowers, incense, sandal paste, *ijyā* or the very act of worshipping the icon and *svādhyāya* or the muttering [chanting] of the *mantra* usual to the particular cult divinity."[4] This *sādhanā* is also called *upāsanā* or *pūjā*. Generally, this *upāsanā* is undertaken as if the image was inhabited by a living being or spirit, a concept developed mainly by the Vaiṣṇava tradition and called *arcāvatāra*. This type of religious experience, subsumed under the larger rubric of *bhakti*, will not occupy our attention, as our aim is to show that the aesthetic experience has a status of its own, even when it comes to *rūpa*, and that it need not be subordinated to the traditional practices of devotion and knowledge. Our position is that a cogniser of *rūpa* can be a *rasika* and need not be a *bhakta*.

In the previous chapter we have focused on how *rasa* arises and develops on the basis of the dramatic situation portrayed in the art object. We now turn from what the art object evokes to its formal structure. The thrust of our argument in this chapter will be that, quite apart from the dramatic situation portrayed by the art object, its sensual form also is replete with meaning. Only that aesthete who has trained the eye and cultivated the mind can respond to these meanings. We will show that, in this sense, just as the content of the art object gives rise to *rasadhvani*, its formal structure becomes the basis of symbolic and suggested meanings. It follows that, since the formal structure of the art object is the basis of resounding meanings that gradually unfold, the outward shape or structure presented to the senses cannot be abandoned or negated in the *advaita* of art. In this sense, it can be said that there is a *rūpadhvani*, just as there is a *rasadhvani*, and a true yoga of art cannot ignore either of these *dhvanis*. The discussion on aesthetic form that follows will apply mainly to sculpture in bas relief, as this, is the most common idiom of classical Indian visual artist, as explained in chapter one.

In the *mārgī* Hindu tradition of visual art, form or *rūpa*, also called *mūrti,* (although the terms *rūpa* and *mūrti* are used synonymously the term *rūpa* will be used in preference to *mūrti* in this inquiry) comes to acquire a definitive meaning and cannot remain a generic term for a multitude of possible forms. Even within the realm of sacred images, *rūpa* stands for the figurative, representational image, and cannot include abstract art such as the *yantras, maṇḍalas* and other abstract art forms, or the multitudinous forms of folk art. *Rūpa* is, and must remain, for those within the tradition, an anthropomorphic concretisation of the cosmic *Puruṣa*. It must be made clear that *rūpa*, in this inquiry, refers mainly to public rather than private art, a form of art that was sponsored by a patron, made by an artist of traditional lineage and that was displayed permanently in public, but was never for personal or private enjoyment. Art and artists in the *mārgī* tradition enjoyed an exalted status, and the traditional *rūpakāra* or image-maker had a certain responsibility to society. There was a constant interaction between the society on the one hand and the artist on the other, the artist leading in a certain sense, by his artistic creations and the society responding and accepting his creations. The Hindu artist thus functioned within the strict confines of his tradition, and at the same time was governed by his potential audience. This made sure that he gave expression in his *rūpa* to the vision of the tradition and never used it solely for self-expression.

The Vedas provide both the concept and the imagery of the cosmic *Puruṣa*, but yet the Vedic Indian showed a considerable amount of hesitancy or inhibition in committing his artistic vision into form. It is interesting to point out that, while the Vedas do not issue any definite proscriptions against the making of visible forms, there are some strong hints at the inhibition of the Vedic tradition in making sacred forms. The ***Śvetāśvatāra Upaniṣad*** says, "there can be no image of him whose name is great glory."[5] Vedic art remained largely aniconic and the only manifestation of Vedic plastic art was the *vedī* or the sacrificial altar. The Vedic altar was considered to be the one form that corresponds, both in its outward strucure and in the symbolism associated with it, to the form of the cosmic *Puruṣa*. It is important to note that the autochthonous[6] Indian on the other hand, at the same period of time, was expressing himself in a variety and profusion of visible forms.[7]

A number of theories could be offered for the inhibition of the Vedic Indian to express himself in plastic form, although a detailed analysis of this question is outside the scope of this inquiry. It could be postulated that the desire of the Vedic Indian to remain aniconic is in keeping with the tradition of keeping sacred knowledge private and for the benefit of the son and the worthy pupil. Such knowledge was not meant to be offered to all and sundry, although it must be admitted that the Vedic *yajña*, which was considered to be the embodiment of sacred knowledge, was by no means private. It does need to be emphasised that the exhibition and display of plastic art was certainly not a Vedic trait. It could also be postulated that the Vedic Indian resisted the ideas and practices of the autochthonous Indian, who was free and uninhibited, when it came to creating and worshipping visual forms and figures. Banerjea points out that "words like *sandṛs*, *pratimā,* etc. might have signified, from a comparatively early date symbolical representations of divinities which were not associated with particular cults. Such use in fact can be found in texts assignable to a period when the cult gods and goddesses had not made their appearance, or even if they had done so, had not been assigned any important position in the religious lives of the higher sections of the Indo-Aryans."[8] According to this thesis, the use of plastic forms as sacred images around which rituals were practised, as well as the public display of such forms, originated with the autochthonous tradition rather than the Vedic tradition.

The ultimate source of *rūpa* is the *Puruṣa Sūkta* of the ***Ṛg Veda***.

It is here that Reality is consecrated as a cosmic *Puruṣa*. The hymn describes the formation of the world from the body of the primordial Man:

> A thousand headed is the Man
> with a thousand eyes, a thousand feet
> encompassing the Earth on all sides
> he exceeded it by ten fingers breadth.[9]

The ***Ṛg Veda***, after having elaborated on the cosmic *Puruṣa*, goes on to give it an archetypal status when it declares, "*rūpam rūpam pratirūpam bhavati*".[10] The *VSU* interprets this verse to signify that all plastic forms are but reflections of the one primal form, and that the only form of artistic merit can be a visual representation of that primal form. Although the original quotation in the ***Ṛg Veda*** refers to Indra, who by the power of his *māyā*, puts forth multiple forms of himself, Pippalāḍa, author of the *VSU*, takes the term '*rūpam*' in the neuter gender, referring to the cosmic *Puruṣa* and to forms in general, and not specifically to the form of Indra.[11]

The conception of the cosmic *Puruṣa* is the basis not only of aesthetics of *rūpa* in the *mārgī* tradition, but also of metaphysical speculation, and in combining the two functions, an indissoluble bond between aesthetics and metaphysics has been made in the Hindu visual tradition. Aesthetics and metaphysics, as far as *rūpa* is concerned, are so closely wedded together that the artist is also at the same time a *sthāpakodgītha* or sacrifical priest.[12] The idea that the aesthetic form points beyond itself to the source of all cosmic forms has wielded a powerful influence on the Indian aesthetic tradition. The following statement of Śrī Aurobindo bears witness to the continuing power of this idea:

> [the] greatness and continuity of Indian sculpture is due to the close connection between the religious and philosophical and the aesthetic mind of the people;[13] the Indian sculptor is concerned with embodying spiritual experiences and impressions, not with recording or glorifying what is received by the physical senses;[14] the Indian sculptor stresses something behind, something

> more remote to the surface imagination but nearer to the soul and subordinates to it the physical form.[15]

Underlying the acceptance by the *mārgī* tradition of the cosmic *Puruṣa* as the archetypal form, is a basic Tāntric idea, "What is here is there. What is not here is nowhere."[16] Although this concept of the homology between macrocosm and microcosm comes to the fore in the Tantras and dominates the Tāntric tradition, its roots lie in the world-view of the Vedas and the Upaniṣads. This fundamental Tāntric idea is at the root of not only the creation of *rūpa*, but also, more importantly, of its appreciation or realisation. The *rūpa* becomes not only a copy of the archetypal *Puruṣa* but a bridge for the correlation of the macrocosm with the microcosm, the *jīvātman* with the *paramātman.*

This idea has profound implications for aesthetics. Since every *rūpa* is considered to be a concretisation of the cosmic *Puruṣa*, it follows that the structural form of every *rūpa* is perceived to be a point of correlation between macrocosm and microcosm. The homologous relationship between macrocosm and microcosm that was first established through the creative sacrifice of the *Puruṣa*, and is reproduced in every Vedic sacrifice, is reflected and reaffirmed in every aesthetic form. In this sense the traditional visual artist imitates the role of the sacrificial priest, the *udgītha.*

From the Veda onwards the image of the cosmic *Puruṣa* is a recurring one and it becomes not a passing but a sustained metaphor. In the ***Bṛhadāraṇyaka Upaniṣad*** a graphic picture of the cosmic *Puruṣa* emerges thus:

> The life of all beings became three-fold, the east was his head, the intermediate quarters on either side (north-east and south-east) his arms, the west was his hind part, the intermediary quarters (north-west and south-west) his thighs, the south and north were his sides; heaven his back; the sky his adbomen, this earth the chest, thus being established in the waters.[17]

In the ***Aitareya Upaniṣad*** the cosmic *Puruṣa* is described thus:

> Fire became speech and entered into the mouth, air

> became breath and entered into the nostrils, the Sun became sight and entered into the eyes, the *diśās* became hearing and entered into the ears, herbs of healing and the plants and trees became hairs and entered into the skin, the Moon became the mind and entered into the heart, death became *apāna* the lower breathing and entered into the navel, the waters became the seed and entered into the organ.[18]

The concept of *puruṣa* in indeed pan-Indian. Terms such as "*ādipuruṣa, virāṭ-puruṣa, ādi-avatāra, virāṭ-prṇa*" occur in the ***Bhāgavata Purāṇa***. The ***Bhagavadgītā*** graphically describes the *Viśvarūpa*.[19]

The significance given to the human form in all these texts is of the utmost importance in understanding both the structural form of the art object, as it is conceived in the *mārgī* tradition and the meaning invested in that form. The human body, by virtue of its individual parts and its organic unity, is considered to be the perfect symbol of the correlation and the harmony between the microcosm and the macrocosm. This explains why most of the art objects of the *mārgī* tradition are based on the human form. This human form that is so familiar to us is invested with infinite worth in the tradition because it is perceived as a microcosmic copy of the cosmic *Puruṣa*. Aesthetically, the cosmic *Puruṣa* establishes the human form as the basis of *rūpa* and the norm of plastic beauty, for as the ***Aitareya Upaniṣad*** says, "*puruṣo vāva sukṛtam*", "Man indeed is well made".[20] Metaphysically, it points to the correlation of the macrocosm with the microcosm. Both these ideas are of cardinal importance to the plastic arts in the *mārgī* tradition. The image of the cosmic *Puruṣa* provides a focus for the traditional artists to relate to the universe, it is the centrepetal force that prevents a scattering of their creative energies, it is the point of rest of creation and creativity, the channel of reintegration of the universal Reality with the reality within. This is the supreme function of visual art in the *mārgī* tradition. Rabindranath Tagore, in his writings, expresses the view of modern Indian aestheticians who follow the tradition in accepting the image of the cosmic *Puruṣa* as the basis of aesthetic form. These modern aestheticians agree that the image of the cosmic *Puruṣa* provides a focus for the traditional artists to relate to the universe, for in the words of Tagore:

> art awakens a sense of the real by establishing an intimate relationship between our inner being and the universe at large, bringing us a consciousness of deep joy;[21] [for] the man who shapes brings the real very close to us, throwing light upon our awareness of the reality within man.[22] What is hidden, veiled in the shadows of unfamiliarity gives no pleasure... [but] by joining himself to the universe...man makes aquaintance of his own inner being.[23] Thus in artistic creation the Real stands before us in all its immediacy.[24]

We have cited Tagore as an example of modern Indian aestheticians who hold the view that the creative energy of the artist is put to use, not for mere individual self-expression, but to attain insights into the nature of Reality and to heighten consciousness.

It is interesting to note that, with the dawn of the modern era in India, sculptors and painters, desiring individual self-expression, have broken away from the orbits of the *mārgī* tradition to a far greater degree than musicians and dancers. Individual self-expression, as understood in the modern sense, was never an issue with the traditional Indian artist. That the *mārgī* tradition did not stifle individuality is witnessed by the variations among *rūpas* that portray the same theme. No two Naṭarājas, for example, are exactly alike. However, for the traditional Indian artist, the ideal of beauty in form continued to be based on the cosmic *Puruṣa*. This concept set the tone for all visual art of the *mārgī* tradition and left but little room for such artistic expressions as portraits and statues of historical persons, or for mere portrayal of landscapes.

Rūpa as opposed to *rasa*, implies a physical formation. For the purpose of understanding the process of art creation, as well as the *mārgī* attitude towards the self-expression of the artist, the creation of the *rūpa* can be broken down into various steps. Although this inquiry does not focus on the yoga of the artist or the artisan, but mainly on the yoga of the aesthete, it is important to understand the creation of the *rūpa*, so that we can better understand the task of the aesthete. For in *rūpa* as in *rasa*, the aesthete's undertaking is the mirror image of that of the artist; remembering of course that the artist very often is also an aesthete. Since the same types of visual forms are created in the *mārgī* tradition generation after generation, it becomes necessary to distinguish between the sage-artist or the pristine artist or *ṛṣi*, who first conceives of a *rūpa*, and others who follow after him. For example, it is theoretically possible to distinguish the sage-artist who first conceived of the form of the Naṭarāja from others who used it as their model. Accordingly, in this inquiry, we distinguish between the *dhyāna* of the sage-artist and the *dhyāna* of those who follow after him. Although there are no references in the texts to historical personages who were sage-artists, it is evident that the *dhyāna* or artistic contemplation that gives birth to an original aesthetic form, must differ from the psychological processes through which others reinterpret this model. Second and subsequent generations of artists, who recreate the same or similar type of *rūpas*, are acting under historical and psychological conditions that differ from that of the sage-artist. The aesthete is to take his cue from the sage-artist, the *ādi śilpī*, rather than from the subsequent generation of artists.

The first step in the evolution of the *rūpa* is the *dhyāna* of the artist. It will be shown that in this first step, the conception of the *rūpa* is dependent on the coming together of the artist's individual genius and inspiration (*pratibhā*) and his discipline of contemplation (*dhyāna*), which has as its focus the traditional imagery of the cosmic *Puruṣa*. It is this step that transforms the *rūpa* from formlessness to form, "*arūpad rūpam*".[25]

Dhyāna, for the Indian artist, was a disciplined activity and one that could be deliberately induced. This *dhyāna* of the artist is not a trance, in the sense of a loss of volitional control, or a contentless ecstasy, but a meditative discipline focused on the cosmic *Puruṣa*, with the express purpose of revealing its form. The artist sees the form of the cosmic *Puruṣa*, in his *dhyāna*, just as the Vedic *ṛṣis* hear the cosmic sounds out of which they compose the hymns. The desire on the part of the sage-artist to visualise the cosmic *Puruṣa* is the key to the entire *dhyāna*. As the *VSU* says,"The intention [to worship] leads to the appearance of a particular form."[26] The sage-artist adores and delights in the form that rises in his mind. This could be called an inner or aesthetic adoration, in contradistinction to the ritual worship, that is performed in front of images. As the *VSU* says, "it is in the process of *dhyāna* that the form becomes clear."[27] The artist prepares himself for his *dhyāna* by his intense training, *śikṣā*, which includes an intimate knowledge of the measurements and proportions prescribed for the *rūpa* by the *śāstras*. It is important to point out that the artist's *dhyāna* differs from that of the *bhakta*, because of his specific purpose of re-interpreting and recreating the *rūpa*. Furthermore, his training has made him an aesthete of the highest order, and his aesthetic sensibilities enter into his *dhyāna*. A *bhakta* on the contrary need not necessarily be an aesthete. On the basis of the sources available to him, Mulk Raj Anand describes the artist's *dhyāna* thus:

> The artist performs purifactory ablutions and sits down to focus his attention on . . . a *dhyāna-mantra*. He then offers flowers, incense and other gifts to the form conceived. The mental picture is thus seen in all its details and the work of art is complete in the mind even before being translated into form. The artist then begins the task of technical elaboration, during which time he must hold fast to the conception evolved through *yoga*. . . The kind of mental state designed to be secured through the practice of *yoga* can also be cultivated by the artisan through tuning up the functions of the body and the mind into perfect obedience to the faculty of intuition and through the deliberate invocation of dreams. . .[28]

Heinrich Zimmer points out that the *mārgī* tradition provides a rich storehouse of *bījamantras* or seed *mantras*, and *yantras* or diagrams, to facilitate the *dhyāna* of the artist who wishes to re-create a proper variant of a primordial *rūpa*. The artist's *dhyāna* is a formal activity, brought into focus by a specific *mantra* or helped by a linear *yantra*. Zimmer notes that, "*mantra*, *dhyāna* and linear *yantra* are three quantities that are congruent in the underlying idea."[29] The rich store of seed *mantras* correspond precisely with images that can be invoked through them, and therefore, they lead to a complete and accurate inner visualisation. Zimmer explains, "it is the power of the syllable (*mantraśakti*), whether whispered or simply inwardly articulated, that can, in the realm of inner vision, produce whatever corresponds to the sound."[30] If a *yantra* is used as the focus of concentration, it is the *dhyāna* that harmonises, "outward sight and inner vision".[31]

A feature of the artist's *dhyāna* is that the image, which appears to his inner vision in its entirety, is in perfect harmony. Zimmer, in his description of *dhyāna* says that:

> no part of the manifestation presented to the inner vision is in motion, and that inward sight does not shift its focus from point to point. All that appears before the inward eye is equally in focus, so that everything present shines forth with equal clarity. Each part is at rest within itself.[32]

Zimmer contrasts our ordinary modes of recalling images that have arisen in our consciousness with the *dhyāna* of the artist. He points out that "our untrained inward sight is generally successful in recalling images that have appeared, only to vanish immediately...".[33] By contrast, in the supra-sensory inner vision of the artist's *dhyāna,* these images remain stable and ensure that they are translated into aesthetic form. It is important to note that the *rūpa* is algebraically, but not arithmetically, complete in the *dhyāna* of the artist. In this sense, the primary creation of the *rūpa* takes place in the mind of the artist. The translation of it into a material medium, by contrast, is a process of construction, calling in the skill of the craftsman. It is important to focus on the *dhyāna* of the artist as it sheds light on the *dhyāna* that the aesthete must undertake.

We have seen that *rasa* arises, not through the portrayal of raw emotion, but through the transformation of emotion within the context of a dramatic situation into a visual form as in *nāṭya.* Similarly, aestheticians of the *mārgī* tradition, stress that the *rūpa* is not a photographic representation, but an aesthetic transformation of the natural visual form. The measurements and proportions presented in the *śāstras* have the purpose of effecting this transformation.

Vātsyāyana in his ***Kāmasūtra*** lists six essential ingredients of *rūpa*. These are: *pramāṇa, rūpa-bheda, bhāva, lāvaṇya-yojana, sādṛśya* and *varṇika-bhaṅga*, that is proportion, perception, emotion, grace, resemblance to reality and the artistic use of implements and materials.[34] Of these *pramāṇa* and *sādṛśya* need further elucidation since they are related to the *mārgī* view that the aesthetic form is a concretisation of the cosmic *Puruṣa*.

Pramāṇa is the very hallmark of *rūpa*. It is by virtue of its harmonious proportions that an aesthetic form achieves organic unity and becomes a reflection (*pratibiṁba*) of the form of the cosmic *Puruṣa*. Mulk Raj Anand makes the illuminating comment that "aesthetic *pramāṇa* expresses in plastic terms the norm of properly directed action (just as) speculative *pramāṇa* expresses the norm of properly directed thought."[35]

It is significant that the proportions prescribed in the *śāstras* are not based on the empirical study of natural forms and shapes but on idealised conceptions in the minds of the creators of aesthetic forms. Thus Śukrācārya asserts that even an ill-made *rūpa* that conforms to the prescribed proportions is to be preferred to the form of man, "however attractive the latter may be, for perchance one (man) in a million has perfect form, perfect beauty."[36] The connotations of this statement will be further explored in the discussion on *sādṛśya*.

Pramāṇa in the Indian visual tradition, signifies not just linear measurements, but also rhythm and harmony. This combination and interrelation of measurement (*māna*) and harmony (*tāla*) is brought out by the term *tāla-māna*. Modern interpreters of the aesthetic tradition have stressed the concept that the measured inner rhythm of the *rūpa* bears witness to the correlation between the microcosm and the macrocosm. Coomaraswamy maintains that, according to the tradition, all rhythm in art corresponds "in the last analysis to cosmic rhythms".[37] Writing on artistic rhythm in the same vein Tagore says:

> It is the magic of mathematics, the rhythm which is the

> heart of all creation which moves in the atom and its different measures fashion the rose and the thorn, the sun and the planets. These are the dance steps of numbers in the arena of time and space which weaves the *māyā*, the patterns of appearance, the incessant flow of change that ever is and is not. It is the rhythm that churns up images from the vague and makes tangible what is elusive. This is *māyā*, this is the art in creation and art in literature which is the magic of rhythm.[38]

It is worth noting that in Tagore's poetic language *māyā* has the double connotation of measurement and magic, and is not used in the sense in which Śaṅkara uses the term.

The inner rhythm of the *rūpa*, based on its proportions, creates the impression of movement, a movement ***in situ***. Niharranjan Ray, in his interpretation of the aesthetic tradition, says that the measured rhythm of the *rūpa* is to be correlated with the rhythm of the life-breath (*prāṇa*) of the universe. As he puts it, the *rūpa* is endowed with "an inner reality of rhythmic vitality and movement (or) *prāṇa* which is its essential form."[39]

The large number of texts dealing with sculpture, the *śilpa-śāstras*, give in exquisite detail the principles of measurement and rhythm by which the sculptor must be bound. While the minutia of these measurements and proportions are of no importance to us in this inquiry, the principle of *pramāṇa* or measurement brings home the fact that mathematical precision is the keynote of *rūpa*, both in its conception, as well as in its execution and realisation. *Pramāṇa* is the *dharma* of the *rūpa*, and it is through this *dharma* that it is perceived as a reflection of the perfect form of the cosmic *Puruṣa*.

The *mārgī* ideal of beauty in form is fulfilled only by a formalised *rūpa* that conforms to certain precisely stated aesthetic principles of harmony and rhythm: hence, in the *mārgī* tradition, only an art form made in accordance with the canon can be called beautiful. Although we are not concerned here with the relationship between the aesthetic tradition and society at large, it is to be noted that the *śāstras* influenced the minds of the artists and the aesthetes alike, so that they could seldom see beauty outside the prescribed models.

In a certain sense, this could be called the tyranny of the tradition, but it was one factor, amongst others, that was responsible for maintaining continuity through the troubled and chaotic periods of Indian history. It must also be remembered that there was a constant cross-pollination between the *mārgī* and the *deśī* traditions, one enriching the other, so that the *mārgī* tradition did not become stale or irrelevant.

When we turn from *pramāṇa* or proportion to the principles of *sādṛśya* or correspondence to reality, it seems at first glance, that these two principles are at variance with each other. As we have noted, the principle of measurement is not based on the study of empirical forms, but seeks to reflect an ideal of perfect beauty inculcated and prescribed by the tradition. *Sādṛśya*, on the contrary, insists on correspondence to an inner empirical reality. How are these two principles brought together, and what is the philosophic basis for the harmonising of *pramāṇa*, which looks beyond this imperfect world, with *sādṛśya*, which turns towards it? In this inquiry we take the position that both *pramāṇa* and *sādṛśya* are based on the concept of the cosmic *Puruṣa*. The principle of *pramāṇa* points to the perfection and transcendence of the form of the cosmic *Puruṣa*, while the principle of *sadṛśya* indicates the immanence of the *Puruṣa* in the world as we know it through our senses. Together, *pramāṇa* and *sādṛśya* seek to indicate the correlation and unity of the macrocosm and the microcosm.

Although *sādṛśya* is accepted as a principle in the *mārgī* tradition, the *VSU* does not elucidate its significance. We therefore turn to modern interpreters of the aesthetic tradition to seek an explanation of what correspondence to reality connoted for the artist and the aesthete.

Modern interpreters, beginning with Coomaraswamy, stress that *sādṛśya* does not signify realism. They maintain that the artist of the *mārgī* tradition does not aim to give a photographic representation of the empirical form. According to these interpreters, the purpose of the principle of *sādṛśya* is to suggest the essential nature of the object and the inner laws of its development, namely its *svadharma*, and to indicate that, by virtue of its *svadharma*, the object is in harmony with the cosmic laws, the *dharma* of the universe. The *rūpakāra* or creator of visual forms depicts the essential nature of the object, as he intuits it in the inner vision of his *dhyāna*, and shows that it is this essential nature which makes it a manifestation (*pratirūpam*) of the cosmic *Puruṣa*. In the words of Śrī Aurobindo, "for the Indian mind form does not exist except as a creation of the spirit and draws all its meaning and value from the spirit."[40]

Modern interpreters, therefore, stress that *sādṛśya* is to be understood at many levels: first, the correlation between the aesthetic form and the intrinsic nature of the object portrayed; second, the correlation between the *rūpa* and the intuitive vision of the artist, and finally, the correlation between the well proportioned form of the *rūpa* and the ideal form, namely, the form of the cosmic *Puruṣa*.

Coomaraswamy points to the correlation between the aesthetic form and the inner vision of the object in the artist's mind, when he speaks of the "indivisible identity of form and content."[41] Stella Kramrisch expresses her agreement with Coomaraswamy when she says that, "the figures of Indian sculpture are based primarily on a reality which is not seen but felt."[42] Kramrisch also elucidates the significance of *sādṛśya* as the correlation between the aesthetic form and the intrinsic nature of the object that it portrays, when she says that "the sculpture does not depict the concrete, gross (*sthūla*) physique as perceived and interpreted, but shows the subtle (*sūkṣma*) reality of life as felt in and through the body."[43]

According to modern interpreters, *sādṛśya* is based on information which is gathered by the eye as a visual organ but which is processed by the inner eye. Stella Kramrisch remarks that "Indian sculptural form then, is neither a record of the appearance nor of the structure of the body. It aims rather to render the inner experience and awareness of life in the body."[44] She correctly says that the whole aim of *sādṛśya* is to "proceed beyond empirical truth to express the metaphysical", but she perhaps goes too far, when she says in the same breath that "Indian sculpture (has) no reality other than in states of inner awareness,"[45] for this statement denies the sensual bonafides of a *rūpa*. *Rūpa* is not photographically descriptive of objects as they are presented to the human senses, but *rūpa* does conform to the manner in which sensory experience is interpreted in the more exalted states of human consciousness. *Rūpa*, as aesthetic form, depicts beauty in its purely physical form and by virtue of its specific and well defined sensual qualities possesses a *sākṣātartha*. It is well to remember that *rūpa* is visual language and just as "language bespeaks itself before it bespeaks God",[46] *rūpa* must have a significant *sākṣātartha*, or significant sensual attributes, before it can lead the onlooker to another level of *artha*. Its sensual beauty however cannot remain a superficial art sensation for the prepared aesthete but must eventually lead to a meaningful epistemic encounter, exalting the senses to a state of *ānanda*. A proper understanding and realisation of the *sākṣātartha* of the *rūpa* cannot but lead the aesthete from the *rūpa* to the *pratirūpa*. On account of its other properties, the *rūpa* hints insistently at the metaphysical, hidden basis of beauty, beauty that will be cognised as *parokṣārtha*. Herein lies its significance for an *advaita* of art.

NOTES

1. Rabindranath Tagore, ***On Art & Aesthetics***. (Bombay: Orient Longmans, 1961) p. 81.
2. *dvidhāto brahma rūpavat bhavati.*
   On account of having two forms [*nirguṇa* and *saguṇa*] *Brahman* acquires form.
   A. Boner *et al.* ***Vāstusūtra Upaniṣad.*** The Essence of Form in Sacred Art (Delhi: Motilal Banarsidass, 1982) (hereafter referred to as *VSU*), 4.3.
3. S. Kramrisch, ***The Hindu Temple.*** (Delhi: Motilal Banarsidass, 1976) Volume 2, p. 342.
4. J.N.Banerjea, ***The Development of Hindu Iconography***. (Calcutta: University of Calcutta, 1956) p. 78.
5. *na tasya pratimā asti yasya nāma mahadyaśaḥ.*
   There can be no image of him whose name is great glory.
   J.N.Banerjea, p.78.
6. The word autochthonous is used synonymously with the term *deśī* in preference to terms such as original or native. The anthropolgical debate as to whether or not the Vedic people were immigrants is an engaging one, and the possibility of regarding the Vedic people as also autochthonous is not ruled out.

7. Personal communication from Smt. Pupul Jayakar. Smt. Jayakar's monograph ***The Earthen Drum*** is perhaps the first attempt to systematically analyse the folk arts.
8. *Ibid.*, p. 39.
9. ***Ṛg Veda*** X.90.1. quoted by K.Vatsyayan.***The Square and the Circle of the Indian Arts.*** (Delhi: Roli Books International, 1983) p.9.
10. *rūpam rūpam pratirūpam bhavati.*
    Every form is an image (of an original form).
    VSU, 1.2.
11. *VSU*, 1.2 gloss.
12. *VSU*, p. 54 fn # 45.
13. Śrī Aurobindo. ***The Foundations of Indian Culture***. Volume 14, (Pondicherry: Sri Aurobindo Birth Centenary Library, 1972) p. 229.
14. *Ibid.*, p. 234.
15. *Ibid.*, p. 203.
16. *yadihāsti tadanyatra, yannehāsti na tat kvacit.*
    What is here is there, what is not here is nowhere.
    Woodroffe, J. ***Śakti and Śākta***.(Madras: Ganesh and Co. Pvt. Ltd., 1965) p. 296.
17. ***Bṛhadāraṇyaka Upaniṣad,*** 1.2.1. quoted by K.Vatsyanan. p. 14.
18. ***Aitareya Upaniṣad***, 1.2.4. Śri Aurobindo.***The Upanishads.*** (Pondicherry: Sri Aurobindo Ashram, 1972) p. 357.
19. The ***Bhagvadgītā***. Chapter XI.
20. *puruṣo vāva sukṛtam.*
    Man indeed is well made.
    Aitareya Upaniṣad, 1.2.3, Sri Aurobindo. ***The Upanishads***. (Pondicherry: Sri Auobindo Ashram, 1972) p. 357.
21. R.Tagore, ***On Art & Aesthetics.*** p. 86.
22. *Ibid.*, p. 84.
23. *Ibid.*, p. 82.
24. *Ibid.*, p. 86.
25. *arūpad rūpam.*
    From form to formlessness.
    VSU, 5.21.
26. *saṇkalpad vikalpa iti viśesaḥ.*
    The intention [to worship] leads to the appearance of a particular form.
    VSU, 5.19.
27. *dhyānaprayoge rūpa sauṣṭhavam spaṣṭam bhavati.*
    It is in the process of *dhyāna* that the form becomes clear.
    VSU, 3.14.
28. Mulk Raj Anand, ***The Hindu View of Art.*** (Bombay: Asia Publishing House, 1957) pp.75-76.
29. H.Zimmer, ***Artistic Form and Yoga in the Sacred Images of India.*** (Princeton: Princeton University Press, 1984) p. 71.
30. *Ibid.*, p. 58.

31. *Ibid.*, p. 53.
32. *Ibid.*, p. 60.
33. *Ibid.*, p. 56.
34. Mulk Raj Anand, p. 85.
35. *Ibid.*, p. 85.
36. *Ibid.*, p. 81.
37. A.Coomaraswamy, ***The Transformation of Nature in Art.*** (New York: Dover Publications, 1956) p. 179.
38. R.Tagore, ***On Art & Aesthetics***. p. 79.
39. N.Ray, ***An Approach to Indian Art.*** (Chandigarh: Punjab University Bureau, 1974) p. 108.
40. Sri Aurobindo, ***The Foundations of Indian Culture.*** p. 211.
41. A. Coomaraswamy, ***The Transformation of Nature in Art***. p. 183.
42. S.Kramrisch, ***Indian Sculpture in the Philadelphia Museum of Art***. (Philadelphia: University of Pennsylvania Press, 1966) p. 29.
43. *Ibid.*, p. 26.
44. *Ibid.*, p. 25.
45. *Ibid.*, p. 24.
46. J.G. Arapura, "Some Perspectives on Indian Philosophy of Language", in ***Revelation in Indian Thought.*** (California: Dharma Publishing, 1977) p. 41.

Chapter 5

Parokṣārtha

> Penetrate deeper to know the truth, know the physical first then the spiritual,
> He who knows the first vital thread, binding all the things formed in shape, colour and words, knows only the physical form of the universe, and knows very little,
> But he who goes deeper and perceives the string inside the string, the thin web binding separate life forces with cords of unity, knows the real entity.
>
> ***Ṛg Veda,*** 8.58.2

Rabindranath Tagore has said that "arts and literature ... in their cadence of lines, colours, movements, words, thoughts, express vastly more than what they appear to be on the surface. They open the windows of our mind to the eternal reality of man.[1] Tagore is referring to the *sūtrasya sūtram* of the ***Ṛg Veda*** and has succinctly summarised the concept of *parokṣārtha* in art. The conception of *śabda* having more than one meaning was established early in the Indian *kāvya* tradition. While Bharata is silent on this, Bhartṛhari's *sphoṭavāda* lays down in clear terms the foundation for Ānandavardhana's *dhvani*. "*dhvanirnāma arthāntaram*".[2] Ānandavardhana's cryptic definition of *dhvani* leaves no doubt that the same word or sentence, and by extension an art object, is capable of providing another or multiple meanings. This dictum has far reaching epistemic implications. Ānandavardhana posits the concept of *dhvani* without referring to any *pramāṇas* indicating that his concern was mainly with *artha* and not with the *pramāṇas*, with the end and not so much the means. Ānandavardhana leaves little doubt when he says that "the question of logical truth and falsity in regard to suggested meanings is entirely futile and that it is ridiculous if one were to indulge in discussions regarding the *pramāṇas*."[3] We feel justified in taking a similar position and postulating a *parokṣārtha* in art, an *artha* which yields a meaning other than the superficial, while retaining both and rejecting none. The *parokṣārtha* in Indian art incorporates Ānandavardhana's *dhvani* but goes beyond to include a number of indirect meanings which are available in verbal and visual arts. It is important to note that Ānandavardhana, like the rest of the *alaṃkārikas* of his period, was dealing solely with *kāvya* and not with art objects in general. An epistemic inquiry, such as ours, which takes its stand on *kāvya* but does not restrict it just to *kāvya*, needs to extend the concept of Ānandavardhana's *dhvani*. When one is investigating meanings in the entire spectrum of the artistic tradition, it is not possible to restrict oneself to one *pramāṇa* or the other as logicians tend to do; neither is it possible to follow strictly the *alaṃkārikas* as they restricted themselves to an analysis of poetry. While recognising the value of the approach of the logician and the *alaṃkārika*, aesthetes need not be bound by them. An aesthete's interest is in procuring the highest, deepest and most exalted *artha*, in probing and enjoying different levels of meanings, without necessarily negating or losing any level of meaning in the true spirit of *advaita*, in an ever expanding vista of meanings, so as to assure himself of a satisfying, enriching, blissful, subjective, aesthetic experience.

Parokṣārtha builds upon and proceeds from *sākṣātartha*, for even after the senses have been saturated with meaning, the limits of meaning are by no means exhausted. Newer, more enriching levels of meaning remain to be explored, carrying the aesthete to not only higher and deeper epistemic levels, but providing hidden visions of beauty in the art object. In letting meaning be obvious as well as hidden, in being overt and at the same time covert, in being superficially expressed and at the same time suggested, the artist is exercising his creativity or *pratibhā* and ensuring a similar recreative function for the aesthete. Yet it needs to be emphasised that in allowing multiple meanings from a single word, sentence, poem or art object, an aesthete in the Indian artistic tradition is expected to stay within the tradition. The concept of levels of meaning does not permit artistic licence either for the artist or the aesthete. This is a pre-condition and forms a part of the *śikṣā* of the artist and the aesthete. If tradition provides the epistemic framework upon which the *parokṣārtha* is to be developed, *sākṣātartha* is the reference point to which *parokṣārtha* must relate. In other words, *parokṣārtha* stems from the *sākṣātartha* and is tied to the tradition on the one hand and *sākṣātartha* on the other. While the *sākṣātartha* touches a certain aspect of the aesthete's psyche, the *parokṣārtha* nourishes other aspects of the aesthetic space of the *rasika*.

The previous chapters have discussed *rasa* and *rūpa* under the aegis of *sākṣātartha*. The point, although made earlier, needs to be stressed, that although *rasa* is suggested, in other words it is *rasadhvani* which is directly perceived and not mediated, a form of *mānasikapratyakṣa*. Having availed himself of *rasa* and *rūpa* through the *pramāṇa* of *pratyakṣa* the aesthete's epistemic task is not complete. He must undertake a *parokṣa* inquiry. This will include an analysis of the *gāthās* and the *kathās* (commonly referred to as myths) that form a foundation of much of traditional Indian art, an understanding of symbols, investigating allegory and finally inquiring into the inner logic of composition. This constitutes the totality of *parokṣārtha*.

Coomaraswamy has drawn our attention to the oft recurring expression *parokṣa prīya iva devaḥ*[4] and also to the origin of the concept of *parokṣa*, commenting that the term *parokṣa* has carried a variety of meanings in the Indian tradition, meanings such as: "indirect, angelic, mystic, esoteric, cryptic, noumenal, universal, abstract & metaphorical."[5] While *parokṣa* and *sākṣāt* are thus to be differentiated from an epistemic standpoint, the tradition also at the same time emphasises "the correspondence between what is known to the Angels in one way, to man in another."[6] What becomes obvious is not just the concept of *parokṣa* as an indirect way of expression and knowing, but also that there exists a correspondence, *anurūpam*, even in the Vedic literature between *parokṣa* and *sākṣāt*, the macrocosm and the microcosm. While the distinction between *parokṣa* and *sākṣāt* is important, what is equally signficant is that it is the *sākṣāt* that leads us to the *parokṣa*; the outer points to the inner, the visible to the invisible, emphasising that at no point is the *advaitic* relationship between the two lost. These ideas are of seminal importance in aesthetics and *parokṣārtha* comes to occupy a significant part in the epistemology of art, uncovering those aspects of the art object which are hidden or *guhā-nihitam*. Beauty, as Coomaraswamy writes, "is invisible and indivisible, only to be known as Deity is known in the heart"[7] the "*antarhṛdaya-ākāśa*" of the Upaniṣads. Coomaraswamy's reference is clearly to the *parokṣa* nature of both beauty and Deity, of which the ***Ṛg Veda*** says, "Only the lowest abodes of these are seen, who exist in supreme and secret places."[8] It is obvious that the epistemic reaches of *sākṣātartha* fall short of the Vedic "*guheyeṣu vrateṣu*"[9] and that only *parokṣārtha* can take us there. *Parokṣārtha* is an umbrella epistemic term, including under it not only the resolution of artistic devices such as symbol, allegory and metaphor, but also the use of certain special aesthetic concepts such as myth and *yantra* which are essential in the creation and cognition of visual art.

While *sākṣātartha* depends largely on *pratyakṣa* as a mode of cognition, inference forms an essential part of *parokṣārtha* and this *pramāṇa* can be termed a *parokṣapramāṇa*. Annambhaṭṭa in ***Tarkasangraha*** defines *anumāna* as "*liṅga parāmarśa anumānam*"[10] or "inference is the subsumptive reflection upon the connection existing between perceptual *sādhanā* (inferential mark) and *sādhya* (the property to be inferred)." That limited definition of *anumāna* acceptable to logicians needs to be extended when it comes to aesthetics. Aesthetic *anumāna* or *parokṣapramāṇa* in a *parokṣa* inquiry illuminates those aspects of the art object that aesthetic *pratyakṣa* missed or failed to uncover. *Parokṣapramāṇa* thus has a wider scope and is to be understood not just as inference but as a type of aperceptive or inner knowing.

The history of the Indian epistemic tradition is filled with debates between various schools as to the validity of *anumāna* and *śabda* as *pramāṇas*. In particular this debate featured logicians of the Mīmāṁsā, Buddhist and the Nyāya-Vaiśeṣika schools. Illuminating and thoroughgoing as it was, the details of this debate which lasted centuries need not detain us here, but one can profitably draw upon some of their arguments without necessarily accepting their positions in toto. Interested as we are in the epistemology of aesthetic experience, our parameters and purpose are not identical with theirs. The one cardinal difference is that the chief concern of these logicians was the reality or otherwise of the perceived word and the value of *anumāna* and *śabda* in verifying that reality, whereas for us as aestheticians the reality of the art object is as given, albeit within another and larger dimension of reality, and is therefore the bonafides of that art object are not debatable; *parokṣapramāṇa* within the bonafides of that art object explores the deeper meaning of that object using not only the process of inference but verbal testimony as well. The situation is similar to the epistemic status of a dream within a dream, for as it has been said that you are closest to waking when you dream within a dream. What is important to us is the value of *parokṣapramāṇa* initially in fixing the meaning of the art object and later its role in the ultimate aesthetic experience, realising of course that meaning is objective and experience is subjective. But we propose to show that *parokṣapramāṇa* not only has an epistemic function and assists in the determining of a *parokṣārtha* which resides in the art object but propels that *artha* to its successful fruition in the aesthete's ultimate *ānanda,* for cognition is an essential but only an intermediate step in the total aesthetic process. While pursuing the arguments for and against *anumāna* and *śabda* we depart company from the rigorous logicians in yet another significant way; for the logician's main concern is with the validity and strength of his arguments on the one hand while paying attention mainly to the *sādhanā* and *sādhya* on the other.[11] While the aesthete, established as he is in the art object, is equally if not more concerned with the locus or the property possessor (*pakṣa*), namely the art object, that prompts the inferential process. In other words the inquiry is artistically grounded and revolves around the art object which is the centre of his attention. This sort of inquiry on the part of the aesthete therefore uncovers those features of the art object which the initial encounter through the aegis of aesthetic perception or *pratyakṣa,* as discussed in the previous chapters, missed or failed to uncover. It becomes obvious that *parokṣapramāṇa* leads the aesthete to a greater awareness and deeper, progressive and more deliberate appreciation of the art object. In this sense the process of *parokṣārtha* could be artistically defined as an epistemic process that makes us see what is unseen at the surface level in the art object, leading to a greater enjoyment of that object. The logician would find it hard to make such a claim.

Early in the Indian tradition *alaṃkārikas* elucidated the three modes of *artha*, namely *abhidhā*, *lakṣaṇā* and *vyañjanā*. *Abhidā* or the primary meaning, either of a *śabda* in particular and of art objects in general, has been revealed to the aesthete through the epistemic process of *pratyakṣa* as discussed in the previous chapters. It is the purpose of *parokṣārtha* to cognise both the metaphorical and suggested meaning of the art object and in this process all three *pramāṇas* may have to be employed. In a *parokṣa* inquiry the aesthete relies heavily on *anumāna*, and this *pramāṇa* can therefore be looked upon as a *parokṣapramāṇa.* This wider, though more artistic, definition and dynamics of *anumāna* as an epistemic mode for *parokṣārtha* does not intend to bypass the classical debate between the *dhvanivādins* such as Ānandavardhana and the anti-*dhvanivādins* such as Mahimabhaṭṭa. The important distinction between *lakṣaṇā* or metaphor and *vyañjanā* or suggestion is by no means meant to be blurred, but by including both under the wider term *parokṣapramāṇa* or aesthetic inference a more holistic approach to art appreciation is intended, an approach that accepts an extension of the art inquiry on the part of the aesthete beyond *pratyakṣa* into *parokṣa* with the express purpose of a richer, more complete meaning. Matilal rightly describes *anumāna* as the outcome of *pramāṇa* and *parāmarśa*, where *pramāṇa* is the knowledge of concomitance between the evidence and the inferable feature and *parāmarśa* is the intellectual judgement justifying the inference.[12] In *parokṣapramāṇa* it is *parāmarśa* that drives the art encounter into becoming a knowledge episode and calls into play the aesthete's *śikṣā* and *saṃskāra* and encourages not just cognition but recognition which is the ***sine qua non*** of Kāśmīr Śaivism. A fundamental feature of Kāśmīr Śaivite epistemology is its insistence on multiple cognitions rather than a single cognition in apprehending an object. The series or layers of cognitions that the process of *parokṣapramāṇa* encourages, provides the ideal epistemic framework in a *parokṣa* type of aesthetic cognition and ultimate experience. The ***Ṛg Veda*** states that, "Intelligence is the most rapid of birds";[13] *parokṣārtha*, in this sense, provides the wings to art appreciation taking it to greater heights in the prepared aesthete.

The seed of inference is *siṣadhayiṣā* or the desire to infer an unknown from a known fact. While this places the onus of aesthetic inference on the aesthete, the need for inference is prompted by the twin concepts of *ākāṅkṣā* or expectancy and *mukhyārthabādha* or breakdown of primary meaning in the art object. *Ākāṅkṣā* as a concept was championed by the Mīmāṁsakas in their relentless inquiry into Vedic exegesis, and therefore directed towards the Vedic *śabda*. However, in keeping with our aim of enlarging the concept of *śabda* to include art objects in general and not just the Vedic *śabda*, *ākāṅkṣā* can also be extended to include *dhvani* or suggested meanings in general. Derived from the root *kāṅkṣ*, 'to desire' *ākāṅkṣā* is "the desire on the part of listeners to know the other words or their meaning to complete the sense."[14] There are two main types of *ākāṅkṣā*, syntactic and psychological, although a third variety where both types coexist is also certainly possible. *Ākāṅkṣā* implies that not only is the *śabda* incomplete as it stands but equally importantly suggests a *jijñāsā* or desire on the part of the listener to complete what is missing in order to arrive at a full and proper *artha*. One has to disagree with Salikanatha of the Prabhākara school that this desire merely stems from curiosity.[15] In our view *ākāṅkṣā* represents the desire on the part of the aesthete to undertake a sustained cognitive effort in order to experience a fuller and richer *artha* and that this desire ultimately stems from the special artistic properties of the art object. Raja is right in pointing out that the "scope of *ākāṅkṣā* depends on the intention of the speaker"[16] and in a larger sense that of the art object, but what he fails to emphasise is that it equally depends on the desire and ability of the listener to conduct an extended, *parokṣa* epistemic inquiry. *Mukhyārthabādha* (e.g. "*gaṅgāyam ghośaḥ*") is the heart of *lakṣaṇa* and is the basic aesthetic device both for the verbal and non-verbal arts, and provokes the aesthete to conduct a more deliberate, deeper inquiry. Both *ākāṅkṣā* and *mukhyārthabādha* are aesthetic attributes or *guṇas* that on the one hand confer beauty on the art object and on the other, lead the aesthete to entertain an extended and therefore more meaningful aesthetic inquiry.

Ānandavardhana's *dhvani* provides a good model for the understanding of *parokṣārtha*. The basic dynamics of *dhvani* is a shift in the meaning, or an *arthāntara,* from a superficial perceived meaning to a deeper, richer inferential meaning. The recognition of *dhvani* was crucial in moving aesthetic *artha* from the perhaps less profound connotation given to the term by Bharata to the inner, deeper, more mystical *rasadhvani* of Abhinavagupta. While *rasa* was developed in the framework of *nāṭya* and later applied to art in general, *dhvani* was formulated in the context of poetry and we are extending it generically to art objects. Ānandavardhana says that it behoves not only the poet but also the aesthete to understand *dhvani*[17] for the best ideas are presented through suggestion and not through expressed words,[18] for endless are the meanings of such poetry[19] and that the soul of poetry is suggestion. Ānandavardhana makes it perfectly clear about the three-fold function of words[20] and that the suggested sense arises from the power of the word "*śabdaśakti*".[21] Ānandavardhana goes on to say that the denotative function of words and the implying function of words are quite different from each other.[22] Implicit in Ānandavardhana's declaration is one fundamental aesthetic principle which is this: that it is the *śabda* itself, having discharged its function of *sākṣātartha* that gives unmistakable hints of a *parokṣārtha*. Stated differently, it means that the primary meaning, the *śākṣātārtha* of an art object has aesthetic significance and is never discarded at any stage. The aesthete in his desire for a deeper and progressive meaning never negates anything and in a true *advaitic* sense adds layer upon layer to meaning. Ānandavardhana's ***Ghaṭapradīpanyāya*** states the position succinctly. Just as the light of the lamp will not recede as soon as the perception of the pot is brought home to the observer, so also the expressed sense will continue to shine even after the suggested sense is apprehended.[23]

It is important at this point to explore the relation between the primary and the ultimate meaning of the art object brought about by *parokṣārtha*. Whereas the shift in meaning in *dhvani* is gradual or *asamlakṣyakrama,* like "a needle going through a pile of lotus leaves",[24] each layer yielding a richer and fuller meaning, in the case of *lakṣaṇa* the shift in meaning is sudden or *samlakṣyakrama.* Without belittling this significant diffference between *lakṣaṇa* and *dhvani*, yet in choosing to subsume both under the rubric of *parokṣārtha*, we take the position that in both instances there is a shift in the meaning, and that it is this shift that produces the *parokṣārtha* and is of cardinal aesthetic importance in the enjoyment and understanding of an art object. To explain the internal relation between the two levels of meanings, Ānandavardhana makes use of two metaphors: *aṅgāṅgibhāva* and *ātmāśarīrabhāva.* Whether the shift in meaning is gradual or sudden, the important first step is the turning away from the primary meaning, a process that becomes the hallmark of *parokṣārtha*. Ānandavardhana points out that "the suggested meaning flashes suddenly across the truth perceiving minds of perceptive critics when they turn away from the literal meaning."[25] In turning away from the primary or incomplete meaning, the aesthete is dipping into his artistic resources and assuring himself of an exalted art experience. Ānandavardhana further asserts that "it (*dhvani*) is not understood by a mere learning in grammar and in dictionary. It is understood only by those who have an insight into the true significance of poetry."[26] And he goes on to say that the "(suggested) meaning remains beyond the understanding of persons with a grounding merely in the science of meanings and words but averse to aesthetic contemplation of the intrinsic significance of poetry."[27] Mammaṭa reminds us that "the expressed (primary meaning) produces a mere comprehension in one who knows the meaning of words, while the suggested sense produces charm in men of taste alone."[28] Amaladass is right in pointing out that there is an "inner unity" between (the primary and the ultimate meaning)[29] and this unity creates not an option but an *advaitic* progression of meanings. *Parokṣārtha* creates a dialectic tension between the primary and the ultimate meaning, for the aesthete's job is not to select one between the two but, while negating nothing and affirming all levels of meaning, to undertake a progressive and deepening artistic inquiry in order to secure for himself the highest reaches of *artha*. The Tāntric overtones in this process are obvious for it emphasises that nothing is to be negated in the aesthete's *advaitic* quest. *Parokṣa* as a *pramāṇa* is unique in this respect in that it opens up levels of meaning, levels that create a new epistemic dimension and provide a deeper insight into the fundamental nature of the art object. At the same time, the exercise of handling more than one level of meaning occasioned by *parokṣa* gives the aesthete a foretaste of what is to occur at the next level of art experience, namely the harmonious blending of the objective meaning with the subjective response. This aspect of art experience will be dealt with in a later chapter.

While on the question of *dhvani* it would be valuable to examine Rabindranath Tagore's comments on the ***Īśa Upaniṣad***. In his characteristic non-sectarian manner he bases his aesthetics on the Upaniṣadic roots of Indian thought. He turns to the ***Īśa Upaniṣad*** to stress the importance of both the sensory realm and the higher levels of meaning that are manifested through it to a responsive person. In his intepretation of the *Īśa,* Tagore says that this *Upaniṣad* makes no cleft between the apparent and the ultimately real as Advaita Vedānta of Śaṅkara does. The ***Īśa Upaniṣad*** reminds us that, "into a blind darkness they enter who follow after the Ignorance, they as if into a greater darkness who devote themselves to the Knowledge alone."[30] By "absolute infinite", Tagore means an utterly transcendent Absolute that is totally untouched by the world of senses. The ***Īśa Upaniṣad*** reminds us once again that "he who knows That as both in one, the Knowledge and the Ignorance, by the Ignorance crosses beyond death and by the Knowledge enjoys Immortality."[31] The world of sensory experience does not constitute unreality or falsity, but is the very means of attaining the ultimate Truth. These words of the ***Īśa*** can be interpreted to signify that this whole universe, as it appears to the senses and all art objects, reverberate with meanings that reach level by level towards the ultimate Truth. That which the senses apprehend is not negated, abandoned or deprived of worth, as the higher level of meaning becomes revealed, for as Tagore says, "when you deprive truth of its appearance it loses the best part of its reality."[32] The Tāntric overtones in this interpretation of the ***Īśa*** by Tagore are too obvious to be missed. He further says that, "there is a point where in the mystery of existence contradictions meet."[33] When the ***Īśa Upaniṣad*** is made the basis of *parokṣārtha* the implications are profound, since we are now in a position to raise the question: do the suggested meanings that reverberate from an art object have a limit or do they extend infinitely? Tagore's answer, on the basis of the ***Īśa***, is that art is that mystery where the "infinite becomes the finite without losing its infinity."[34] If one seeks to experience this mystery, the sensory form of the art object and its *sākṣātartha* should never be abandoned, for without them the suggested meanings of *parokṣārtha* can neither arise nor rise towards infinity. It becomes clear why artists and aestheticians have difficulty with the *māyāvāda* of Śaṅkara and opt for a system or an interpretation of reality where one can move from ecstasy to ecstasy, not *neti neti*, but *iti iti*. The beauty and the bliss of aesthetic experience is the transformation of the *vācyārtha* or the expressed meaning into the *vyaṅgyārtha* or the suggested meaning; without the former there would be no art, without the latter there would be no aesthetic experience. Once again in the words of the ***Īśa Upaniṣad***, "neither the transitory nor the eternal has any meaning separately. When they are known in harmony with each other only then, through the help of that harmony, we cross the transitory and realise the immortal."[35] On the basis of the Īśa it can be said that the art object provides this harmony, this meeting of the *sākṣtartha* and the *parokṣārtha*, the finite and the Infinite.

The need to undertake an extended inquiry on the part of the aesthete prompted by *ākāṅkṣa* and *mukhyārthabādha* forms the basis of *parokṣārtha*. Admittedly this extended inquiry could be conducted on psychologic, social or historical lines, lines of inquiry that would yield information about the socio-historical factors that pertain to the art object. Our concern however is primarily epistemic, and it is in that direction that we wish to extend the aesthetic inquiry; in that context we are interested mainly in the dynamics of *parokṣārtha* as it relates to converting an art encounter into a knowledge episode. Kumārila in the ***Mīmāṁsādarśana*** makes it quite clear that one should spare no effort in arriving at the meaning of a sentence when he says:

> The meaning of a sentence could extend beyond the limits of its syntactical structure. If the required meaning cannot be found in the word itself then one should look for it in some other word in the sentence. If it is not found within the sentence then one should go to some other sentence. If it cannot be found in another place too then one should go to some other (relevant) context and if it is not found there then one should look for it in the wide world. And if you cannot find it even there you should decide that there is no other meaning of the word or utterance and take the utterance to have conveyed a complete meaning.[36]

Bhartṛhari echoes the same idea when he says that "The meanings of words are determined by (their) syntactical connection (in the sentence), situation, context, the meaning of another word, propriety, place and time, and not from their mere form."[37] "*Na rūpadeva kevalam*" or not by form alone becomes the theme for the aesthete as he undertakes an extended inquiry under the aegis of *parokṣa*, realising as he does that mere surface form is unable to give him a full and total meaning.

Thus both Kumārila and Bhartṛhari admit the need for this extended epistemic inquiry without which the verbal testimony is likely to be incomplete and even erroneous. Admitting, as we have, the *vākya* to be the unit of meaning, it is important to note that it is unable to contain within its physical limits the totality of an idea. The same physical limitations apply to art objects whether it be in the visual or performing field. But even apart from physical limitations, there is a distinct artistic merit in leaving the sentence artistically, if not syntactically, incomplete in order to confer beauty on the *śabda*, thereby provoking the aesthete's mind and leaving room for aesthetic inference. In letting the meaning be implicit rather than explicit, covert rather than overt, suggested rather than expressed, the artist exercises an aesthetic privilege and opens up for the aesthete the creative joy of aesthetic inference adding a new dimension, ensuring a richer and fuller aesthetic exprerience. In aesthetics, as opposed to logic, inference is an integral and enjoyable part of the total art process and pertains to both artistic creation and aesthetic experience.

Having established the validity of *parokṣapramāṇa* as a valid epistemic entity in *parokṣārtha*, the next problem that needs to be addressed is what is it that is inferred, or what is the *anumeya*? Grounded as are in the art object, aesthetic inference in the process of *parokṣārtha* reveals the essential nature of the art object, revealing those aspects that *pratyakṣa* failed to reveal, bringing to light some deeper and fundamental features of that object ensuring a more complete cognition of that art object. Abhinavagupta makes it quite clear that "determinate cognition entirely depends on the use of words. And the word (*śabda*) is the very life of this determinate knowledge."[38] This is in keeping with Bhartṛhari's doctrine that "the meaning of a linguistic expression is to be identified with *vikalpa*, the constructed image which is assumed as external reality."[39] It is *parokṣa* rather than *pratyakṣa* that can bring in *vikalpa* and therefore lead to a fuller cognition. For the Kāśmīr Śaivites *savikalpa jñāna* is knowledge ***par excellence.***

An important part of the discipline of logical inference is the question of error so that "we may not attach psychological certainty to a false awareness".[40] Here once again we part company with the logicians. Matilal himself concedes that "psychologism is not always a crime"[41] and this is certainly true in aesthetic inference. However, in general terms aestheticians would have no difficulty in accepting the "triple-character of reason"[42] or *hetu* as enunciated by Diññāga.

Thus *ākāṅkṣā* and *mukhyārthabādha* form the heart of the mythic or metaphoric image both in the verbal and the non-verbal arts, an image that lacking nothing in surface beauty yet provokes the aesthete to the process of aesthetic *anumāna* and then on to *parokṣārtha*. While the epistemic process of *pratyakṣa* has assured the aesthete of *artha* when it comes to *rasa* and *rūpa* as discussed in the previous chapters, it is insufficient in handling some types of verbal and visual images that form such an important part of any art tradition, specially Indian, for which he must rely on *parokṣapramāṇa* and proceed to a *parokṣārtha*. These images are richly laden not only with specific symbols but form a part of a whole symbol system in the tradition and are set in the framework of traditional *gāthās* and *kathās*. In essence *parokṣapramāṇa* then is the epistemic process that is necessary for an aesthetic handling of images, for "pictures invite the eye not to rush along, but to rest a while and dwell with them in enjoyment of their revelation".[43] For this revelation is subtle or *parokṣa* and available only to the inquiring mind, to the prepared aesthete who is committed to penetrating the superficial and undertaking a sustained cognitive effort, one who is ready to open the door and enter the world of hidden and suggested meanings in the images, one who is not satisfied with a superficial art encounter but who insists on making that encounter a knowledge episode.

When it comes to visual images, and in particular *rūpa*, it is important that we make a clear distinction, as far as it is possible, between its aesthetic and religious meanings, for the approach in both cases would be different. *Parokṣārtha* limits us to an epistemic enjoyment of the image and in this sense makes available the aesthetic and excludes the religious. It is interesting to note that while a religious approach incorporates at least what is superficially aesthetic, the purely aesthetic cannot support the religious. For the aesthete an image, be it sacred or secular, is a visual *kāvya*, an object of cognition for aesthetic enjoyment, and must be epistemically treated as such.

Myth, which includes in its wider implication allegory, understood as the traditional *gāthās* and *kathās*, provides the foundation of much of Indian verbal and visual art. Fortunately the word myth in the Indian tradition has not been devalued and has not acquired the meaning of fantasy or fiction but continues to enjoy an unbroken acceptance and credence. For the Indian psyche, both of the artist and the aesthete, the truth of a myth is never in question, for it has always enjoyed an inner consistency or coherence. Myth remains for us in India an integral part of the larger reality of life and does not need any defence, and the large number of Western studies on mythography undertaken mainly from an anthropological standpoint are not only irreverent but irrelevant as well. What however is relevant in our inquiry is the study of the dynamics of myth from an aesthetic standpoint and to investigate the role of *parokṣārtha* in the enjoyment of that myth and therefore of the image. Myths operate at various levels even within the tradition and serve many functions, but our interest lies solely in their epistemic status. The Indian mind has shown preference to myth rather than to *itihāsa,* for history is a mere chronicle of human events, and no historical analysis or portrayal is capable of pointing to a reality other than its own. The structure of history is too concrete, its concerns too limited, its contents too prosaic, to excite the Indian artistic mind which is quintessentially poetic. Indian artists therefore have shown scant interest in depicting the historical through their visual or verbal images, choosing instead mythic or metaphoric images to convey their vision. For only myth provides a language that can at once remain beautiful on the surface and contain a vision at another level, that can hint at cosmic rhythms although striking an earthly drum, that concerns itself with the universal while being involved with the particular, that leads the subject to a better understanding of objectivity, that addresses itself to the individual and yet draws on the collective consciousness of the society, that can suggest order while depicting chaos, which can point to the ultimate while being grounded in the immediate and which converts profane time into Great Time. As Eliade rightly points out "Living a myth then implies a genuinely religious [*alaukika*] experience since it differs from the ordinary experience of everyday life."[44] It is no wonder that the Indian tradition has a treasure of countless myths and that the Indian artist has fathomed into this treasure to fashion his images.

The role of *parokṣapramāṇa* in dealing with a myth is two-fold. In the first place the tradition expects the aesthete to be fully conversant with the myths of the tradition. This is part of the *śikṣā* of the aesthete who is expected to bring with him the entire myth when he is enjoying an image. Very often this is taken for granted. At other times, the myth is portrayed in its entirety as in a narrative scroll image, and in some instances a couplet from an epic poem is inscribed on the image as in a Kṛṣṇa miniature painting. This aspect of aesthetic inference is so fundamental that some would even deny this process as inferential. The real aesthetic inference is the capacity of the aesthete to handle a myth, fix the meaning of the image by penetrating the surface of the myth, analysing its components but yet not destroying its artistic unity, enjoying the abstract while not losing the concrete, in other words living the myth at least in an epistemic sense. Aesthetic *anumāna* calls for the enjoyment not explanation, realisation not fragmentation, of a myth. The dramatic aspect of a myth can be understood under the aesthetic dynamics of *rasa* for the epistemic process is mainly emotive. Thus the battle of Durgā with the demon Mahiṣa, of Kṛṣṇa with the serpent Kāliya and countless other mythic accounts can be enjoyed at their dramatic level and are revealed by aesthetic *pratyakṣa* and will not need *kāvyānumāna.* However *rasa* is only one component of a myth, important but not exclusive, for an equally important feature of a myth is its *dhvani* or suggestiveness, and it is in the enjoyment of the suggested meaning of a myth that aesthetic inference plays a major role. The amorous relationship of Rādhā and Kṛṣṇa in the many Kṛṣṇa myths is a good example. The dalliance of the two in the enchanted Vṛndāvana assumes quite a different meaning when Rādhā is understood as the *jīvātman* seeking the *paramātman* and the *abhisārika nāyikā* ceases to remain just a love lorn damsel, the *rājhaṃsa* flying across the sky in a miniature painting can hardly be looked as just another bird and the *latā* that winds around a tree trunk not just another creeper and the *āliṅgan* of Śiva not just an amorous clasp. Zimmer rightly points out that the:

> mythical symbols of India resist intellectualisation and reduction to fixed significations. Such treatment would only sterilise them of their magic. In the myths of India we are brought the intuitive, collective wisdom of an ageless, anonymous and many sided civilisation. The myths are effective primarily on a subconscious level, touching intuition, feeling and imagination ... [they] soak down and shape the deeper stratification of the psyche.[45]

There is thus a superficial, outer aspect of a myth, beautiful even at the initial artistic encounter but yet incomplete without its inner, deeper, almost secret meaning that is available to the initiate through aesthetic *anumāna*. One would have no difficulty in agreeing with Śrī Aurobindo that "if these (Vedic) words could be interpreted symbolically ... the progression of thought (becomes) more perfect, more luminous, more coherent and the sense of the hymn in its entirety (can be) victoriously completed".[46] Inherent in Śrī Aurobindo's statement is the fact that without this interpretation the Vedic hymn would remain incomplete. The basis of Vedic myths according to Śrī Aurobindo is the Vedic word which is *śruti*, a "divine Word that came vibrating out of the Infinite to the inner audience of man",[47] and the cardinal feature of this *śruti* is *śleṣa* or the rhetorical figure of double entendre. Vedic Sanskrit is ideally suited for the verbal aesthetic device of *śleṣa*, a language that permits transformations in meaning, an outer material profane meaning at one level and an inner spiritual sacred meaning at another, and the resolution of *śleṣa* needs not logical but aesthetic reasoning. There is no doubt that the "word for the Vedic Rishi is ... a living thing, a thing of power, creative, formative. It is not yet a conventional symbol for an idea but itself the parent and former of ideas."[48] The Vedic word has a life of its own that does not concretise meaning within its confines but permits the growth, expansion and explosion of meaning within itself. Śrī Aurobindo cites several examples of Vedic words with multiple meanings, words such as *gauh, aśva, ghṛta, agni* that permit beautiful poetry at the surface but which yield a rich treasure of meaning in their depths; he further explains at length in the ***Secret of the Veda*** various Vedic myths. Śrī Aurobindo rightly points out that the root *vid* not only means to know but also to find[49] and in aesthetics *parokṣārtha* is the finding of what is hidden, the discovering of what is suggested, "bringing to birth ... the light out of the darkness."[50] It becomes obvious that the Vedic *ṛṣis* through the device of *śleṣa* in the hymns created poetry that not only had an outer and an inner meaning but that this hierarchy of meanings was accompanied by a difference in purpose, one for the outer ritualistic activity and the other, inner, for the initiate. This was to lay the foundation not only of aesthetic *anumāna* in the Indian tradition but also of Tāntric epistemology. The Vedic hymns were to lay down what present-day scholars call the "structures of a symbol"[51] for symbols, if that word should at all be used, in the Indian tradition are not mere sterile images but images pregnant with meaning, created with a language that is not only beautiful on the surface but that carries within it seeds of *dhvani*. As Eliade rightly points out "symbolism adds a new value to an object or to an action without however disturbing their own proper and immediate values."[52] He further points out that "the interdependence of the valences of a symbol and the homology of its different contexts ought not to be understood as a monotonous repetition of the same message on different levels."[53] Each level of meaning in a myth is new but vibrates in consonance with the overall meaning. Eliade is equally right in pointing out that "the meaning of ... symbolism ... becomes comprehensible to us only in the measure that we succeed in grasping the structure in its entirety."[54] While the process of *kāvyānumāna* in the understanding of a myth lets us move back and forth from one level of meaning to another, at no time does this movement fragment the myth, each level of meaning is held in dynamic equilibrium, asserting the interdependence of one level on the next. It is important to note that a myth translates a "human condition into cosmological terms ... but reciprocally discloses the interdependence between the structures of human existence with cosmic structures."[55] In understanding myths we not only become mythopoeic ourselves but "open ourselves to the objective world, (and) at the same time succeed in leaving our unique condition and acceeding to a comprehension of the universal."[56] The language of a myth belongs to the society and not to an individual and by participating in a myth through the art object the aesthete assures himself of a wider and richer experience. This epistemic dynamic in the understanding, enjoying and resolution of a myth constitutes the *parokṣapramāṇa*.

If myth is the aesthetic basis of images, both visual and verbal, in the Indian tradition, a *yantra*, also sometimes called *pañjara* provides the aesthetic undergirding of all plastic arts notably *rūpa* and *vāstu* and therefore also of *nāṭya* which is the immediate source of *rūpa*. The cardinal purpose of *parokṣapramāṇa* is to move the art experience from a superficial encounter to a deeper and epistemologically meaningful process, and the aesthetic concept of *yantra* provides that inner movement to the outer aesthetic experience of *rūpa*. While the cognitive process of *pratyakṣa* provides valuable sense data there are certain aspects of *rūpa* that remain untouched, aspects that are necessary for a complete aesthetic understanding and enjoyment of the image and which may be of passing interest to a casual observer of the art object but not to the aesthete. A *yantra* in its basic sense is an instrument. Understood aesthetically it is the basic geometrical analogue or equation of an image which forms an indispensable part of the artist's *dhyāna* and which equally must form an essential component of the aesthete's *dhyāna* as well. For perception reveals the superficial sensual aspects of the form, but it is only a *yantra* through its geometrical forms that provides an equation and which can uncover and make available the inner logic of composition. In the words of Woodroffe, "The dynamic graph or the diagram of forces which can be represented ... is called the *yantra* of that thing."[57] The words "dynamic" and "forces" capture the essence of a *yantra* for a *yantra* imparts a dimension of movement, both in time and space, to what otherwise would remain a static visual experience. While aesthetic perception has conveyed the *rasa* of the image and nourished the emotional aspect of the aesthete's experience, cognition is still at a superficial level and only a *yantra* can penetrate the surface to uncover the "primary spiritual essence"[58] of the *rūpa* to touch a deeper and more fundamental aspect of the aesthete's psyche. It is important to realise that the *yantra* is not an art form in itself but an instrument consisting of geometrical shapes for the adept, shapes that are used to create yet another dimension of realisation of the art object in the aesthete's mind. In order to do this the *yantra* must "speak a language different from the one familiar to the eye"[59] for after all the *yantra* is meant for the eye of the eye. The *yantra*, which by its very nature is saturated with meaning, has a specific purpose, and is not an "autonomous construct of the creative imagination but ... a functionally determined utensil for a spiritual, sacramental rite."[60] The use of a *yantra* requires the mediation of reason and thus it becomes clear why the process of utilising a *yantra* in aesthetic experience is a *pramāṇa* of the nature of *anumāna* and is indispensable in the realisation of *parokṣārtha* of images both visual and literary.

Boner is right in pointing out that "with the creation of the fire altar [*vedī*] the integration of man into cosmic order has perhaps for the first time found a clear and explicit expression" in the Indian tradition.[61] The geometrical features of the *vedī* are too obvious to be missed and can be considered the earliest examples of a *yantra*. The correlation of the microcosm of the *yajamāna* with the macrocosm of the universe, in other words of the *puruṣa* with the *Puruṣa,* takes place through the *yantra* of the *vedī* and provides the foundational experience of the *yajña* and remains the prototype for all later *yantras* in the Indian plastic tradition. The *anurūpam* or micocosm-macrocosm correlation is provided by the Vedic sacrifice in a number of different ways; our interest lies primarily in the anthropocosmic efficacy of the geometrical shapes of the Vedic fire altars acting as intermediaries between man and the cosmos, with the ultimate objective of establishing a communication between the finite and the Infinite, the mutliplicity of forms and the formless, the *rūpa* and the *arūpa,* a process of considerable aesthetic importance. Vātsyāyana rightly points out that the "*yajña* is not a simple sacrifice but is instead a meticulously constructed system of correspondences and identifications between concrete physicality and abstract metaphysics."[62] It provides for the first time in the Indian tradition geometrical motifs which can express speculative thought and which "in turn guide the destinies of Indian art for centuries."[63] This geometrical vocabulary initiated in the Vedic sacrifice is continued in the Upaniṣads although it moves from being anthropocosmic to being anthropocentric and from an outer to an inner plane of sacrifice, from *yajña* to *yoga*. The concept of the *yantra* is further strengthened in the many unmistakable geometric images of the Upaniṣads, images such as the wheel with its hub and its spokes. In the ***Bṛhadāraṇyaka Upaniṣad*** there is the striking image of a spider at the centre of its web of concentric circles issuing and reabsorbing its threads, emphasising that "the point of origin of the supreme consciousness is simultaneously an infinite reservoir of collective energy from which everything issues and into which everything returns."[64] It is not difficult to see how the spider of the Upaniṣad becomes the *bindu* of later *śilpa* texts and is a pointer to the *yantra* of later plastic art. Vātsyāyana has dealt at length on the subject of these and other geometric motifs in the Upaniṣads conveying the basis of speculative Indian thought. These geometric motifs of the Vedas and later of the Upaniṣads emphasise that all forms have a gross outer structure and a subtle inner structure; in particular, they reveal the inner cosmic basis of forms and shapes and become a harbinger of the later *yantras*, which in a similar way reveal the inner essence of *rūpa* and which therefore must form an integral part of their aesthetic understanding and enjoyment.

Khanna has pointed out that *yantras* are an amalgam of three principles: the form principle (*ākṛti rūpa*), the function principle (*kriyā rūpa*) and the power principle (*śakti rūpa*).[65] As aesthetes our concern is with the first two principles and less so with the third, as the *śakti rūpa yantra* has magico-religious implications which are of no value to us as aesthetes. While the *ākṛti rūpa* yields the inner, cosmic or hidden form of the *rūpa*, the *kriyā rūpa* acts on the psychic level and functions as "revelatory symbols of cosmic truths and as instructional charts of the spiritual aspect of human experience. All the primal shapes of a *yantra* are psychological symbols corresponding to inner states of human consciousness through which control and expansion of psychic forces are possible."[66] A *yantra* thus serves as a cross-over point from the aesthete to the artist, from the microcosm to the macrocosm, from the outer sensual beauty of the *rūpa* to the inner logic of its composition and must form an important part of the inferential process of the aesthete.

While the iconometric and iconographic details of *rūpa* are dealt with extensively in the *śilpa* texts of the tradition, it is not easy to explain why, with the exception of texts such as ***Śilpaprakāśa*** and ***Vāstusūtra Upaniṣad***, the texts are silent on the *yantras* of *rūpa*s. However, modern writers such as Boner, Zimmer and Vātsyāyana have refocused our attention on the importance of *yantra* for the aesthete. It becomes obvious that there are two alternatives for the aesthete. He could either start ***de novo*** and derive his own *yantra* based on well established aesthetic principles or resort to the *yantras* already provided in the tradition as an aid to a fuller and deeper realisation of the image. Zimmer is right in pointing out that "in most cases the initiate is his own priest and therefore is, on the whole, dependent on himself for the devices required for the act of worship".[67] When Zimmer talks of "worship" he is obviously referring to an aesthetic enjoyment of the image. The term "worship" for us in this inquiry connotes throughout aesthetic rather than ritual worship.

The geometrical elements that constitute a *yantra* are the line, circle, square and the triangle each with its special meaning, and of these the circle and the line seem the most important as between them they "embrace the whole display of visible forms in the universe."[68] Boner has said that "every *pañjara,* the geometrical diagram of every image of divinity is like a universe in miniature, the totality and quintessence of a universe, where all powers are potentially present."[69] The ***Vāstusūtra Upaniṣad*** (hereafter referred to as *VSU*) lays special emphasis on the line and states that it is the *rekhā* or "the line that conveys the *bhāva* of the image",[70] and that "the knowledge of the line is to be known as all-comprehensive."[71] The role of *rekhā* is strongly emphasised by the

VSU, for it says, "the lines are the Truth, and the lines are the cause of form,"[72] and "the line is the support of the composition",[73] and even more emphatically equates *rekhā* with sacrificial offerings. The *VSU* describes three types of lines: vertical or *agni rekhā* which conveys a feeling of elation, horizontal lines or *ab rekhā* which conveys a feeling of longing, and diagonal lines or *vāyu rekhā* which imparts a feeling of energy. The main vertical middle line is likened to the "post of Meru, the backbone in the animal, the marrow of the tree, the soul in living beings."[74] With horizontal lines, the *VSU* explains, the panel is divided first into ten and later into fourteen compartments. At every step in the progressive evolution of the *rūpa* as manifested in the *yantra* the interconnection between the microcosm and the macrocosm is never forgotten. Tagore admits his indebtedness to lines when he says that "they seize the mind because of some distinctive quality inherent in them."[75]

If the *rekhā* in a *yantra* displays the emotional character of the image, the *bindu* or the focal point is the source of the image's artistic energy. For we are told, "*bindu brahmeva*",[76] the *bindu* is *brahman,* and further, "it is the *bindu* that imparts glory and harmony to the image."[77] The *bindu* ensures that the *rūpa* does not remain a static art form but gives the impression of a dynamic art process. The *yantra* through the *bindu* gives the impression of at least two types of movement: a dynamic physical movement like that through the axis of a wheel, and more importantly, a psychic centripetal movement, gathering toward itself forces that it liberates, making sure that the physical centre of the art form is also the metaphysical centre of the art experience. In her interpretation of its centripetal movement, Kramrisch writes that "the urge towards form at any movement has an outward direction but it becomes form only by the corresponding countermovement."[78] In a *yantra* no movement exists without its countermovement. The appearance of balance of movements creates harmony with the *yantra* and makes it a symbol of cosmic harmony. By the balancing of centrifugal and centripetal forces, the *bindu* creates the ambience of rest in the midst of action and of serenity in the midst of dramatic tension, features that are the hallmark of *rūpa* that come to light in a *yantra*. With the *bindu* comes the actual or implied circle. The gloss on the *VSU* says, "The circle is the All. The breath of life is contained in its form as the mind is in Man. The circle is time according to Vastuveda."[79] The conception of the circle limits the compositon in a physical sense, while at the same time endowing it with the attributes of wholeness and organic unity. The circle is also symbolic of cosmic unity. Moreover, the concept of circularity gives to the *yantra* the dimension of time. By means of the circle in the geometric grid, the dramatic situation depicted in the *rūpa* is set within the framework of time and is given a cosmic dimension. The circle also gives to the *rūpa* its stability by ensuring that it will maintain a centripetal rather than a centrifugal force. Boner explains that not only the circle or the periphery but "every circle with a constant curvature is part of a circle and has in itself the tendency to close into full circle ... it gathers up movement as a pool gathers up the inflowing waters."[80] The *vṛttam* or circle is, more often than not, an imagined or invisible periphery, sometimes suggesting itself by an arc or a curve, and at other times by a semi-circle, but in no uncertain terms calling attention to itself by the *bindu* of the *yantra*. In her interpretation of the geometry of the *rūpa*, Vātsyāyana argues that it is the function of the *bindu* to ensure that the "one breaks into the multiple and the configuration of the mutiple invariably returns to the unity of the one."[81] The breaking up of the whole into parts and then bringing together of the parts is not a meaningless exercise like putting parts of a jig-saw puzzle together, but is meant to "evoke a psychic state."[82] This is the essential function of a *yantra*.

The *VSU* makes it amply clear that these basic geometric shapes, namely the circle, square, the triangle and the lines, or the basic grammar of the *yantra* are not mere abstract or arbitrary shapes but cosmic shapes, reminding one of the Vedic *yajña*. As Vātsyāyana puts it "these geometric motifs and figures have their own logic and meaning and the (*rūpakāra*) uses them with extraordinary sensitivity and understanding"[83] and which are available to the avid aesthete only through the *yantra*. The human body in the Indian tradition is reduced to the point of geometrical abstraction so that the *rūpa* may become, not just another form in the world of forms, but a fit receptacle for the form and feeling of the cosmic *Puruṣa*. This idea becomes evident only in the *yantra* of the *rūpa*. It is the function of the geometric forms to manifest the causal and the subtle components of consciousness. The interplay of these geometric shapes in the *yantra* ensures that the "panel is a microcosm reflecting all the elements of the Macrocosm". Finally, it is the interplay of these basic cosmic forms that creates the "*mahā-chandas*", the principle of order and rhythm. That these *chandas* are not only metre in poetry but a principle of order and rhythm in all arts is shown in the ***Aitareya Brāhmaṇa*** where the term '*chandomaya*' is applied to all kinds of art. It is only when, through *parokṣārtha*, that the geometric underpinning of *rūpa* is realised that a firmer, more deliberate appreciation of form, a "*dhāraṇā*" can take place.

It is amply clear that only when an aesthete comes under the influence of a *yantra* that he realises that the outer sensual aspects of the *rūpa* are only a threshold to the inner geometric form reminding one of the Ṛg Vedic declaration that "as one mounts peak after peak there becomes clear much that still has to be done."[84] The inferential process of converting an image to its *yantra* leads the initiate to what Vātsyāyana calls an "ordered inner vision"[85] and a "complete and accurate visualised diagram of the deity in the worshipper's heart",[86] converting outer sight into inner vision. It is important to note that the two levels of cognition, an initial perceptual and a later inferential through the *yantra*, move together and feed each other, "unifying the outer fire with the fire of knowledge"[87] creating a richer, more fuller cognition of the image. Khanna has rightly pointed out that *yantras* are:

> visual metaphors through which we move beyond our material order, they serve as cosmic cross-points by means of which our contact with nature at large can be expanded, to tap higher and more unified levels of experience. They provide halting places, sites of rest and support when the seeker gains an awareness of the universe it its totality and discovers his inner identity with the single, immutable centre.[88]

The ***Kulārṇava Tantra*** leaves no doubt about the importance of *yantras* when it says that "as body is to the soul and oil is to the lamp a *yantra* is to the deity."[89] It must be pointed out that generally a *yantra* cannot be isolated from its system of sound dynamics, in other words its *mantra.* "The *yantra-mantra* complex is basically an equation that unites space, *ākāśa* which in its gross form appears as shapes, and vibrations, and which in their finite forms occur as the spoken or written word."[90]

One of the best applications of the epistemology of *dhvani* under the rubric of *parokṣārtha* is to the understanding of symbols. The term 'symbol' can be ambiguous and is very often used interchangeably with the term 'sign'. Thus a word can be called a symbol for what it stands for. In art, however, a symbol must possess certain essential, surface qualities of beauty and point to a reality beyond itself; in other words it should possess both a *sākṣātartha* and a *parokṣārtha*. It is important to remember that the Indian visual artist does not copy the natural object but renders it into an aesthetic form filled with symbolic meanings. A modern interpreter of the tradition says of Indian art "it is not so much an illustration as a translation of a reality."[91] He further comments that in the process of this "translation of a reality" the *rūpa* acquires a visionary character", and he goes on to say that "Indian art is generally synaesthetic—a mixture of media combined in a manner which resembles, but is not identical with, oneric experience;"[92] "a kind of recollection in tranquillity of the rapture of visionary experience."[93] It is this visionary character of Indian art that is created by the use of symbols and which demands not just a superficial, but deep and penetrating understanding. The Indian visual artist depicts form not as the ordinary human eye sees it, but as the *devas* see it with the divine eye. It is in this sense that Coomaraswamy translates the following statement of the ***Aitareya Brāhmaṇa*** as "it is in imitation of the angelic works of art that any work of art is arrived at here."[94] Modern commentators have also stressed that the symbolism that pervades the entire specturm of *rūpa* must be understood, not in any superficial or token sense, but as a highly evolved, integrated and sophisticated language of symbols. As Coomaraswamy explains, "symbolism is a language and a precise form of thought, a hieratic and metaphysical language and not a language determined by somatic or psychological categories."[95]

We shall begin this inquiry by restricting the discussion on symbols to the type of symbols found in traditional performing and visual art, namely in *nāṭya* and *śilpa,* both of which can be subsumed under the rubric of *rūpa*. The origin of the use of symbols, understood in this sense, can be traced at least as far back as *mudrās* in *nāṭya.* "Where the hand goes so do the eyes, where the eyes go the mind follows"[96] is the foundational *sūtra* of the value and function of *hastamudrās* in *nāṭya.* It stresses the two step process of *mudrās*. In the first place the *mudrās* have to be attractive and beckon the eyes; having achieved that and touched the mind, they must then become a source of knowledge. Most *mudrās* are taken from the ordinary gestures of daily life, refined and stylised and then incorporated into the repertoire of classical dancing, pointing quite clearly that the *lokadharmī* and the *nāṭyadharmī* are intimately related. *Mudrās* employ predominantly the hands but the *hastamudrā* forms an integral part of the entire body of the dancer and the *rūpa* which includes *abhinaya* and *āṅgika*. While the entire *śāstra* of the *mudrās* need not detain us here what is worth stressing is that *mudrās* can have both a superficial, initial *sākṣātartha* and another deeper *parokṣārtha*, and that both types of meaning are held in an unbroken *advaitic* chain of meanings and that at no point does one need to sacrifice one for the other and destroy the integrity of the *mudrā*. *Mudrā*, like myth and *yantra* discussed earlier, satisfies the basic premise of *dhvani* and is a type of *parokṣārtha.* If *nāṭya* provides the foundation, Theravāda Buddhism gives the hagiographic basis to symbols in the Indian tradition. The account of Śākyamuni Buddha's response as to how he wished to be represented after his passing away is so well-known that it is considered historical and need not be recounted here in any detail. Of greater importance to us as aesthetes, is the fact that the Buddha felt that his chosen symbol, the tree, would serve the purpose of contemplation rather than prayer, and lead his students to gnosis rather than religious adoration. This has seminal aesthetic importance, for symbols not only have surface beauty but more importantly promote *parokṣārtha.* Much has been written about the use of a tree by the Buddha as his symbol, for it has numerous implications. However, what interests us is its impact on visual art, especially plastic art and equally on aesthetics. It established the use of symbols in plastic narrative as well as representational anthropomorphic art and conferred on symbols not only a visual but an intellectual credibility. Symbolism, as Coomaraswamy writes, became not only a language but a precise form of thought.[97] Indian artists developed not only individual symbols but a whole symbol system, drawing from the common objects of nature such as trees, creepers, forests and rivers, birds and flowers as well as weapons and objects of daily use such as mace, conch, trident, drum, bell and so on. These symbols then became the treasure of the community and were not private to any one artist or school. Buddhism ensured that a symbol is not a mere object of transubstantiation but a visual theophany. R. Panikar contends that a "symbol is a thing as it appears and ... as it expresses and manifests itself ... and is one of the ways to reach a supreme experience ...Through a symbol such as a *mudrā* one is led to perceive the essence of things."[98] A symbol thus becomes an essential mediator between object and subject, consciousness and being, language and reality, stressing the inner *advaitic* unity between the two levels of meaning and becomes a source of new insight. There is thus a double movement from the expressed to the suggested and from the suggested to the expressed, from the *bodhi* tree to the *dharma* and from the *dharma* back to the *bodhi* tree, from *ḍamaru* to creation and from creation back to the *ḍamaru* and so on. This double movement is the hallmark of a symbol understood and enjoyed aesthetically rather than religiously. This freedom of double movement is not possible in a strict religious use and understanding of a symbol. In *bhakti* epistemology there is only one way movement from the symbol to what is symbolised and reaching the latter the former is jettisoned by the *bhakta.* The onus of this movement lies on the outer superficial aspect of the symbol, for it has the sensual capacity to lead the onlooker to another level of meaning entirely on the basis of its sensual properties, or what Ānandavardhana would call *vācyasāmarthyakṣiptah.* Amaladass is right in stating that knowledge from symbols is "knowing the unseen from what is seen, reaching the inner significance from external realities ... from what is perceived at the space-time level towards an apperceptive level of reality."[99] A symbol through a process of *sphoṭa* in the mind of the aesthete conveys far more than what a *śabda* can and leads to an altogether different, deeper and richer kind of knowledge for the aesthete and is a good example of *parokṣārtha.* It is the function of symbols in Indian visual art to be interrelated forming a symbol system. The right hand of Naṭarāja relates to what the left hand touches, and the uplifted left leg must relate to the firmly grounded right leg, and so on with every limb and part of the Naṭarāja's *rūpa.* When even a single symbol of the *rūpa* yields its *parokṣārtha* the whole image catches fire, as it were, and becomes one whole symbol. As Kramrisch says, "no phase of Indian art exists apart from the whole, so are the various aspects, forms and figures interconnected."[100] This dynamic coherence, intrinsic connectedness and inner rhythm are mainly brought about by the symbols. For, in the inner world of *parokṣārtha*, we are no longer tied to what is sensually real, but we are in a world of higher reality, we are participating in the inner life of the *rūpa* where time and space have been transcended. The various components of the *rūpa* not only blend into a harmonious whole but the inner harmony of the *rūpa* acts as a catalyst in the transformation of the aesthete. This inner harmony is a feature of *parokṣārtha.* When Kramrisch states that "the urge towards form at any moment has an outward direction, but it becomes form only by the corresponding countermovement",[101] she is referring, in unmistakable terms, to the *parokṣārtha* of the image. One can assert with Khanna when she says that "all Indian images are symbols of the Supreme Principle and vary only in degree of abstraction. Consequently, the outer form of an image should always be perceived in relation to its symbolic value."[102] Symbolism in *rūpa* demands a resolution not by the eye, but by the "eye of the eye".[103] Coomaraswamy reminds us that the traditional symbols are never the invention of the particular author "but are of immemorial antiquity"[104] and are rather the treasure of the tradition. It therefore becomes clear why both the artist and the aesthete need to be steeped in the tradition. The symbolism of the *rūpa* links it not only with the myths of the Purāṇic tradition but also with the *yajña* of the Vedas. Pippalāḍa emphasises that sculpture is indeed a *yajña* and the sculptor a *sthāpaka* or a priest of art. The strong connection between *rūpa* on the one hand and *yajña* on the other is further underlined by the *VSU* when it says: "it is from the knowledge of form that sacrifice originates in the world."[105] In equating *rūpa* with *yajña* Pippalāḍa gives Indian sculpture its pedigree, points to the principle of the *yantra* and connects it unquestionably with the Veda itself.

In a prepared aesthete, who is undertaking a *parokṣa* inquiry, the *rūpa* cannot remain a mere piece of art, useful for its superficial sensual artistic qualities, qualities that have been cognised in its *sākṣātartha,* but by the very nature of its *parokṣārtha*, breaks out of its form to reveal the formless, much as in the artist the formless *pratibhā* gives rise to form. In many ways, the *dhyāna* of the aesthete is a mirror-image of that of the *dhyāna* of the artist; in the former, it is the formless that gives rise to form, in the latter, it is the form that proceeds to the formless. There is ample evidence in the texts to establish that *rūpa* like *vāk* has a function and meaning beyond its outer form. The *VSU* says that "whatever one attains through word the same they can attain through form."[106] A *rūpa* has for the prepared aesthete not only a superficial but a deeper meaning as well, not just *sākṣātartha* but a *parokṣārtha* The *śilpakāra,* like the *kavi,* uses artistic devices, "*vakratah*"[107] to suggest this second meaning. In suggesting another level of meaning, it is important to note that the surface aesthetic qualities of the *rūpa* are never jeopardized or abandoned. For *rūpa* is no ordinary form but a *surūpa* or perfect or ideal form. And it is this perfection of form in the *rūpa* that leads to "*divyatvam*".[108] In order to effect this transformation to divine nature, the first requisite of *rūpa* is that it leads to "*pramoda*"[109] or pleasure in the beauty of the image, for, from this pleasure will arise love and from love contemplation, which in turn ensures "the very nature of *brahman*".[110] Pippalāḍa declares in a sentence that sums up our entire argument when he declares that "the higher and ultimate understanding of artistic form is none other than metaphysics",[111] making the unequivocal connection between aesthetics and metaphysics. It is importrant to note that no where does Pippalāḍa mix *bhakti* and aesthetics, or the holy and the beautiful, or magic and meaning, or *arca* and *artha*. For an aesthete the bonafides of *artha* are never subordinated to that of *arca*. Instead, he leaves us with the very definite impression that a purely aesthetic appreciation and realisation of the *rūpa*, through both a surface and deeper *artha*, is a valid artistic activity fully capable of leading the prepared aesthete to ineffable *ānanda*. The *rūpa*, though mute, is a "*vyaktarūpa*"[112] that gives insistent visual hints of a *parokṣārtha*, hints that encourages a calmer, more deliberate understanding of its form. Such continually deepening understanding is what Pippalāḍa calls *rūpaprajña*. We have the support of the ***Viṣṇudharmottara*** when it says, "*hetumca tadākara*",[113] form indeed has a purpose and a meaning, both *sākṣāt* and *parokṣa*.

NOTES

1. Rabindranath.Tagore, ***The Religion of Man.*** (London: Unwin Books, 1975) p. 94.
2. *dhvanirnāma arthāntaram.*
   Dhvani is just another meaning.
   Ānandavardhana, ***Dhvanyāloka.*** K. Krishnamoorthy (ed.) (Delhi: Motilal Banarsidass, 1982) 1.13.
3. *kāvyavisaye ca vyaṅgyapratītinām satya asatya nirūpanasya aprayojakatavam eva iti tatra pramāṇa antara vyāpara parīkṣa upahāsāya eva sampadyate.*
   As a matter of fact, the question of logical truth and falsity in regard to suggested meaning is entirely futile.
   Ānandavardhana, ***Dhvanyāloka.*** III.33. pp. 222-23.
4. A.K.Coomaraswamy, ***The Transformation of Nature in Art.*** (New York: Dover Publications, 1934) p. 138.
5. *Ibid.*, p. 137.
6. *Ibid.*, p. 129.

7. *Ibid.*, p. 174.
8. *dadṛsa eṣāmavamā sadāmsi, pareṣu ā guhyeṣu vrateṣu.*
Only the lowest abodes of these are seen, who exist in supreme and secret places.
Ṛg Veda, III.54.5.
A.C.Bose, ***Hymns from the Vedas.*** (Bombay: Asia Publishing House, 1966) p. 297.
9. *Ibid.*, p. 297.
10. Annambhaṭṭa in ***Tarkasaṅgraha***. p. 22.
taken from S. Kuppuswami Sastri (ed.) ***A Primer of Indian Logic***. (Kuppuswami Research Institute, Madras, 1961).
11. B.K.Matilal, ***Logic, Language & Reality.*** (Delhi: Motilal Banarsidass, 1985) p.64.
12. B.K.Matilal, ***Journal of Indian Philosophy.*** Volume 16, Number 2, June 1988.
13. ***Ṛg Veda***. VI. 9.5. quoted by M. Eliade, ***Myth and Reality***. (New York: Harper & Row Publishers, 1963) p. 4.
14. K.Kunjunni Raja, ***Indian Theories of Meaning.*** (Madras: The Adyar Library and Research Centre, 1963) p. 157.
15. *Ibid.*, p. 157.
16. *Ibid.*, p. 158.
17. *ityuktalakṣaṇo yo dhvanir vivecyah prayatnataḥ sadbhiḥ, satkāvyam kartum jñātum vā samyagbhiyuktaiḥ.*
Principal suggestion which we have defined hitherto should be attentively studied not only by all poets who aspire after writing good poetry but also by all critics who aspire after understanding it well.
Ānandavardhana, ***Dhvanyāloka.*** III.45, pp. 260-61.
18. *prasiddhi śrevamastyeva vidagdha vidvatparisatsu yad abhimatataram vastu vyangyatvena prakaś'yate.*
In polished literary circles it has indeed become a convention of wits to communicate their best ideas only through suggestion and not at all by expressed words.
Ibid., IV. 5. gloss, pp. 280-81.
19. *vācaspati sahasrānām sahasrair api yatnataḥ, nibaddhāpi kṣayam naiti prakṛtir jagatāmiva.*
Like the resources of primordial Nature herself, the infinite possibilities of poetic themes can never be drained off even by a million Bṛhaspatis composing with all their might simultaneously.
Ibid., IV. 10 pp. 292-93.
20. *tadevam śabde vyavahāre trayaḥ prakārāḥ vācakatvam guṇavṛtti vyañjakatvam ca.*
Thus it is clear that the function of words are three-fold: denotation, indication and suggestiveness.
Ibid., III. 3233 pp. 206-07.

21. *śabdasāmarthyapratiprasavabhuteti śabdas'aktimūlam kalpyate.*
Though the apprehension of the suggested is thus produced by sense alone, it is still regarded as based on the power of the equivocal word itself.
Ibid., III.32-33 pp. 194-95.

22. *tasmād bhinna viṣayatvād bhinna rūpatvācca svārthā abhīdayitvam arthāntarāvagama hetutvam ca śabdasya yattayoḥ spaṣṭa eva bhedaḥ.*
Since the scope and natures of the two functions are thus quite different, it is clear that the denotative function of words and the implying function of words are quite different from each other.
Ibid., III. 32-33 pp. 198-99. Also see pp. 220-21.

23. *yathaiva hi pradīpdvāreṇa ghaṭapratītau utpannāyām na pradīpaprakāśo nivartate tadvat vyaṅgyapratitau vācyāvabhāsaḥ.*
Just as the light of the lamp will not recede as soon as the perception of the pot is brought home to the observer, so also, the expressed sense will continue to shine out even after the apprehension of the suggested sense has been achieved.
Ibid., III. 32-33 pp. 200-01.

24. *padmapatraṣatavyatibhedanayena.*
This original quotation by Abhinavagupta has in turn been quoted by all commentators including Mammaṭa and Viśvanātha.
see Mammaṭa, ***Kāvyaprakāśa***. Vol 1. p. 62.

25. *tadvat sacetasām so artho vācyārtha vimukhātmanām. buddhau tattvārtha darśinyām jhatyevāvabhāsate.*
The suggested meaning flashes suddenly across the truth perceiving minds of perceptive critics when they turn away from the literal meaning.
Ibid., I.12 pp. 18-19.

26. *śabdārtha śasana jñāna mātrenaiva na vedyate, vedyate sa tu kāvyartha-tattvajñāireva kevalam.*
It is not understood by a mere learning in grammar and in dictionary. It is understood only by those who have an insight into the true significance of poetry.
Ibid., I.7 pp.14-15.

27. *atha ca vācya-vācakalakṣaṇa mātra kṛta śramāṇām kāvyatattvārtha bhāvanā vimukhānām.*
But the fact is that the meaning remains beyond the understanding of persons with a grounding merely in the science of meanings and words but averse to aesthetic contemplation of the intrinsic significance of poetry.
Ibid., I.7 gloss pp. 14-15.

28. *boddhṛmatra vidagdha vyapadeśayoḥ pratitīmātra camatkṛtyośca kararāt kāryasya.*
The expressed meaning produces a mere comprehension in one who knows the meaning of words while the suggested produces charm in men of taste alone.
Mammaṭa, ***Kāvyaprakāśa.*** R.C.Dwivedi (ed.) (Delhi: Motilal Banarsidass,

1967)
V.134 gloss, pp. 174-75.

29. A. Amaladass, ***Philosophical Implications of Dhvani.*** (Vienna: E.J.Brill, 1984) p. 160.
30. ***Īśa Upaniṣad***. 1.9.
Śrī Aurobindo, ***The Upaniṣads.*** (Pondicherry: Sri Aurobindo Ashram, 1972) p. 65.
31. ***Īśa Upaniṣad***. 1.11.
Śrī Aurobindo, ***The Upaniṣads.*** p. 66.
32. Rabindranath Tagore, ***Personality.*** (London: Macmillan and Co., 1959) p.56.
33. *Ibid.*, p. 44.
34. *Ibid.*
35. ***Īśa Upaniṣad.*** 1.14.
Rabindranath Tagore, ***Personality***. p. 61.
36. Kumārila, ***Mīmāṁsādarśanam.*** (Pune: Anandashram Edition). ***Tantravārtika*** on 2.1.48.
37. Bhartṛhari, ***Vākyapadīya.*** II.314.
38. Abhinavagupta, ***Īśvara Pratyabhijña Vimariśinī.*** (Delhi: Motilal Banarsidass, 1986) Volume III pp. 142-43.
39. B.K.Matilal, ***Logic, Language & Reality***. p. 33.
40. *Ibid.*, p. 73
41. *Ibid.*, p. 72.
42. *Ibid.*
43. J. Campbell. ***The Mythic Image***. (Princeton: Princeton University Press, 1974.) p. xi.
44. M. Eliade, ***Myth & Reality.*** p. 19.
45. H. Zimmer, ***Myths and Symbols in Indian Art and Civilisation.*** (New York: Harper Torch Books, The Bollingen Foundation, 1946) p. 41.
46. Śrī Aurobindo, ***The Secret of the Veda***. (Pondicherry: Sri Aurobindo Ashram, 1971) p. 39.
47. *Ibid.*, p. 8.
48. *Ibid.*, p. 51.
49. *Ibid.*, p. 145.
50. *Ibid.*
51. M. Eliade, ***Myth & Reality.*** p. 6.
52. *Ibid.*, p. 6.
53. *Ibid.*, p. 14.
54. *Ibid.*, p. 12.
55. *Ibid.*
56. *Ibid.*
57. A.Boner, ***Principles of Composition in Hindu Sculpture***. (Leiden: E.J.Brill, 1962) p. 16.
58. *Op. cit.*

59. H. Zimmer, ***Artistic Form and Yoga in the Sacred Images of India.*** (Princeton: Princeton University Press, 1984.) p. 124.
60. *Ibid.*, p. 124.
61. Boner, p. 22.
62. K. Vatsyayana, ***The Square and the Circle of Indian Arts***. (New Delhi: Roli Books International, 1983.) p. 24.
63. *Ibid.*, p. 33.
64. M. Khanna, ***Yantra***. The Tantric Symbol of Cosmic Unity. (London: Thomas and Hudson, 1979) p. 9.
65. *Ibid.*, p. 11.
66. *Ibid.*
67. H. Zimmer, ***Artistic Form and Yoga in the Sacred Images of India.*** p. 145.
68. A. Boner (ed.) ***Vāstusūtra Upaniṣad***. (Delhi: Motilal Banaridass,1982.) p. 27. Hereafter referred to as *VSU*.
69. *Ibid.*, p. 27.
70. *Ibid.*, 2. 20.
71. *Ibid.*, 2. 26.
72. *tathā rekhā hi satyam, rekhā rūpasya kāraṇam.*
    The lines are the Truth and the lines are the cause of the form.
    VSU, 4. 26 gloss.
73. *rekhā nyāsasyādhāro sā dhāreva.*
    The line is the support of the composition.
    VSU, 2.8 gloss.
74. The line is the backbone in the animal, marrow of the tree, soul in the living being.
    VSU, 4.26 gloss.
75. R. Tagore, ***On Art & Aesthetics.*** (Bombay: Orient Longmans, 1961) p. 108.
76. *bindu brahmeva brahma dhruvam.*
    The *bindu* is like *brahman*, *brahman* is immovable.
    VSU, 6.11.
77. *brahmabindvavalambanena rūpagani saubhāgani bhavanti.*
    It is by adopting the centre that the limbs of the image become harmonious.
    VSU, 6.13.
78. S. Kramrisch, ***Indian Sculpture***. (Delhi: Motilal Banarsidass, 1981) p. 58.
79. *vṛttam iti Viśvam tadrūpaprāṇah yathā puruṣasya manah sa vṛtta-kālaḥ eṣa vāstuvede.*
    The circle is the All. The breath of life is contained in its form even as the mind is in Man. The circle is Time according to Vāstuveda.
    VSU, 2.6 gloss.
80. A.Boner, ***Principles of Composition in Hindu Sculpture***. (Leiden: E.J.Brill, 1962) p. 46.
81. K.Vatsyayana, p. 48.
82. *Ibid.*, p. 49.
83. *Ibid.*, p. 56.

84. *yat sānoh sānumāruhat bhūryaspaṣṭa kartvam*
Ṛg Veda, 1.10.2.
Quoted by S.Shankarnarayanan, ***Sri Chakra***. (Pondicherry: Dipti Publications, 1979) p. 85.
85. K. Vatsyayana, p. 106.
86. H. Zimmer, ***Artistic Form and Yoga in the Sacred Images of India.*** p. 142.
87. *jñānagnim bāhyāgnim ca ekīkṛtya prapūjayet.*
S. Shankarnarayanan, p. 95.
88. M. Khanna, ***Yantra***. p. 10.
89. *yantra mityahare tasmin detah prīṇāti pūjitah śariramit jīvasya dīpasya snehavat priye.*
Kulārṇava Tantra, V.86. Quoted by M. Khanna, p. 12.
90. M. Khanna, ***Yantra***. p. 34.
91. R.Lannoy, ***The Speaking Tree***. (London: Oxford University Press, 1971) p. 29.
92. *Ibid.*, p. 21.
93. *Ibid.*, p. 24.
94. A. Coomaraswamy, ***The Transformation of Nature in Art.*** p. 126.
95. R.Lipsey, (ed.) ***Coomaraswamy***. 1:***Selected Papers,*** Traditional Art and Symbolism (Princeton: Princeton University Press, 1977) p. 174.
96. *yato hastaḥ tato dṛṣṭiḥ, yato dṛṣṭiḥ tato manah. yato manah tato bhāvo, yato bhāvah tato rasah.*
Nandikeśava, ***Abhinayadarpaṇa.*** 37.
M. Ghosh (editor) (Calcutta: Manisha Granthalaya, 1981).
97. R.Lipsey, *op. cit.*, p. 174.
98. A. Amaladass, p. 164.
99. *Ibid.*, p. 160.
100. S. Kramrisch, ***Indian Sculpture***. p. 132.
101. *Ibid.*, p. 139.
102. M. Khanna, ***Yantra***. p. 132.
103. *śrotrasaya śrotram manaso mano vad vāco ha vācam sa u prāṇasya prāṇah caksuṣah caksuḥ ...*
Kenopaniṣad 1.2.
It is the ear of the ear, the mind of the mind, the tongue of the tongue and also the life of the life and the eye of the eye.
104. R.Lipsey, *op. cit.,* p. 173.
105. *rūpa-jñanad yajñaḥ prabhavati loke*
It is from the knowledge of form that sacrifice originates in the world.
VSU, 6.25.
106. *yat kiñca vācā tad rūpeṇa vijñānavaca prapannena ācaranti. sa evam veda.*
Whatever one attains through [sacred] word the same they can attain through form.
VSU, 4. introduction.
107. *lakṣaṇa-prakāśārtham śilpavidyā.*

The science of sculpture is mainly to manifest the attributes (of the deities as revealed in the myths)
VSU, 6.3.

108. *surūpad divyatvam upalabhante manuṣyāḥ.*
Men can obtain divine nature through perfect form.
VSU, 3.1 gloss.

109. *pramodāt ratirhi prasarati.*
From pleasure (in the images) arises love.
VSU, 6.15.

110. *sā eṣā rūpaprajña brahma sākṣātkāra ānanda iti.*
From understanding the image [comes] the very realisation of *Brahman.*
VSU, 6.15 gloss.

111. *yathā brahmavidyā tathā rūpaprajña.*
The higher and ultimate understanding of artistic form is none other than metaphysics.
VSU, 2. 10 gloss.

112. *yad rūpasya hāvabhāvādi pratyakṣam tad vyaktarūpam.*
When attractive and other states become visible in the image, that is the manifest form.
VSU, 3.13.

113. *hetum tadākara.*
From indeed has a reason.
Viṣṇudharmottara Purāṇa. Third Khaṇḍa, Priyabala Shah (editor), (Baroda: Oriental Institute, 1961) p. 46.

Chapter 6

The Epistemology of Aesthetics

bhogo yogayate sākṣāt patakam sukṛtayate,
mokṣayate ca saṃsarah kuladharme kuleśvari
Kulārṇava Tantra, 2/24

Chapters two, three four and five explored the dynamics of *sākṣātartha* and *parokṣartha* of a *rasa* and *rūpa* experience, with the emphasis on the art object, as exemplified by *kāvya* and *śilpa*. It was shown how these art forms, which are repositories of artistic information, yield this information to the aesthete. The emphasis in the preceding chapters was primarily on the art object. This chapter will examine the epistemology of aesthetic experience and shift the attention from the art object to the aesthete, from the object to the subject. We are concerned here with the processes that occur in the mind of the aesthete who receives and responds subjectively to the objective *artha* of the art object. In applying epistemological methods to the examination of aesthetic experience, our purpose is to expand and clarify our argument that aesthetic experience is not merely sensory knowledge but a form of *āgamic* or intuitive knowledge.

Both aesthetic emotion and aesthetic form in the *mārgī* Hindu tradition, are artistic creations, created within the strict confines of the tradition, embodying in the one case a feeling, and in the other a vision, giving outer expression to a sense of beauty and delight, exalting the senses and leading, almost demanding, the aesthete to enter into his inner resources, to bring the experience to a transcendent culmination. Śri Aurobindo is right in saying that:

> the whole basis of Indian artistic creation perfectly conscious and recognised in the canons, is directly spiritual and intuitive", and that "its highest business is to disclose something of the Self, the Infinite, the Divine."[1] He further comments that the Indian artist does not depend on "an idea in the intellect, a mental imagination, an outward emotion" but instead dips into an "idea, image, emotion of the spirit". He continues, "This is the distinctive character of Indian art and to ignore it is to fall into total incomprehension or into much misunderstanding...And it is because of this that the ordinary aesthetic instinct will not suffice, a spiritual insight or culture is needed if we are to enter into the whole meaning of Indian artistic creation.[2]

Śrī Aurobindo's statement has been given in full because it emphasises that the word 'meaning' or *artha* sums up the entire undercurrent of the *mārgī* artistic activity. Aesthetic meaning is to be grasped not by the senses or the intellect alone but by direct intuition as well; and, unless the aesthetic emotion or form is propelled to its ultimate meaning, the artistic encounter remains sterile, incomplete and superficial, perhaps not moving beyond a superficial, hedonistic experience. Hiriyanna puts it succinctly when he says that, "the beautiful as a value needs to be striven for and achieved (*sādhya*) no matter whether one approaches it as an artist or as a spectator."[3] Thus, the creation and equally the appreciation of beauty in art is, in essence, the intuitive and deeper understanding of the meaning of the art object, and such understanding is not only a discipline or *sādhanā* but a yoga. Stated differently, it is the function of the aesthete to seek and realise artistic meaning up to the fullest.

A sound epistemology of aesthetic experience must be grounded in a metaphysics that provides first, a firm support for objective experience as exemplified by aesthetic experience, and second, an ontological basis for affirming creativity and creation as values that are not denied or negated at any point. We need to place art experience within the orbits of a system of thought that gives credence both to the creator as well as to the connoisseur, the artist as well as the aesthete, art creation as well as aesthetic experience. In the major *darśanas* or schools of Indian philosophy, the question of the relationship betweeen the subject and the world of objective experience is set within the framework of the quest for ultimate Reality. Radhakrishnan sums up the problem when he says, "When we divide the subject from the object the question of building the bridge from one to the other becomes difficult. Either we have to hold that the object is the creation of the subject or that there is no object at all."[4] The epistemology of aesthetics must not only provide a validity for the art obejct and an understanding of objective experience as exemplified by art experience, and at the same time, explain creation and creativity.

Art precedes aesthetics, and the proper understanding and realisation of what is created cannot be done in isolation from the creative process itself. The major schools of Indian thought set their examination of the nature, value and significance of creative processes also within the framework of the quest for ultimate Reality. From our perspective, it is important to note that a metaphysical system which considers creative processes to be either ultimately unreal or of little value cannot provide a firm basis for artistic experience, for an aesthete is as much of a creator as an artist. We have already pointed out that Abhinavagupta and many aestheticians who followed him, found in Kāśmir Śaivism a firm metaphysical basis for their aesthetic theory. In this chapter we will show that Kāśmīr Śaivism, both in its metaphysics and its epistemology, offers a strong support to artistic experience, both for the artist and the aesthete. Abhinavagupta maintains that the schools of Realism, which include Sāṃkhya, Nyāya-Vaiśeṣika, Mīmāṁsā and Cārvāka, cannot provide a satisfactory basis for art. It is true that all these schools of thought, except Cārvāka, accept consciousness as an ultimate metaphysical category, but they do not perceive creativiy to be an ultimate value within consciousness. In Sāṃkhya, for example, all creative processes stemming from human consciousness, including art creation, are seen as happenings within *saṃsāra*, governed by *kārmic* or current psychological causes. If pushed, this school may offer a psychological explanation for the artist's activity, but it does not perceive conscious acts of creativity to be of any ultimate value for the soul, the *puruṣa*. Abhinavagupta takes the position that for those who are content with the superficial and the momentary, these Realistic systems of thought are sufficient. He implies that, for those who seek to give an ultimate meaning to the objective world, and in particular to art objects, these schools of thought will not suffice.[5]

From the Idealist schools of thought, we only need to consider seriously the epistemology of Śaṅkara's Advaita Vedānta, for this was the exalted system of Indian thought in Abhinavagupta's time, and is our *pūrvapakṣa*. The Viśiṣṭādvaita of Rāmānuja is an important school of thought, as far as Hindu aesthetics is concerned, for it gave a prominent place to *kāvya, saṅgīta, nāṭya* and all forms of visual art, but only within the auspices of the temple. Chronologically, Rāmānuja came much later than Abhinavagupta and therefore, we do not have Abhinavagupta's evaluation of Viśiṣṭādvaita and of the practices of *bhakti* associated with this school of thought. From our perspective, Rāmānuja's system offers only qualified support for a yoga of art, and not at all for the *advaita* of art. The major obstacle in Rāmānuja's Viśiṣṭādvaita, from the aesthetic point of view, is the fact, that for Rāmānuja, *bhakti* is the overriding ***modus operandi***, and all epistemic experiences must be subordinated to it. A pure aesthetic experience, devoid of *bhakti*, would be unacceptable to Rāmānuja However, it is to be noted that Viśiṣṭādvaita, considered purely as a metaphysical system, can offer a firm ontological basis for establshing the ultimate value of aesthetic experience. Viśiṣṭādvaita affirms the reality of the world and the validity of objective experience, by regarding this world as the 'body of God'. It establishes the value of all creative processes by granting them an ontological basis in the creative energy of God. And, above all, it grants ultimate value to beauty by perceiving it to be an essential attribute of God. But, by the same token, in practice, the followers of Rāmānuja insist that the perception of beauty should be subordinated to *bhakti*, thereby denying the art object an objectivity of its own. Strictly speaking, the object in the epistemology of Viśiṣṭādvaita, becomes part of the subject and no real subject-object transaction can take place, denying *bhakti* its epistemic credence, and certainly under no circumstances allowing it to be considered *advaitic*. And in this lies the problem for aestheticians interested in pursuing art as *advaita*.

Śaṅkara recognises the objective world of name and form as provisionally real, and further recognises that the perception of this objective world is a function of all beings. For Śaṅkara,[6] this world of manifold perceiving subjects, and objects of perception, has no existence apart from *brahman*. In his metaphysics, Śaṅkara recognises the world as provisionally real, and in his epistemolgy, he strongly argues that the world of objects is not a creation of the subjective mind, thereby distinguishing his view from that of the *Vijñānavādins*. Nevertheless in the end, he would have us insist that the universe is ultimately unreal, an appearance maintained by ignorance (*avidyā*), and superimposed on *brahman*. Correspondingly, in his epistemology, there is a sharp break between the perception of objects and the knowledge of *brahman*. To use his own analogy, there is no way, whereby the truth of the rope and the illusion of the snake, can be upheld at one and the same time. In the light of ultimate truth the reality of the universe is contradicted and consequently, objects of perception are divested of ultimate value. The mind that rests in the contemplation of *brahman* and the universe of objects are "adrift like two logs in the ocean", never to meet again. From the perspective of Abhinavagupta's criticism, there are major problems in accepting Śaṅkara's metaphysics as a framework for aesthetics. Śaṅkara's *māyāvāda* ultimately rejects the world of objects and, therefore, cannot give ultimate value to the art object. Further since Śaṅkara's *brahman* does not include the world of objects and is essentially passive and *nirguṇa,* as a consequence, all creative processes, whether in material nature or in human consciousness, including art objects, are relegated ultimately to the status of *māyā*.

Abhinavagupta worked within the framework of Kāśmīr Śaivism, for it was important for him not only to enunciate his theory of aesthetics, but to show that art experience was a form of higher realisation. He found in the metaphysics of Kāśmīr Śaivism the most suitable framework for his theory of aesthetics. Kāśmīr

Śaivism is a generic term for a number of heterodox, *advaitic* systems of thought brought together under the umbrella of Śaivism. Believed to have been systematised and developed in the Kāśmīr valley, in the tenth century, it had a number of exponents, but the high priest of them all was indeed Abhinavagupta. It is not necessary to outline this system of thought in any great detail, in particular we need not consider its rituals and cults. Our interest lies in its epistemology, with special reference to aesthetic experience.

The transcendent godhead of Kāśmīr Śaivism, called *parāsaṃvid* or *anuttara* resembles the *brahman* of Śaṅkara, and is something about which nothing can be said, an entity therefore beyond words. The Śaiva *śāstras* declare that "it is undefinable in terms of everyday life",[7] which is similar to the Vedāntic declaration that, "there the eyes do not reach, neither speech, nor the intellect."[8] However the fundamental difference between the two systems is that Kāśmīr Śaivism does not recognise the *māyā* of Śaṅkara but instead postulates the concept of *ābhāsa.* Etymologically meaning "reflection", Abhinavagupta defines *ābhāsa* as "all that appears, all that forms the object of perception or conception, all that is within the reach of the external senses or the internal mind, all that can be said to exist in any way and with regard to which the use of any kind of language is possible, be it the subject, the object, the means of knowledge or knowledge itself, is *ābhāsa.*"[9] Several metaphysical implications follow from the concept of *ābhāsa*. First and foremost, *ābhāsa* affirms the reality of the manifested world, without negating the non-duality and the transcendence of the Absolute. *Ābhāsa* allows differentiation without duality and affirms the ultimate reality and value of creation without compromising the integrity of the creator. According to Abhinavagupta, "Śiva first manifests the world of *bheda* as the *pūrvapakṣa* and then again brings it to the *uttarapakṣa* of *abheda.*"[10] Stated differently duality and difference is the freedom of *advaita.* The Śaiva *śāstras* explain the significance of *ābhāsa* with the analogy of one flame lighting another, where the first flame remains intact when the second arises, and both flames are identical in essential nature, though manifestly distinguishable. The ***Chānogya Upaniṣad*** hints at the concept of *ābhāsa* when it declares, "That is whole, this is whole; from the whole the whole becomes manifest. From the whole when the whole is negated, what remains is the whole."[11] The concept of *ābhāsa* is central to Tāntric epistemology, and it enables one to understand creativity and the understanding of what is created as an integral activity. It is *ābhāsa* that assures the ontological ***bonafides*** of the art object. The concept of *ābhāsa* signifies for the Kāśmīr Śaivas that the world manifestation arises out of a free and a spontaneous creative activity or *spanda* in the Absolute. Furthermore, *ābhāsa* connotes that creativity is the spontaneous self-expression or self-projecion of the Absolute: the created world displays the very nature of the Creator and therefore by the same token the art object reflects the essential nature of the artist. In Kāśmīr Śaivism, therefore, creativity and freedom are of ultimate value because it has its ontological basis in the Absolute. Abhinavagupta leaves no doubt when he asserts that "true knowledge consists in the equal predominance of both consciousness (*bodha*) and freedom (*kartṛta*).[12] *Svāntantrya* is the very essence of Kāśmīr Śaivism and one which differentiates it from Advaita Vedānta. The concept of *ābhāsa* or emanation has, as its correlative, the idea of levels of reality. Each lower level is a manifestation or *ābhāsa* of the one above it. All the levels are correlated and at each level a form of differentiation is displayed without the negation of non-duality. At every level there is the differentiation into subject and object, but this differentiation is based in, and unified by, the non-duality of consciousness. In this sense *ābhāsa* signifies the "self-projected reflection of consciousness".[13] In making it dependent, ontologically on consciousness itself, *ābhāsa* is not an illusion of the Śaṅkara variety but like a "dream within a dream." The real illusion for the Kāśmīr Śaivite is the appearance of duality.[14] The analogy of a dream should not be taken as a reversion to the *māyāvāda* of Śaṅkara, or as the espousal of subjective Idealism. For Kāśmīr Śaivism, this universe of individual subject and objects is the true self-expression or real emanation of the consciousness of Śiva. In this sense the world is Śiva's dream. Similarly, the subjective awareness and objective experience of the individual is the dream of self-expression of individual consciousness. The individual's dream is included and transcended in Śiva's dream. In questioning the reality or otherwise of *ābhāsa*, the Tāntric would argue, "are you real"? For, if you are real, the Tāntric would further argue, that the *ābhāsa* is also real. It is important to note that the Kāśmīr Śaivite affirms the reality of *ābhāsa* at three levels. In the first place, appearance as appearance is real; secondly, appearance as self-projection is real and finally appearance inasmuch as it provides a value is real.[15] This is particularly true of art objects. As Tagore writes, "the fact of their [the art object's] existence enkindles in us the awareness that we also exist."[16] The reality of the objective experience reinforces the perceiver's subjective reality, in cognising and proclaiming its own reality, the art object encourages a realisation of the aesthete's reality. The onus in the dialectic about reality, for the Tāntric, is always on the subject and not the object, objective experience merely reinforcing subjective reality. The object merely asks the questions, it is for the subject to provide the answers, and as this question and answer proceeds cognition and higher realisation takes place. Aesthetic cognition and experience is none other than the dialogue of Śiva and Pārvatī, realising that it is none other than Śiva who divides himself into the questioner and the answerer, and that the whole dialogue takes place within Śiva. As Abhinavagupta writes:

> Self who is the natural state of all existents, who is self-luminous, amusing Himself with question-answer which is not different from Himself, and in which both the questioner (as *devī*) and the answerer (as *bhairava*) are only Himself, enjoys self-reflection.[17]

The concept of *ābhāsa* implies that the artist's creative self-expression is a reflection or a manifestation, at the human level, of Śiva's creative self-expression. As the world reflects Śiva's consciousness, so the art object reflects the consciousness of the artist. The aesthete's enjoyment of art is a reflection of Śiva's spontaneous enjoyment of the world.

What is noteworthy in the Tāntric argument is that at no stage does it allow any sense of duality, for the Tāntrics argue that any sense of duality in an experience is a source of ignorance. No level of experience is abandoned as untrue, no type of experience is negated; every experience, on the other hand, is included and transcended in a higher level of experience, every level of *ābhāsa* used to activate the otherwise passive self into a state of cognitive alertness. It is Pārvatī who ensures that Śiva is energised for a joyous epistemic and ecstatic union.

The immanent godhead of Kāśmīr Śaivism is termed *prakāśa-vimarśamaya* indicating that the Absolute is now beginning to display its two constituent parts, which were preserved ***in potentia*** in the transcendent state as unity-in-diversity; *prakāśa* also called Śiva *tattva* or *aham*, signifying subjectivity or the substratum of manifestation, and *vimarśa* or Śakti *tattva* or *idam*, denotes that power of manifestation which gives rise to self-awareness, will, knowledge and action. Stated differently, *prakāśa* is the 'I' and *vimarśa* the 'myself', both being held in dynamic equilibrium, an example of reflexive consciousness, which is a cardinal feature of this variety of Indian thought. *Vimarśa* or reflexive consciousness is the active component of the immanent godhead, as compared with *prakāśa* which is the passive and dormant. It is *vimarśa* that provides content to what would otherwise be an empty godhead. The Kāśmīr Śaivites point out that *vimarśa* acts spontaneously and with freedom, it posseses not an act of will but play, not the expression of a lack, but the display of fullness, its action termed *kriyā* or *spanda* or *svāntantrya*, meaning spontaneous and free action rather than *karma* or volitional action. The concept of *vimarśa* is the key to the understanding of not only creativity and creation on the one hand, but the appreciation of what is created, or aesthetics on the other. In making *vimarśa* a part of the immanent godhead the Kāśmīr Śaivites opened the door to objective realisation as a form of higher experience. *Vimarśa* is no *māyā* or illusion, it is a *līlā* and therefore it is epistemically real. At the human level, constituting what the Vedāntins would call the *ātman*, the same *prakāśa-vimarśamaya* principle operates at the core of the human personality, with one important difference, namely that *prakāśa* which is of the essence of knowledge at the human level, is not capable of self-awareness, since it is dormant, and therefore needs the activity of its *vimarśa* aspect. While the cosmic Śiva is capable *savikalpa pratyakṣa* is a matter of observation and is given in introspection. We become aware of it not as it arises but in a second knowledge termed *anuvyavasāya*"[26] The Kāśmīr Śaiva interpretation of the cognitive process provides the epistemological framework to explain the union of the aesthete and the art object through the aesthetic experience. Thus *vimarśa* through *savikalpa pratyakṣa*, rendered as a multi-layered, open-ended, determinate cognitive step, becomes vital to the development of an epistemology of aesthetics. It is this determinate cognition or *samvṛtti*[27] that "consumes objects of sense just as fire set ablaze consumes fuel."[28] At every step Abhinavagupta reminds us that "the immanent Self is to be realised by looking outwards and not within," in other words through *vimarśa* and not just *prakāśa*."[29] As he beautifully puts it, "slender rain falling continuously is not visible in the far-spreading sky but it is clearly visible in juxtaposition with the tree of the forest or the eaves of the roof of a house."[30] Abhinavagupta's statement that, "the chief characteristic of *pramāṇa* is its power to produce determinate knowledge ... and *śabda* is the very life of this determinate knowledge... determinate cognition entirely depends on the use of words",[31] is reminiscent of Bhartṛhari's position. It is very easy to be misled into believing that determinate cognition, through the faculty of *vimarśa*, because of its outward tendency leads to a scattering of different cognitions. However *vimarśa* has both a centrifugal as well as a centripetal force, it leads to diversity but at the same time is responsible for maintaining epistemic unity, it leads the subject out but equally draws the object back to rest on the subject, and at no point does it cease to be *advaitic*, for "the divine dialogue is, in the ultimate analysis, a spiritual monologue, a sort of self-reflection, self-recollection".[32] This will become clearer in the discussion on *viśrānti*. Unlilke Advaita Vedānta the determinate knowledge of Kāśmīr Śaivism through *vimarśa* is "that which is not proved to be false at a later stage."[33] Abhinavagupta thus relentlessly establishes the importance of *vimarśa* and determinate knowledge on the one hand and credibility of the objective world on the other, stating that "perfection consists in being full of the objects of the universe."[34] If it be so of the everyday objective world, how much truer it would be of art objects and aesthetic

Śiva and Pārvatī, and it is only in that state of unity and full activity of both that there can be *ānanda* or bliss. The process of *viśrānti* not only assures the culmination of cognitive experience in *ānanda*, but at the same time removes the gulf between the subject and the object, so that the subject looks upon the object as "identical with one's own self", beautifully depicted by the mirror in the hand of Pārvatī. The mirror in the hand of Pārvatī is held such that Śiva sees himself in it. It is for this reason that Kāśmīr Śaivites consider cognition a recognition, and this system of thought is also sometimes called *pratyabhījña* or remembrance. It is, as it were, the cognising self, as a result of the cognising experience, remembers the identity between the subject and the object which has existed all along, but which was temporarily hidden. Śiva's initial cognition reveals Pārvatī but a second or subsequent cognition reveals himself in the mirror. In this sense, it can be said that the aesthetic experience has not added any new knowledge, but has merely uncovered existing knowledge.

An important part of any epistemic inquiry must be the question of error, its recognition and prevention, a problem that does not exempt aesthetes in their pursuit of an aesthetic experience. For, in his quest for artistic truth, an aesthete must ensure that he be not privy to artistic untruth. Each school of philosophy puts forth its own theory of error, and the Abhivanagupta theory which we shall explore is a corrollary of Śaiva metaphysics. According to Abhinavagupta error is *apūrṇakhyāti* or incomplete knowledge, for he clearly states that "*apūrṇakhyātirūpa akhyātireva bhrāntitattvam*";[50] a cognition in which "the object does not continue to figure in as perfect form as it should be up to the time of final judgement."[51] Abhinavagupta further clarifies that, "The means of right knowledge is that because of which the object shines determinately ... and which is free of spatial and temporal limitations and which is not contradicted."[52] In keeping with Śaiva metaphysics Abhinavagupta does not posit the source of error either in the subject or in the object but in the *pramāṇa*. Abhinavagupta is an absolutist and does not accept the problem of error in a negative sense, for according to him error also is a form of knowledge, for he states:

> If it be said that *akhyāti* or ignorance is that which never appears (that is which is never experienced) then knowledge alone remains. If it be said that *akhyāti* does appear (that is it is experienced) then knowledge alone remains.[53]

In Kāśmīr Śaivism thus there is no illusion of the Śaṅkara variety, as the bonafides of the object are never questioned, but there is only imperfect penetration of the object by the *pramāṇa*. In doing so, the Kāśmīr Śaivite parts company from the Buddhists and the Vedāntins who posit the source of error either in the subject or the object. If error, according to the Śaivites, is *apūrṇakhyāti* the prevention of erroneous cognition lies in sustained and determinate cognition. As Rastogi states quite correctly, "for Abhinavagupta nacre cognition is thus not a negation of silver cognition, it is an improvement upon and fulfilment of silver cognition."[54] The correction, relative to the immediate past experience, is itself a cognition.[55] Abhinavagupta is quite consistent in his insistence on determinate cognition, for it is that alone that reveals the essential nature of objects, and thus leads to full and total cognition.[56] The prevention of erroneous cognition lies in "*vimarśabala*"[57]: the strength of determinate cognition.

The aesthetic implications of these statements by Abhinavagupta are of considerable import. The source of error is neither in the art object nor in the subjective aesthete. The truth seeking aesthete must ensure that his *pramāṇas* are right. This emphasises not only repeated and sustained cognition to avail oneself of the *sākṣātartha* but also the importance of seeking and cognising a *parokṣārtha* of the art object, for it is this latter *artha* that encourages a determinate cognition, which in turn eliminates erroneous cognition. Not to recognise the presence of a *parokṣārtha* is the chief source of aesthetic error. Built into the Tāntric epistemology is the step-ladder approach, a process that takes the aesthete from knowledge to greater knowledge, a position particularly suited to cognition of art, for art incorporates two levels of *artha*. Nothing is negated by the Tāntrist as he embraces art objects and elevates the cognition to a transcendent experience, who tastes emotion only to transform it into *rasa*, who is not content with mere form but seeks its inner sense, the *rūpaprajña*. It is only *apūraṇakhyāti* that would introduce a sense of duality in the art cognition and experience, and duality is the very source of ignorance, for the Tāntrists assert "it is the sense of duality that becomes an obstacle in (right) knowledge",[58] and by its implication it is only an *advaitic* approach that can lead to artistic truth.

Aesthetically, the question arises whether every form of cognition leads to *ānanda*. Abhinavagupta states that, "to the liberated in life the entire objective world appears as a mere reflection on the self, and therefore, as really non-different from it."[59] "He looks upon the entire objective world that is reflected on him as his own manifestation."[60] Such a person is a *jīvanmukta* and to such a person the diversity of the objective world which is ordinarily looked upon as bondage, appears as identical with one's own self. In the case of such a person even the cognition of an earthen jar would lead to *ānanda*; the aesthete however would need an encounter with art objects to lead him to *rasānanda* and *rūpānanda*. Perhaps this is one of the reasons why it is said that *rasānanda* resembles *brahmānanda*, like a twin brother, but is not identical with it.

The origins of yoga are prehistoric but it was Patañjali who systematised the concepts and objects of yoga and his concepts are still seminally valid. When it comes to its methods and ultimate objectives Tāntric yoga, however, parts company from Patañjali's yoga. Patañjali's yoga calls for the eventual withdrawal from the objective world and can be termed the "yoga of alienation", while the Tāntric yoga is the "yoga of integration".[61] Tāntrists have no difficulty in accepting the basic postulates of Patañjali as preparatory steps. Patañjali worked within the Sāṃkhya tradition and the end point of his yoga was *kaivalya* or *kevala Puruṣa* or a state in which the *puruṣa* is self-contained and uninvolved with *prakṛti*. *Kaivalya* is said to be a state of pure subjective consciousness, transcending the duality of subjective and objective modes of experience. This position is obviously unacceptable to Tāntrists for whom the objective experience is a means of realising the transcendent subject and cannot be eliminated even at the last stages of a transcendent experience.

Abhinavagupta regards six components as essential to his yoga, viz. *prāṇāyāma* or breath control, *dhyāna* or contemplation, *pratyāhāra* or restraint, *dhāraṇā* or concentration, *sattārka* or logic and *samādhi* or the merging of the consciousness with the Ultimate.[62] Abhinavagupta eliminates *yama* or self-control, *niyama* or ritual observances and *āsana* or postures from the basic eight of Patañjali. Thus, contemplation, restraint and concentration form a part of the Tāntric yoga. Aesthetically speaking, it emphasises the basic discipline required of an aesthete, who approaches the art experience, with a sense of dedication and purpose, devoid of egoity and after proper preparation. Any superficial or hedonistic artistic activity would not qualify for a true aesthetic experience in the *mārgī* tradition. The disciplines prescribed by Abhinavagupta have much in common with the disciplines prescibed for the aesthete in the *mārgī* tradition. The non-acceptance of *yama* or self-control by Tāntrists is not hard to understand, as Tāntric yoga requires a seeking out, embracing and participating in objective experiences and not an introspective withdrawal which is a feature of Patañjali's yoga.

The main feature of distinction between Tāntric yoga and Patañjali's yoga is the concept of *sattārka*. It is *sattārka* that brings about self-recognition, by uprooting the apparent distinction between the subject and the object, grasping "the true subjective nature of what appears to be objective."[63] *Sattārka* is the understanding that in every act of cognition the subject projects himself into the object, so that objective experience is always a reflection of the nature and attributes of the subject. In Tāntric yoga it is *sattārka* that permits a seeking out of objective experiences and making it a part of higher realisation.

The term *bhoga*, even within the Tāntric tradition, is capable of several interpretations. Although we have restricted its use to aesthetic enjoyment, for a Tāntrist, any objective experience that leads to higher realisation can be called *bhoga*. For those who prefer to follow the left handed Tāntric rituals, the *pañcamakāras* or the five 'Ms' namely *mithuna, madirā, māṃsa, matsya* and *mudrā* become *bhoga*. Since the cornerstone of Tāntric yoga is *bhoga*, and *bhoga* itself is so protean, no consistent definition of yoga is possible in the Tāntric framework. Mishra is right in pointing out that "unlike the ***Yogasūtras*** of Patañjali there is no systematic treatise on the Tāntric yoga".[64] Different interpreters of Tantra offer various definitions. Mishra suggests that Tāntric yoga is the "unfolding of the *Kuṇḍalinī*."[65] Abhinavagupta in the ***Tantrasāra*** states that "yoga is a form of experience which is of the nature of perceiving unity with that form",[66] 'that form' referring to the ultimate nature of Śiva. Tāntric *śāstras*, as opposed to Patañjali's ***Yogasūtras***, remain rather imprecise about yoga, and leave its concepts rather amorphous.

Tantra has been called the right system for the present age or Kali *yuga*. It has been said that, "in the Kali age the fool who seeks to attain *siddhi* by the paths shown in other *śāstras* is like a thirsty man who digs a well on the very banks of the Jāhnavi."[67] For no other system can incorporate *bhoga* or pleasure and *mokṣa* or liberation, no other ideology can claim to be "*bhuktimuktikārānika*"; and no other practice would "make it possible to attain in one life or in one week that which was rarely attained even by *devas* like Indra."[68] There is yet another reason why Tāntric *yoga* is the *yoga* for this age. The ***Tantralokaviveka*** states, "[Tāntric yoga] permits one to be a Kaula within, a aivite outside and a Vaidika amongst the people, like a coconut which keeps its nectar-like juice hidden inside."[69] This *sūtra* brings out at least two important features of Tāntric yoga. Firstly, the *sādhaka* is enjoined to keep the Tāntric practices personal and private, almost a secret to himself, making this kind of yoga a private rather than a public yoga. Secondly, it permits the *sādhaka* to be an ecclectic, and prevents his aesthetic *sādhanā* from becoming a cult. Thus a practitioner of the yoga of art has indeed great freedom; he need not change his outward religious and social practices, and does not get into any conflict with other traditions. It is for this reason that art and aesthetics do not set up any social and sectarian boundaries, and it is for the same reason that *bhakti* aesthetics cannot be included in the *advaita* of art. Thus, *bhoga* leads to freedom without necessitating withdrawal from the world. The aesthete is promised that, "even while he is busying himself with sense-objects he can become *samaviṣṭa*, a *yogin* of the highest type."[70] This signifies that, by accepting the Tāntric principle of *bhoga* the artist and the aesthete alike, can aim to develop a life style of personal and artistic freedom and yet lay claim to an exalted state of being, the whole activity remaining outside the scope of religion as previously defined.

In conclusion, we return to the question with which we began our inquiry. Can aesthetic experience be seen as an independent form of yoga? The concept of *ānanda* pervades the entire Upaniṣads and Bharata hints at the exalted nature of *nāṭya* when he says that, "what final goal the scholars of Veda reach, what final goal the performers of *yajña* reach, what final goal the benefactors reach, that same goal is attainable (by the ***Nāṭyaśāstra***)". He has further said that "the gods will not be propitiated as much when they are worshipped with sandal and garlands as they will be when they are by the praises contained in the enactment of the drama."[71] However, it remained for medieval aestheticians like Abhinavagupta to fully expound this view that art experience points to a transcendent goal. Understood in this sense, one is able to affirm the Upaniṣadic *mahāvākya*: '*tat tvam asi*', 'that thou art', through the *advaita* or the yoga of art, and exclaim, pointing to the art object: *Śivo'ham.*

While art in India is pre-historic and has had an almost unbroken tradition through millennia, aesthetics came into its own only with the *alaṃkārikas* and more fully with the Tāntric aestheticians. Not only did Tāntric aestheticians legitimise aesthetics as a form of higher realisation, but they succeeded in giving aesthetics a status of its own, independent of religious implications, the term 'religion' being used in a ritualistic sense. Aesthetics for the Tāntrists and especially the Kāśmīr Śaivites, was an artistic or poetic truth to be realised through a process of knowledge, and not as an appendage of *bhakti*, as it in fact became when the *bhakti* cult spread across the country in medieval India. The ***Mahānirvāṇa Tantra*** which elaborates on the "*tatasthalakṣaṇa brahman*" or the *brahman* that is objectively realised from its earthly forms, clearly states, "That same *brahman* which is known from His external signs...for those who would know Him through these external signs, for them *sādhanā* is enjoined."[72] That is, the same *brahman*, who may be known in its inner nature by the real or direct knowledge (*svarūpajñāna*) of Self, may also be apprehended through the senses, from its manifestation in the created world. Thus Tantra does not disclaim the introspective, indeterminate contemplation of the self as advocated by Śaṅkara and Patañjali, but points out that objective determinate contemplation based on sensory experience, or *bhoga*, can also lead to the same results. Following Abhinavagupta, there were a spate of aestheticians, who wrote exhaustively on various aspects of aesthetics but Abhnivagupta remains the high priest of aesthetics. What is also important to note is that the twin concepts of *bhoga* and *viśrānti* of aesthetic experience can be subsumed under an *advaitic* epistemology. Niharranjan Ray rightly points out that "in the matter of cognition and creation, subject and object are one and the same, there being no dichotomy between the two. In other words, intrinsic perception and knowledge are impossible so long as the object is considered as something external to the subject."[73] This *advaitic*, biune, relationship of *bhoga* and *viśrānti* is possible because aesthetic experience is essentially a knowledge episode.

Of the modern Indian aestheticians there are two that are worthy of special note, namely, Śrī Aurobindo and Rabindranath Tagore. It is they, from amongst many others, who have preserved the Indian tradition of keeping aesthetics within the realm of philosophy, rather than under the rubric of art history or religion. They themselves were artists first and aestheticians next. On examining their ideas, it is interesting to note that the influence of Tāntrism on them seems obvious. It is important to stress the contribution of these modern aestheticians, in order to show that the influence of Tāntrism was not just short lived or local, but that it has fully pervaded Indian culture. When Tagore says, "I dive down into the depth of the ocean of forms, hoping to gain the pearl of the formless" [74], or "Ever in my life have I sought thee with my songs,"[75], or "In this playhouse of infinite forms I have had my play and here have I caught sight of him that is formless",[76] he is defining the basic postulate of Tāntric yoga, that one may ascend "from form to formless". And then again when Tagore says that, "deliverance is not for me in renunciation. I feel the embrace of freedom in a thousand bonds of delight. No I will never shut the doors of my senses. The delights of sight and hearing and touch will bear thy delight",[77] he indeed is speaking of *bhoga*.

In opting for *bhoga* as a sustained aesthetic principle, the door opens up for breaking away from tradition and bringing in its wake the acceptance of modern and secular art. For *bhoga* lays down no ritual, does not limit itself to sects, accepts no barriers and works without boundaries. Tagore says this in no uncertain terms:

> Art is not a gorgeous sepulchre, immovable brooding over a lonely eternity of vanished years. It belongs to the procession of life, making constant adjustment with surprises, exploring unknown shrines of reality along its path of pilgrimage to a future which is as different from the past as the tree from the seed. If today we have a living soul that is sensitive to ideas and to beauty of form, let it prove its capacity by accepting all that is worthy of acceptance, not according to some blind injunction of custom or fashion, but in following one's instinct for eternal value.[78]

Śrī Aurobindo has stressed the supra-rational nature of art creation and art appreciation:

> But as with truth of religion, so with the highest and deepest truth of beauty, the intellectual reason cannot seize its inner sense and reality...its secret inner law of beauty and harmony... can be seized by vision, not by intellectual analysis; great art...seeks for a deeper and original truth which escapes the eye of the mere sense or the mere reason...Where the greatest and most powerful creation of beauty is accomplished and its appreciation and enjoyment rise to the highest pitch, the rational is always surpassed and left behind.[79]

Indian art, from its pre-historic beginnings to its contemporary state has evolved and changed, but yet remains a palimpsest, where the past is not totally erased, it is a confluence, a *saṅgam* where folk and classical traditions have mingled, an upside down tree "*ūrdhvamūlam vṛkṣa*",[80] which has sent its branches in every direction in a celebration of life, but has kept its roots above. Aesthetics, in the *mārgī* Hindu tradition is the domain of the "supra-rational aesthetic soul",[81] and "to find highest beauty is to find God."[82] We have given an exalted position to art, aesthetes and aesthetics in India, for it was none other than Bharata who said that "music and singing are more holy and beneficial than thousands of religious baths and incantations."[83]

Art in India is a spiritual adventure, both for the artist and the aesthete, *advaitic* in its methods and postulates, driven by a quest for delight, a source of transcendent knowledge and indeed a yoga.

NOTES

1. Śrī Aurobindo, ***The Hour of God and Other Writings.*** Centenary Edition, Volume 17, (Pondichery: Sri Aurobindo Birth Centenary Library, 1971) p. 198.
2. *Ibid.,* p. 211.
3. M. Hiriyanna, ***Art Experience.*** (Mysore: Kavyalaya Publishers, 1954) p. 23.
4. K.C. Pandey, ***Abhinavagupta An Historical and Philosophical Study.*** (Varanasi: Chowkhamba Sanskrit Series Office, 1963), p. 401.
5. *Ibid.,* p. 382.
6. S. Radhakrishnan (editor), ***A Source Book in Indian Philosophy.*** (Princeton: Princeton University Press, 1973), pp. 509-43. This chapter on 'The Non-Dualism of Śaṅkara' is taken from the ***The Vedanta Sutras*** with the Commentary by Sankara, translated by George Thibault.
   Śaṅkara's position has been explained at length as Abhinavagupta directed his critique mainly at Advaita Vedānta and it remains our *pūrvapaksaḥ.*
7. *na vidyate uttaram adhikam yataḥ.*
   Than which there is nothing more.
   Abhinavagupta, ***Parātriśikā-Vivaraṇa.*** (Delhi: Motilal Banarsidass 1988) Jaideva Singh (editor), p. 20.
   Abhinavagupta explains the term *anuttara* in sixteen ways.
8. *na tatra cakṣurgacchati no vaggacchati na mano na vidmo na vijānīmo...*
   There the eyes do not go, neither the mind, nor the intellect...
   Tavalkāra Upaniṣad. 1.3 in K.C.Pandey, p. 323.
9. K.C.Pandey, p. 320.
10. *pūrvapakṣatayā yena viśvamābhāṣya bhedataḥ abhedottarapakṣāntarnīyate tam stumaḥ śivam.*
    Śiva first manifests the world of duality as the *pūrvapakṣa* and then again

brings it to the *uttarapakṣa* of non-duality.
Abhinavagupta, ***Īśvara Pratyabhijña Vimarśinī.*** (Delhi: Motilal Banarsidass, 1986) R.C. Dwivedi (editor), 1.2.1

11. *pūrṇam adaḥ pūrṇamidam pūrṇātpūrṇamudacyate. pūrṇasya pūrṇamādāya pūrṇmeva avaśiṣyate.*
That is whole, this is whole; from the whole the whole becomes manifest. From the whole when the whole is negated what remains is again the whole. This is an invocatory verse from the Upaniṣads. Swami Chinmayānanda includes it in ***Discourses on the Chandogya Upanisad.*** (Madras: Chinmaya Publication Trust, date not given) p. 67.
12. *mukhyatvam kartṛtāyaśca bodhasya ca cidātmanaḥ.*
True knowledge consists in the equal predominance of both consciousness and freedom.
Abhinavagupta, ***Īśvara Pratyabhijña Vimarśinī.*** Vol. II. p. 256.
Also Mishra stresses that freedom is the essence of determinate action. (*parāmarāśalakṣaṇam tu svātantryam.*) Personal communication and forthcoming in his ***Kāśmīr Śaivism: The Central Philosophy of Tantrism.*** (unpublished)
13. K. Mishra, ***Significance of the Tāntric Tradition.*** (Varanasi: Ardhanarisvara Publications, 1981) p. 135.
14. *dvaitaprabhā tadajñānam tucchatvād bandha ucyate.*
Abhinavagupta, ***Tantrāloka.*** 1.30.
quoted by K. Mishra pp. 135-36.
15. K. Mishra. Personal communication and forthcoming in his ***Kāśmīr Śaivism: The Central Philosophy of Tantrism.*** (unpublished)
16. R. Tagore, ***On Art & Aesthetics.*** (Bombay: Orient Longmans, 1961) p. 108.
17. *svātmā sarvabhāvasvabhāvaḥ svayam prakāśmānaḥ svātmānameva svātmavibhinnena praśnaprati vacananat praṣṭr-prativaktṛ svātmamayena ahamtaya camatkurvan vimarśati...*
Self who is the natural state of all existents, who is self-luminous, amusing Himself with question-answer which is not different from Himself, and in which both the questioner (as Devī) and the answerer (as Bhairava) are only Himself, enjoys self-reflection.
Abhinavagupta, ***Parātriśikā-Vivaraṇa.*** p. 48.
18. K.C.Pandey, p. 417.
19. *iti sarvo grāhako viśvaśarīraḥ śivabhaṭṭarakaḥ eva.*
Thus every subject is identical with revered Śiva whose body is the universe.
Abhinavagupta, ***Pratyabhijñāhṛdayam.*** (Delhi: Motilal Banarsidass, 1987) Jaideva Singh (editor), p. 57.
20. *citireva cetanāpadādavarūḍha cetyasankocinī cittam.*
Truly speaking *citta* (individual consciousness) is not anything else, rather it is the exalted *citi* (universal consciousness) itself.
Abhinavagupta, ***Pratyabhijñāhṛdayam.*** p. 59.
21. *tena śabdārthacintāsu na śavasthā na yaḥ śivaḥ.*

Hence whether in the word or object or mental apprehension there is no state which is not Śiva.
Abhinavagupta, ***Pratyabhijñāhṛdayam***. p. 58.

22. *iha jñānamatayaḥ antaḥ sūtrakalpaḥ svasamvedanātmā pramātā jīvitabhūtah iti upapāditam prāk.*
It has been established earlier that the sentient knower (cogniser) whose essence is self-awareness, which is like the inner thread of the garland of cognitions.
Abhinavagupta, ***Īśvara Pratyabhijña Vimariśinī.*** p. 131.
23. *Ibid.*, p. 412.
24. *Ibid.*
25. *padma patra śata vyati bheda nayena.*
(like) a needle going through a pile of lotus leaves.
This original quotation by Abhinavagupta has been quoted in turn by all major commentators including Mammaṭa and Viśvanātha.
see Mammaṭa, ***Kāvyaprakāśa.*** Vol 1. (ed.) R.C.Dwivedi (Delhi: Motilal Banarsidass, 1967) p.62.
26. M.Hiriyanna, ***Outlines of Indian Philosophy***. (London: George Allen & Unwin Ltd., 1932) p. 251.
27. *evam samvṛtiḥ vikalpabuddhiḥ.*
Thus *Samvṛti* is determinate cognition.
Abhinavagupta, ***Īśvara Pratyabhijña Vimarśinī***. Volume III p. 132.
28. *yathā vahnirudodhito dāhyam dahati, tathā viṣayapāśān bhaṣkayet.*
Just as fire set ablaze consumes the fuel, even so should one consume the objects of sense which act like fetters.
Abhinavagupta, ***Prtayabhijñāhṛdayam.*** p. 90.
29. *parāñci khāni vyatṛṇat svayambhūstasmāt parān paśyati nāntarātman.*
The self-existent one pierced the openings (of the senses) outward. Hence one looks outward, not within one's Self.
Abhinavagupta, ***Pratyabhijñāhdayam.*** p. 97.
30. *vitata eva nabhasya viccidaiva pratanu patanna vibhāvyate jalaudhaḥ. upavanataruveṣmani grabhāgā dhrupadhi vaśena tu lakṣyate sphuṭam saḥ. tadvat parabhairavo'ti saukṣmyād anubhavagocaram iti naiva jātu. atha deśakṛtikāla sannivesa sthiti saṁspandita karakatvayogaha. janayantya anubhāvini citti te jatiti nyakṛt bhairaviyabodhāha.*
Slender rain falling continuously is not visible in the far-spreading sky but it is clearly visible in juxtaposition with the tree of the forest or the eaves of the roof of a house. Even so, the Supreme Bhairava, being too subtle, never appears in the range of experience. Under the circumstances, it is only by its connexion with means which depend on space, form, time, pattern and state that consciousness is generated instantaneously in them in whom the awareness of Bhairava is subdued—the consciousness that is indicative of thy presence O Lord!
Abhinavagupta, ***Parātriśikā-Vivaraṇa***. p. 22.
31. *iti abhedah pramāṇaphalayoha vimarśabalena ca yataḥ pramāṇam*

vimarśasca śabdajīvitaḥ śabdaśca ābahāsantarai.
The chief characteristic of *pramāṇa* (the means of right knowledge) is its power to produce the determinate knowledge. And the word (*śabda*) is the very life of this determinate knowledge (because) the only difference between the determinate and indeterminate knowledge is that while in the case of one we cannot use any word, in that of the other we can.
Abhinavagupta. ***Īśvara Pratyabhijñā Vimarśini***. Volume II p. 75.

32. So the divine dialogue is, in the ultimate analysis, a spiritual monologue, a sort of self-reflection, self-recollection.
Exposition by Jaideva Singh on Abhinavagupta's, ***Parātriśikā-Vivaraṇa*** p. 48.
33. *mitirvastunyabādhitā.*
Abhinavagupta, ***Īśvara Pratyabhijña Vimariśinī***. Volume II p. 121.
34. *icchāspandodayasphuṭa sphurita viśvabhāvanirbharatātmanaḥ.*
Perfection consists in being full of the objects of the universe, clearly manifested because of the rise of the stir, the power of will.
Abhinavagupta, *Ibid.* Volume II p. 142.
35. *bhogo yogāyate sākṣāt pātakam sukṛtāyate, mokṣyate ca samsāraḥ kuladharme kuleśvarī.*
O! Kuleśvarī, in this path of Kula, the objective worldly enjoyment becomes the means of yoga, what is normally taken as a vice becomes a virtue, and the world, which is ordinarily a cause of bondage, becomes a means of liberation.
Kulārṇava Tantra. 2/24 in K.Mishra, p. 49.
36. K.Mishra, p.79.
37. *Ibid.*
38. *Ibid.*
39. K.C.Pandey, p. 539.
40. *ātmani ātmabhāvo vilīyate.*
Destruction of the sense of the notself, not being the self.
Abhinavagupta, ***Tantrasāra***. (Bombay: Nirnayasagar Press, 1918) 5.40.
41. *gītādi viṣyāsvādā samasaukhyaikatātmanaḥ, yoginastanmayatvena manorūdhesta tadatmana.*
When a yogin mentally becomes one with the incomparable joy of song and other objects, then of such a concentrated yogin, there is identity with that because he becomes one with it.
Abhinavagupta, ***Pratyabhijñāhṛdayam***. p. 102.
42. *bhairavīya mudrān anupraveśaya yuktya bahiḥ prasaraṇam.*
This technique of inner absorption with external expansion on the senses is known as *bhairavīmudrā*.
Abhinavagupta, ***Pratyabhijñāhṛdayam***. p. 98.
43. See note 29.
44. Tagore, Rabindranath, ***Gitānjali***. (London: Macmillan, 1967), song # 75.
45. Indian artists have artistically depicted the concept of *prakāśa-vimarśamaya* by showing Śiva and Pārvatī as an amorous couple.

46. K.C. Pandey, p. 539.
47. *uktā ca śaiva viśrāntih sarvāpekṣā nirodhataḥ, svātantryamatha kartṛtvam mukhyam īśvarata api ca.*
This resting (within oneself) is what is called sovereignty of will, primary lordship because of the cancellation of all relational consciousness and of dependence on anything outside oneself.
Abhinavagupta, ***Pratyabhijñāhṛdyam.*** gloss. p. 109.
48. *na jane kutrayam dhvanir anupatet samsṛtiriti.*
Indeed I do not know what the sound 'world' is supposed to refer to.
Abhinavagupta, ***Pratyabhijñāhṛdyam.*** p. 32.
49. J.Woodroffe, ***Principles of Tantra.***Part I (Madras: Ganesh & Co. Private Ltd., 1969) p. 94.
50. *apūrṇakhyātirūpa akhyātireva bhrāntitattvam.*
This not shining of the object in a perfect form as it should upto the time of ascertainment is the essential nature of error.
Abhinavagupta, ***Īśvara Pratyabhijña Vimarśinī.*** Vol. II. p. 123.
51. N.Rastogi, Theory of error according to Abhinavagupta. ***Journal of Indian Philosophy***. Volume 14, 1986 (D. Reidel Publishing Co.) p.1.
52. *idametadāgityevam yadśādyavatiṣṭhate, vastu pramāṇam tatso'pi svabhāsobhinavodayaḥ, soantastatha vimarśatma desakāladhbhedeni, ekabhidhāna viṣaye mitir vastu nyabadāhitā.*
The means of right knowledge is that because of whose power the object shines determinately as "this" and of "such and such nature". That is also self-luminous and rises fresh every moment. That (*pramāṇa*) as determinately cognising within itself an object, for which a single expression stands and which is free from temporal and spatial limitations, is the cognition (*miti*) provided that it is uncontradicted.
Abhinavagupta, ***Īśvara Pratyabhijña Vimarśinī.*** Volume II. p. 68.
53. *akhyātir yadi na khyāti khyātir evāvaśiṣyate, khyātiścet khyātirūpatvāt khyātirevāvaśiṣyate.*
If it be said that nescience is that which never appears, i.e. which is never experienced, then appearance, or knowledge alone remains. If it be said that nescience does appear i.e. is experienced (in some form) then (obviously) being of the nature of knowledge, knowledge remains.
Abhinavagupta, ***Pratyabhijñāhṛdayam***. 4. p. 57.
54. N. Rastogi, p. 19.
55. *tatraiva kāle 'nedam rajatam abhut iti hi uttaraḥ parāmarśo na tu uditapratyastamitayam satahṛdayamiva idānīmeva idam na vimarśā.*
Abhinavagupta, ***Īśvara Pratyabhijña Vimarśinī.*** Volume II. p. 123.
56. *tataśca bhrāntyā abhave bādhānupappateh kimartham uktam mitirvastunyabādhitā.*
Determinate knowledge is that which is not proved to be false at a later stage.
Abhinavagupta, ***Īśvara Pratyabhijña Vimarśinī.*** Vol II. p. 121.
57. *svarūpam ca pratyavamarśabalād ekam eva bahyantarādāvapi.*

And the essential nature is the same in the state of internality as well as that of externality because the determinate cognition is the same in both cases. Abhinavagupta, ***Īśvara Pratyabhijña Vimarśinī.*** Vol. II. p. 120.

58. J. Woodroffe, ***Principles of Tantra.*** Part I (Madras: Ganesh & Co. Private Ltd., 1969) p. 94.
59. K.C.Pandey, p.688.
60. *Ibid.*
61. K.Mishra, p. 139.
62. K.C.Pandey, p. 538.
63. *Ibid.*, p. 535.
64. *dvaitapratha tadajñānam tucchatvād bandha ucyate.*
It is the sense of duality that becomes an obstacle in (right) knowledge. Abhinavagupta ***Tantrāloka***. 1/30 in K.Mishra, ***Significnce of the Tantric Tradition.***p. 136.
65. *Ibid.*, p. 142.
66. *Ibid.*
67. *tat svarūpam anusandhānātmavikalpaviśeso yogaḥ.*
Yoga is a form of experience which is of the nature of perceiving unity with that form [of Śiva].
Abhinavagupta, ***Tantrasāra.*** 4.27 quoted by K. Mishra, *Ibid.*, p. 142.
68. J. Woodroffe, ***Principles of Tantra.*** Vol 1. p. 115.
69. *antah kaulo bahih śaivo lokācare tu vaidikaḥ, sārmādāya tiṣṭheta nārikelaphalam yathā.*
[Tantric yoga] permits one to be a *kaula* within, a Śaivite outside and a *Vaidika* amongst the people, like a coconut which keeps its nectar-like juice hidden inside.
B.N.Pandit, ***Aspects of Kashmir Saivism.*** (Srinagar: Utpal Publications, 1977) p. 230.
70. *tatra ca bahyād grasyamānāt viṣayagrāmāt antaḥ parasyām citibhūmau grasanakrameṇaiva praveśaḥ samāveśo bhavati.*
The *sādhaka,* the *yogin* of the highest type, becomes *samavista,* i.e., one who has realised the unfolding of the highest Śakti even while he is extroverted, i.e., even while he is busying himself with senseobjects.
Abhinavagupta, ***Pratyabhijñāhṛdayam***. 19. p. 104.
71. *yā gatirvedavidusām yā gatiryajñakārinām yā gatirdānaśalinam tām gatim prāpnuyat hi sah. na tathā gandhamālyena devāstusyanti pūjitāh, yathā nāṭyaprayogasthaih nityam tusyanti mangalaiḥ.*
What final goal the scholars of Veda reach, what final goal the benefactors reach, the same goal is attainable by [the *Nāṭyaśāstra*].
Bharata, ***Nāṭyaśāstra.*** 37.27.
na tathā gandhamlyena devāh tuṣyati pūjitaḥ. yathā nāṭya prayogasthaiḥ nityam tuṣyati manglaiḥ.
The gods will not be propitiated as much when they are worshipped with sandal and garland, as they will be when they are by the praises contained in the enactment of the drama.

Bharata, ***Nāṭyaśāstra.*** 37.29.

72 . J. Woodroffe, ***The Great Liberation. Mahānirvāṇa Tantra***. (Madras: Ganesh & Co. Private Ltd., 1963) pp. 32-33.

73. N. Ray, ***An Approach to Indian Art.*** (Chandigarh: Punjab University Publication Bureau, 1974) p. 67.

74. R.Tagore, ***Gitanjali.*** song # 100.

75. *Ibid.,* song # 101.

76 . *Ibid.,* song # 96.

77. *Ibid.,* song # 73.

78. Tagore, Rabindranath, ***On Art & Aesthetics.*** p. 62.

79. Śrī Aurobindo, ***The Human Cycle***. (Pondicherry: Sri Aurobindo Ashram, 1971) pp. 135-37.

80. S. Radhakrishnan, (translator),***The Bhagvadgītā***. (London: George Allen & Unwin Ltd. 1960) 15.1 "As the tree originates in God, it is said to have its roots above." p. 326.

81. Śrī Aurobindo, ***The Hour of God and Other Writings***. Centenary Edition, Volume 17. p. 224.

82. Śrī Aurobindo,***The Human Cycle.*** p. 135.

83. *snānajāpyasahasrebhyaḥ pavitram gītavāditam.*
music and singing are more holy and beneficial than thousands of religious baths and incantations.
Bharata, ***Nāṭyaśāstra.*** 36.26.

Chapter 7

Aesthetic Implications of Divine Consortship

śivabhyam astoka-tribhuvana-śivabhyam hrdi punar
bhavaybhyam ānandasphurad anubhavabhyam natiram.
Śaṅkara. ***Śivānandalaharī,*** 1

The concept of the mother goddess is all-pervasive in the Indian tradition existing in an unbroken continuity from times pre-historic to the present. Its manifestations have been protean and its influence going deep in the Indian psyche. From among the many manifestations of the Mother goddess, of special interest to aestheticians is its aspect as a divine consort.

Divine consortship is an important part of the Hindu tradition and can be understood at many different levels. Purely at a psychological level it makes the Hindu gods more human and brings them closer to man. From a religious standpoint it has established a strong cult of mother goddess worship that has played an important part in every period of Indian civilisation. Art historians write with excitement and enthusiasm about its various artistic forms and its diverse manifestations. Sociologists read much into the matrimonial aspects of the consorts. Important as all these considerations are, they fail to address and bring out the important aesthetic implications of divine consortship which is where our interest lies.

This chapter will examine the aesthetic implications of two

independent consortships in the Hindu tradition, that of Rādhā and Pārvatī. In doing this, the study will steer clear of theological and doctrinal considerations, features that would normally fall under the rubric of religion, but instead focus exclusively on its aesthetics, and show that aesthetic considerations are equally, if not more important, than all others.

The name Rādhā is found in popular poetry as early as the sixth century AD, and appears rather tentatively in the early Purāṇas, the ***Harivaṃsa*** (2nd century AD) and the ***Viṣṇu Purāṇa*** (3-6 century AD). From these amorphous beginnings she assumes some importance in the ***Bhāgavata Purāṇa*** (6-9 century AD) and the ***Subodhinī*** of Vallabhācārya where she is mentioned cursorily as Kṛṣṇa's favourite *gopī.* Though the ***Bhāgavata Purāṇa's*** religious leanings are hard to miss, for it overtly promotes Kṛṣṇa *bhakti* and for which reason it became the primary text of the cult of Bengal Vaiṣṇavism, the aesthetic orientation of this Purāṇa, albeit in a seminal form, cannot be dismissed. Notice this verse, "Therefore the Lord danced here and made the *gopīs* dance likewise, so that the *rasa* which was lying dormant in every part of their bodies might make itself clearly manifest."[1] Vallabhācārya and his son Viṭṭhala pick up and exegisise these aesthetic implications and in the ***Subodhinī*** we find frequent mention not only of the word *rasa*, along with a "continual consciousness of the arts of the day both performing and plastic",[2] but direct references to the classical aesthetic theory. For instance, Viṭṭhala says in no uncertain terms that the "love-making ...was His gift of the joy of His own form ...for His own form has *rasa* as its very essence."[3] And when he says that "a fire that is already blazing can kindle the fire that is latent in everything,"[4] he is making an obvious reference to well established principles of *alaṃkāraśāstra.* This has rightly prompted Redington to suggest that Vallabha saw Kṛṣṇa's life partially as fulfilment of Sanskrit aesthetic theory.[5] Both in the ***Bhāgavata Purāṇa*** and the ***Subodhinī*** consortism is still diffuse and generic and involves *gopīs* as a group.

It is not until the twelfth century when Jayadeva made Rādhā the central *nāyikā* in his ***Gītagovinda*** that Rādhā assumes an aesthetic dominance. This aesthetic dominance of Rādhā was to intersperse itself with an outpouring of *bhakti* poetry for almost five hundred years as exemplified by the works of Mīrā, Sūdrās, Vidyāpati and Caṇḍīdās and many others. Along with the *bhakti* poetry there was a concretisation of the theology of Rādhā and it was in a thirteenth century text ***Brahmavaivarta Purāṇa*** that an extensive and elaborate theology of Rādhā emerges. The *bhakti* poetry of Rādhā should be considered in tandem with the rise of Bengal Vaiṣṇavism, a popular and fervent religious movement that was initiated by Caitanya and one that was to spread and take root in many parts of India. In both *bhakti* poetry and Bengal Vaiṣṇavism, religious doctrine and theology predominated over the aesthetic, and *śṛṅgāra rasa* was subordinated to *bhakti rasa*. It may be noted that the celebration of *bhakti* and *sṛṅgāra rasa* in tandem, and in the same work of art, occurs for the last time in the Indian tradition in the ***Gītagovinda***, after which the two *rasas* were bifurcated. The dynamics of *bhakti rasa* are significantly different from those of *śṛṅgāra rasa* and one cannot ignore the fact that *bhakti rasa* was not included in the initial eight *rasas* of Bharata. The Bengal Vaiṣṇavites go to great lengths to defend the *parakīya* status of Rādhā and the *gopīs* and exalt the *virahinī* over the *saṃyoginī*. The consortism of Rādhā developed by the *bhakti* poets and the Bengal Vaiṣṇavites, although aesthetically based, gets intertwined with fervent theology and cannot remain in the pure aesthetic domain and cannot occupy our attention as aestheticians.

After the ***Gītagovinda*** the next development of aesthetic importance takes place with the rise of what is called *rīti kāvya,* a genre of poetry in Hindi, in which Rādhā once again assumes aesthetic predominance, and "Krishna ousts...the courtly lovers who previously had seemed the acme of romance."[6] A good example of this is the ***Rasikapriyā*** of Keśav Dās of Orchha. The rich love poetry, both in Sanskrit and Braj *bhāṣā*, was later to become the inspiration and moving force for the delightful miniature paintings of western India and Punjab hills, which from an aesthetic viewpoint can be considered visual poetry.

For the purpose of this inquiry, which will focus solely on the aesthetic, and not theological, aspects of the consortship of Rādhā, the ***Gītagovinda*** and the ***Rasikapriyā*** will be taken as the prototype of Rādhā poetry, although much of what will be said can be easily applied to most other poetry in this genre.

Jayadeva's ***Gītagovinda*** is rightly considered a landmark in the Indian poetic tradition in more ways than one. Rādhā emerges for the first time as a triumphant *nāyikā* and not merely as a love lorn *gopī*, and the "poignant cry of anguish present in the *viraha* poems of the *bhakti* tradition is largely absent"[7] in the ***Gītagovinda*** and the *rīti kāvya*. As Dimock remarks, "to the orthodox Vaiṣṇavas...true love is love in separation",[8] but not so for Jayadeva. Not only is Jayadeva's poetry unmatched in its literary attributes but it is perhaps for the first time that a mythic theme has been treated secularly. Jayadeva dispenses with the distinction between sacred and profane, moves the artistic experience outside religious constraints, and produces a sensuous, lyrical love poem of the highest order. Jayadeva sets out to produce neither a *Purāṇa* nor a *śāstra* but "joyously evokes the essence of existence."[9] Jayadeva leaves little doubt that *bhāvasāram* is nothing different from "the erotic mood and sacred truth."[10] The essence of life, the meaning of Kṛṣṇa, for Jayadeva is none other than *śṛṅgāra rasa* in all its artistic richness and its manifold aspects. Rādhā is *dhāra*, an outpouring, a stream, a perfect form of *śṛṅgāra rasa* and in Jayadeva's hands she attains *jaya*, victory, unlike the poignant and unrequited love of the *gopīs* of the Bhāgavata, while Kṛṣṇa is "*śṛṅgāramūrtimān*"[11] the very embodiment of the erotic mood. The fact that in the ***Gītagovinda*** Kṛṣṇa is conquered by Rādhā is of singular aesthetic importance, for were it not so, the total and uninhibited dynamics of *śṛṅgāra* could not evolve. It is in the fitness of the aesthetic that Jayadeva does not place a halo around either Rādhā or Kṛṣṇa, for to do so would be to resolve the ambiguity of Rādhā and destroy the beauty of the *rasa*. The Rādhā of Kṛṣṇaite devotional religion is quite different from the Rādhā of courtly love, the former is a symbol of the true *bhakta*, the latter the quintessence of *rasa*. Schomer is right in pointing out that, "Rādhā of *rīti* poetry was not primarily a devotee or divine consort, but rather the supreme model of the woman in love, the *nāyikā* par excellence."[12] Miller points out that in the ***Gītagovinda*** Kṛṣṇa is "referred to (not by religious) but by standard forms of address given for the dramatic hero in Bharata's

Nāṭyaśāstra such as *kānta, dayita, priya, vallabha, kiṭava* and *sakhā*" and he is "both the object of Love's attack and the embodiment of Love's creative sensuality."[13] In the ***Gītagovinda*** and the *rīti kāvya* Kṛṣna and Rādhā interchange as the *ālambana* (object which arouses the emotion) and *āśraya* (the subject in whom it is aroused) of *śṛṅgāra rasa*. The language throughout is poetic, the tensions dramatically delightful, the situation entirely human, the artistic devices purely secular and the ambience is one of unexpurgated undiminished *śṛṅgāra rasa*, pointing to nothing but to itself, and "intellectual contemplation gives way to aesthetic participation"[14] reminding us that Rādhā is "a revelation of what is at the heart of the universe, at the centre of being where our existence culminates and life is most real."[15] Jayadeva points out in no uncertain terms the object of his ***Gītagovinda*** when he says that "(with) each verse...let emotion rise to a joyful mood of love in sensitive men!"[16] When we are told by the poet that "Jayadeva's singing doubles the power of Kṛṣṇa's adornments"[17] it is merely an assertion of accepted aesthetic theories, for *rasa* is not mere emotion but the expression of that emotion in an art object, and therefore needs an outward expression to be enjoyed, appreciated and understood. Without an outward expression of words or images in the form of a *kāvya* or *citra* there can be no *rasa*.

Jayadeva with consummate poetic artistry sensually portrays Rādhā in the eight traditional love situations, the *aṣṭanāyikās* of *śṛṅgāra rasa*, broadly divided into love in separation, *vipralambhaśṛṅgāra* and love in consummation, *sambhogaśṛṅgāra*. Jayadeva unleashes the power of aesthetic rapture to lead Kṛṣṇa and Rādhā to a final aesthetic bliss, and Kṛṣṇa finds his "deep-locked emotions breaking", and Rādhā sees "her passion reach the soul of Hari's mood."[18] This is the climax of the *rasa* experience, when both Rādhā and Kṛṣṇa, *kavi* and *sahṛdaya, āśraya* and *ālambana*, lose their duality and yet maintain their identity as they are joined together in an aesthetic embrace, tasting the same *rasa*, "like a dark lotus root wrapped in veils of yellow pollen",[19] or "like an autumn pond when wagtails mate in lotus blossom hollows".[20] This is the meaning of Rādhā as Kṛṣṇa's consort. The right question for the aesthete then to ask, is not "who is Rādhā?", but "what is Rādhā?"

And the right answer is that Radhā is *raseśvarī*, the embodiment of *śṛṅgāra rasa*.

Although Rādhā and Kṛṣṇa of the ***Gītagovinda*** are purely secular, and the Rādhā of Jayadeva had not assumed any theological importance in his day, yet Kṛṣṇa's divinity was accepted and part of the tradition even at the time of Jayadeva. The amorous and erotic Kṛṣṇa of the ***Gītagovinda*** cannot be entirely separated in the mind of the *rasika* from the sacred and the divine Kṛṣṇa of the ***Bhāgavata Purāṇa***. The Kṛṣṇa of Brindāvan is one and the same Kṛṣṇa who had tamed Kāliya and lifted Mount Govardhana. The apparent tension between the two Kṛṣnas, the sacred on the one hand and the secular on the other, serves only to heighten the *rasa* experience of the ***Gītagovinda*** and the *rīti kāvya*. Jayadeva could easily have chosen a Lailā and Majnu or a Nala and Damyantī for his *rasa kāvya*, for there is evidence to show that "the love-poetry of the early Indian middle ages had been partly paralleled by actual courtly or village practice."[21] But it adds to the aesthetic relish of the aesthete to know that the *nāyaka* and *nāyikā* of his *rasa* experience are no ordinary mortals.

If Rādhā as *raseśvarī* the divine consort of Kṛṣṇa is the perfect embodiment and expression of *rasa*, Pārvatī as the consort of Śiva, can be understood as *vimarśinī* or free and spontaneous objective consciousness, illustrating yet another fundamental aesthetic principle. There is no better place to start an examination of Pārvatī *vimarśinī* than the myth of the seduction of Śiva.[22] That well-known myth goes as follows:

> Śiva was absorbed in meditation when Parvata Raja arrived, offering flowers, fruits and his daughter to serve the Lord. Śiva saw Pārvatī in her great beauty. Regaining control over his nascent passion and lust and closing his eyes asked Parvata not to bring his daughter with him. Pārvatī undaunted addressed the Yogi: "Śiva, you practice arduous austerity because you have the energy to do so. That energy is Prakṛti, the cause of all action. How can the great Lord of the *liṅga* exist without Prakṛti. Everything at all times is held together by

> Prakṛti. What you hear, what you eat, what you see and what you are are all the activity of Prakṛti. I am Prakṛti and you are Puruṣa." Pārvatī undertakes severe penance and arouses Śiva. Śiva still not satisfied tests Pārvatī and then eventually marries her.

The myth then continues to describe the marriage of Śiva and Pārvatī. This beautiful myth is the foundation of much of Śiva-Pārvatī art.

While Rādhā as *raseśvarī* is artistically represented by *rasakāvyas* and the miniature paintings of the Punjab hills and Rajasthan, Pārvatī *vimarśinī* is best seen artistically in the stone and bronze sculptures of Śiva and Pārvatī of which the *ardhanārīśvara*, the androgyn figure representing Śiva on the right side and Pārvatī on the left, the latter holding a mirror in one of her hands is the most beautiful. Equally significant are the beautiful Śiva-Pārvatī images which depict Pārvatī and Śiva together in a variety of amorous poses which while being exquisitely sensuous emphasise the more important attribute of the togetherness of Śiva and Pārvatī. All too often the androgyn figure and the Śiva Pārvatī images are interpreted as demonstrating the equality of sexes in the Indian tradition, while some art historians remark that the mirror held by Pārvatī is a sign of feminine vanity. Iconologists such as Banerjea suggest that the *ardhanārīśvara* image "symbolises (a) syncretic ideology" bringing together the sometimes opposing cults of Śaivism and Śaktism.[23] Both these views offer somewhat limited socio-psychological explanations of this important and significant image. What such and other explanations ignore is that there is a deeper and more central underlying aesthetic idea behind these androgyn images, namely that the androgyn figure of *ardhanārīśvara* is a perfect visual representation, a symbol of the *pratyabhijña* system of epistemology of Kāśmīr Śaivism. No causal relationship is attributed between the *pratyabhijña* system and the image of the *ardhanārīśvara*, but the image leads to a better enjoyment of the concept of *pratyabhijña* and the concept in turn lets us celebrate the image even more.

In essence, the *pratyabhijña* school puts forth the unique concept of cognition through recognition. This has been dealt with in detail in the previous chapter. In its barest terms the Kāśmīr Śaivites admit the reality of the objective world and posit cognition not as a solitary, but a series of perceptive events, with each succeeding cognition leading to remembrance and thence realisation on the part of the cognising subject. Abhinavagupta defines recognition as "shining as facing oneself (*abhimukhyena*) of what was forgotten" and "unification of what appeared once with what appears now,"[24] and as a "reflection on the mirror".[25] Stella Kramrisch considers "the mirror... a symbol and restatement of Śiva's being. The objects seen in the mirror are neither separate from each other nor from the mirror."[26] The first step in the cognitive process is *nirvikalpa pratyakṣa* or indeterminate cognition and the next step is *savikalpa jñāna* or determinate cognition. While *nirvikalpa pratyakṣa* is the direct result of the interaction between the object and the senses of the subject, *pratyabhijñāvāda* postulates that *savikalpa jñāna* is the creation of the mind consisting of "a reaction of the mind on the sense data recorded on the Buddhi...and adding (to it) something from the old store of memory and ...giving it a definite shape and name."[27] As Radhakrishnan points out "Mind is immanent in all cognitive experience as an active process which gives objective form to knowledge. It does not stand in a transcendent relation to an extraneous object which it passively contemplates."[28] Thus it is that cognition is really recogniton, that the initial *nirvikalpa pratyakṣa* of Pārvatī as an object of cognition eventually leads to the *savikalpa jñāna* in the subjective Śiva.

Pratyabhijña therefore implies the two-fold and distinct function of consciousness in cognition, also called the Śiva *tattva, jñāna, prakāśa, aham* or 'I' and the Śakti *tattva, kriyā, vimarśa, idam* or 'this'. In the Tāntric tradition *vimarśa* also called *spanda* is to be distinguished from *karma*, for unlike *karma* it is free and spontaneous. Cognition in Kāśmīr Śaivism is the result of Śakti consorting with Śiva, a consortism which beautifully illustrates the principle of *bheda-abheda* or "seeing non-difference in difference".[29] For, as in any amorous relationship, one is initially attracted by another, an attraction not unmixed with some doubt as well as desire, but having overcome the doubt and uncertainty, one that leads to courtship, an embrace, enjoyment and then finally union. The amorous relationship of Śiva and Śakti, so beautifully depicted in the Śiva-Śakti art, illustrates the basic *pratyabhijña* principle that "self-luminosity of cognition consists in making itself so manifest as to make others also manifest",[30] such that both the "knower and the known, in their distinctive nature, shine in the subject."[31] Cognition as *pratyabhijña* is objective and not just merely subjective and therefore always "implies two",[32] an "awareness of another thing which is of the opposite nature".[33] Underlying the *pratyabhijña* process, as Abhinavagupta rightly points out, is the "intensity of desire"[34] on the part of the subject, the desire arising from the fitness of the object to be desirable, the onus being equally divided between the subject and the object. Notice how in the myth of the seduction of Śiva, Pārvatī had to take the initiative and that Śiva's initial attraction of her was almost lustful. The consortism of Śiva and Pārvatī is a perfect artistic model for the *pratyabhijña* system of Kāśmīr Śaivism. While *pratyabhijña* applies to all forms of cognition it is particularly applicable in understanding aesthetic experience, where a deliberate, repetitive and penetrating experience brings out the manifold levels of meaning in the art object, and leads ultimately to the *ānanda* of aesthetic realisation. This is the meaning of Pārvatī urging Śiva to consort with her, for it was she who realised that without this consortism there could be no *ānanda* or *jñāna* for Śiva. *Ānanda*, as the Kāśmīr Śaivites understand it, is *prakāśa-vimarśamaya* and can only result from the perfect marriage of Śiva and Pārvatī, the dynamic harmony of the subject and the object.

It is important to distinguish recognition or *pratyabhijña* from memory. *Pratyabhijña* consists in the unification of past and present experiences and differs from memory in the sense that while the object of previous experience is absent in the case of memory, it is present in the case of recognition. *Pratyabhijña* in this sense is a refined and penetrating cognition. Pārvatī *vimarśinī* is not to be confused with the forgotten Damayantī of Kālidāsa. It is this refined cognition as advocated by Kāśmīr Śaivites that leads to self-knowledge. As Sharma rightly points out "epistemologically ... all recognition is in fact self-recognition."[35] Herein lies the significance of Pārvatī holding up the mirror to Śiva. The concepts of the mirror, light and reflection feature prominently in Kāśmīr Śaivism and for this reason it is also referred to as *bimba-pratibimbavāda*.

The other notable feature of the *ardhanārīśvara* image is the perfect harmony and equilibrium or *sāmarasya* of Śiva and Pārvatī, each maintaining its own identity, yet dependent on the other, one not overpowering or overshadowing the other, but yet one being implied in the other, a case of identity in difference, *bheda-abheda*, unlike the Vedāntic identity by fusion (*bhakti*) or identity by rejection (*māyā* of Śaṅkara). The consortship of Śiva and Pārvatī illustrates yet another fundamental Tāntric principle, namely that the transcendent incorporates the immanent, the ultimate does not annihilate the immediate, and that ultimate Reality is the perfect equilibrium of two aspects of consciousness, the *prakāśa* and the *vimarśa*. If the *ardhanārīśvara* is the visual representation of the concept of *sāmarasya*, an equally beautiful representation of the same concept is provided by the many amorous bronze and stone sculptures and a mural in Ajanta depicting the betrothal and the marriage of Śiva and Pārvatī and *āliṅgan* of Pārvatī by Śiva.

While the *ardhanāriśvara* is the perfect visual paradigm of the Kāśmīr Śaivite epistemology, Pārvatī *vimarśinī* in her role as Śiva's consort provides a perfect illustration of the *bimba-pratibimbavāda*. Kāśmīr Śaivism departs company from other *advaitic* systems in the Indian tradition in insisting that the *pratibimba* is vital to any knowledge episode, justifying not only Pārvatī's objectivity but bringing into focus her consortship.

The essence of the Śiva-Pārvatī consortship is captured by the words "*etad guhyam mahāguhyam*",[36] a beautiful relationship the meaning of which is hidden and subtle as "the grass and the leaves on the path of someone who passes on in a chariot",[37] and which leads to a dialogue between the divine pair themselves. The questioner is Pārvatī and her respondent is Śiva, for the quintessence of the divine consortship is the quest for knowledge. The epistemic process, it should be noted, is a dialogue and not a monologue, and that is *advaitic*, for as Abhinavagupta explains that this process is nothing but a form of self-reflection, an "intellectual sport",[38] a dialogue that leads to the blissful silence of *annutara*.

But until that silence is reached, the questioning in search of ultimate reality must continue, for this is the "*paramārthamaya*",[39] the basis of the divine consortship.

The objectivity of Pārvatī rests entirely on her being able to seek the subject while sustaining the subject-object dialogue, for Pārvatī is *gocarī, dikcarī, vyomacarī and bhūcarī*, seeking not only to establish objectivity but bringing it to fulfilment in "*khecarīsamatā*".[40] There in this divine consortship a double movement from Śiva to Pārvatī and back to Śiva again, a movement from the subject to its mirror image and from that image back to the subject. As Abhinavagupta explains from *a-ha-m* to *m-ha-a* and back to *a-ha-m*, where a represents Śiva, *ha* represents Śakti and *m* represents the *anusvāra* or *bindu* which unites the two. The evolution and involution of *aham* is the central feature of Tantra, for "Śiva is that whose very nature consists in the expansion of His Śaktis,"[41] and in that expansion is Śiva's delight, creativity, freedom and spontaniety; and Śakti is *kulanāyikā* because it is she who brings into manifestation all objects of experience, the experience itself and the experients. Translated in aesthetic terms, the consortship of Śiva and Pārvatī gives credence not only to art objects but equally to aesthetic experience and in the end to the experiencer himself. The movement from and to *aham* constitutes the core of the *bimba-pratibimbavāda*, from illumination to its reflection and from the reflection back to illumination again, succinctly and beautifully exemplified by the mirror held by Pārvatī, for in this scheme of knowledge the *prameya* (object) has to surrender itself to *pramāṇa* (the means of knowledge) and the *pramāṇa* to the *pramātā* (knower) for its final fulfilment, just as the mirror image surrenders itself to the mirror and the mirror to the subject. It is only because of this outward and inward movement that Śiva, the eternal subject, can say *aham*. Pārvatī's mirror in reflecting Śiva illustrates yet another important feature of the *bimba-pratibimbavāda*, and that is that the *pratibimba* though similar to the *bimba* is not identical with it. Śiva's consortship with Pārvatī stems from Pārvatī's distinct identity, *bheda*, leading to an erotic coming together with Śiva, *abheda*, the resulting union representing the epistemic concept of *bheda-abheda*. The strongly romantic metaphor in this epistemic process is hard to miss and one that has been utilised by artists in creating the numerous amorous representations of Śiva and Pārvatī, exquisitely sensuous in its *sākṣātartha* but providing a *parokṣārtha* to the prepared aesthete. The close similarity between romanticism and epistemology is brought out by the *ardhanārīśvara* image and equally by the *āliṅgan* of Śiva.

While the consortism of Lakṣmī is a favourite subject of artists, it is interesting to note that Vaiṣṇava iconography portrays the marriage of Viṣṇu and Lakṣmī, and the relationship of Viṣṇu and Lakṣmī is anything but amorous. The unique Śaivite concept of ultimate Reality, and especially that in Kāśmīr Śaivism, which is the ecstatic and harmonious coming together of *prakāśa* and *vimarśa*, is best depicted by the artistic model of consortism featuring Pārvatī wooing, being betrothed and married, sitting romantically next to or on the knee, amorously embraced by and ultimately being part of Śiva. In all these works of art the sensual feminine beauty of Pārvatī fulfils itself only in its togetherness with Śiva. It is important to point out that the Naṭarāja is an androgyn figure, the left earring giving away a hint of its feminine aspect. The joyous, ecstatic, amorous relationship of Śiva and Pārvatī is unique to the Śaiva tradition and is underpinned by the equally unique concept of *pratyabhijña* of Kāśmīr Śaivism. Even Śaṅkara in his ***Śivānandalaharī*** describes Śiva not only as "*nīlagrīvam*" or blue throated but equally as "*umāśliṣṭavapusam*"[42] or one whose body is embraced by Umā. Art historians who very eloquently point out the sensuous beauty of Pārvatī fail to bring out the aesthetic underpinnings of this art and especially that of Pārvatī's amorous relationship with Śiva. If Śiva is *ānanda*, Pārvatī is the *hlādinī śakti*, if Śiva is *prakāśa*, Pārvatī is *vimarśa*, if Śiva is the *aham*, Pārvatī as the divine consort is the *idam*, if Śiva is *jñāna* Pārvatī is *kriyā*.

It is well to remind ourselves of the words of Śrī Aurobindo that *prakāśa* and *vimarśinī*, Śiva and *vimarśinī* Pārvatī, *cit* and *cit-śakti*, *ānanda* and *hlādinī-śakti*, *jñāna* and *kriyā* "are not really something dual and separate, it is biune."[43] "In the superconscient truth. . . these two are fused and implied in each other, one and indistinguishable, but in the spiritual-pragmatic truth of the dynamism of the universe, they emerge and become active."[44]

It has been suggested that the role of Śrī as consort in Śrī vaiṣṇavism, seems to parallel the role of Pārvatī *vimarśinī*. Though this may be true to a certain limited extent, there are definite and sharp differences between the two traditions that need to be stressed. The amorous relationship of Śiva and Pārvatī which is a hallmark of Śiva-Śakti art is never a feature of Viṣṇu and Lakṣmī art. The role of Lakṣmī is that of a chaste and devoted consort, as seen in the popular depiction of *śesaṣāyī* Viṣṇu where Lakṣmī is seen tending Viṣṇu's feet. The only vague hint of an androgyn representation of Viṣṇu and Lakṣmī is the depiction of Lakṣmī in the form of a *tulsī* leaf on the breast of Viṣṇu. Nowhere in the Vaiṣṇava artistic tradition does one find the kind of representation of divine consortism that occurs in the Śaiva tradition, and based on this alone it is possible to assert that divine consortism in the Vaiṣṇava tradition does not reflect the *prakāśavimarśa* aspect of consciousness which is a central feature of Śiva-Śakti art.

To accept and grant an independent status to divine consorts would amount to a truncation and a superficial artistic appreciation of this art; a true aesthetic realisation should involve an appreciation of Śakti in her biune state with Śiva, remembering "*na śivena vinā śaktiḥ, na śakti sahitaḥ śivah*" As Śrī Aurobindo says:

> The human mind shut in the prison of its half-lit obscurity cannot follow the many-sided freedom of the steps of the Divine Shakti... Follow your soul and not your mind, your soul that answers to the Truth, not your mind that leaps at appearances.[45]

It is only the tethering of Śakti to its consort that can lead to the proper understanding of Śakti and thence to the *advaita* of art.

NOTES

1. James D. Redington, ***Vallabhācārya on the Love Games of Kṛṣṇa*** (Delhi: Motilal Banarsidas, 1983), p. 257.

2. Redington, p.5.
3. *svarūpasya rasātmakatvāt rasarītyā svarūpanandanam eva.*
   Love-making... was His gift of the joy of His own form ... for His own form has *rasa* as its very essence.
   Redington, p.85.
4. *udgato agniḥ sarvatraiva agnim līnam janayitum śaknoti*
   A fire that is already blazing can kindle the fire that is latent in everything.
   Redington, p. 264.
5. Redington, p. 1.
6. A.G.Archer, ***Loves of Krishna*** (London: George, Allen and Unwin, 1957) p. 62.
7. Karine Schomer, ***The Divine Consort*** Rādhā and the Goddesses of India. (John Stratton Hawley and Donna Marie Wulff, editors) (Boston, Beacon Press, 1982) p. 95.
8. Edward C. Dimock, ***Krishna: Myths, Rites and Attitudes.*** Singer, M. (editor) (Honolulu: East West-Center Press, 1966.) p. 61.
9. *sukhadam śubhadam bhavasāram.*
   ...joyously evokes the essence of existence.
   Gītagovinda 1.15.
10. *śṛṅgarottara satprameya.*
    ...the erotic mood and sacred truth.
    Gītagovinda 1.3.
11. *śṛṅgāramūrtimān.*
    the very embodiment of the erotic mood.
    Gītagovinda 1.46.
12. Schomer, p. 92.
13. Barbara Stoller Miller, ***The Gītagovinda of Jayadeva*** Love Song of the Dark Lord. (Delhi: Motilal Banarsidass, 1984.) p. 25.
14. Shrivasta, Goswami, ***The Divine Consort*** p. 85.
15. Norvin Hein in ***The Divine Consort*** p. 117.
16. *janayatu rasikajanesu manoramati rasabhāva vinodam.*
    (with) each verse... let emotion rise to a joyful mood of love in sensitive men!
    Gītagovinda 12.9.
17. *śrijayadeva bhaṇitavibhava dviguṇīkṛta bhūsaṇabhāram.*
    Jayadeva's singing doubles the power of Krishna's adornments.
    Gītagovinda 11.31.
18. *vikasitavividhavikāravibhaṅgam.*
    (Radha sees) her passion reach the soul of Hari's mood.
    Gītagovinda 11.24.
19. ***Gītagovinda*** 11.26.
20. ***Gītagovinda*** 11.27.
21. A.G.Archer p. 73.
22. Stella Kramrisch, ***The Presence of Śiva*** (Princeton: Princeton University Press, 1981) p. 353.

23. Jitendra Nath Banerjea, ***The Development of Hindu Iconography*** (Calcutta: Calcutta University Press, 1956) p. 552.
24. *pratipam ātmābhimukhyena jñānam prakāśah pratyabhijñā". "pratyabhijñā ca bhātbhasamāna rūpānusandhānātmikā." "iti pratisandhanena abhimukhībhūt vastuni jñānam.*
Recognition consists in the unification of what appeared once with what appears now.
Abhinavagupta, ***Īśvara Pratyabhijña Vimarśinī.*** K.A. Subramania Iyer and K.C. Pandey (editors) (Delhi: Motilal Banarsidass, 1986) Vol.I pp. 36-37.
25. *biṁbapratibiṁbavat saṅkrāntiḥ.*
the meaning of the treatise on the system is reflected in the consciousness of the deserving disciple, as a reflection on the mirror...
Abhinavagupta, *Ibid.*, Vol. I. p. 44.
26. Stella Kramrisch, ***The Presence of Siva.*** p. 449.
27. Abhinavagupta, ***Īśvara Pratyabhijña Vimarśinī.*** II.p.103.
quoted by K.C. Pandey, ***Abhinavagupta an Historical and Philosophic Study*** (Varanasi: Chowkhamba Sanskrit Series Office, 1963) p. 409.
28. S. Radhakrishnan, ***The Idealist View of Life*** (Bombay: Goerge Allen & Unwin Ltd., 1976) p. 10.
29. *sarvathā tāvadatra prameye bhagavat eva bhedena ca abhedena ca svātantryam...*
(Cognition) initially conceals the unitary bliss of pure Self-Consciousness and then reveals it.
Abhinavagupta, ***Īśvara Pratyabhijña Vimarśinī*** Vol. II. 129.
30. *paraprakāśanatmaka nijarūpaprakāśanameva hi svaprakāśatvam jñānasya bhaṇyate.*
Self-luminosity of congnition consists in making itself so manifest as to make others also manifest.
Abhinavagupta, ***Īśvara Pratyabhijña Vimarśinī.*** Vol.I p. 127.
31. *tanmaya draśyate dṛṣṭoyam sa ityāṃrśatyapi, grāhyagrāhakatā bhinnavarthau bhatah pramātari.*
Both the knower and the known, in their distinctive nature, shine in the subject.
Abhinavagupta, *Ibid.*, p. 187.
32. *nāsau vikalpaḥ sa hyukto dvapekṣī viniścayaḥ*
Cognition... is objective and not subjective and therefore implies two.
Abhinavagupta, *Ibid.*, p. 302.
33. *vikalpa eva sa parapratiyogyāvabhāsajaḥ.*
Awareness of another thing which is of the opposite nature.
Abhinavagupta, *Ibid.*, p. 313.
34. *arthitātiśayat.*
Intensity of desire.
Abhinavagupta, *Ibid.*, p. 162.
35. L.N. Sharma, ***Kāśmir Saivism*** (Varanasi: Bhartiya Vidya Prakashan, 1972)

p. 76.

36. *etad guhyam mahāguhyam kathayasva mama prabho.*
Tell me this secret, this greatest secret, O Lord who are my very Self. Abhinavagupta, ***Parātriśika Vivaraṇa.*** (Delhi: Motilal Banarsidass, 1988). Jaideva Singh (editor) p. 53.

37. *bhāvamapyabhāvena rathyāgame tṛṇaparṇādivat.*
So though present, it is as if non-present, just as the grass and leaves on the path of someone who passes on in a chariot.
Abhinavagupta, *Ibid.*, p. 58.

38. *camatkurvan vimarśate.*
The questioner (as Devī) and the answerer (as Bhairava) are only Himself, enjoys self-reflection.
Abhinavagupta, *Ibid.*, p. 48.

39. *paramārthamayatvāt.*
So, the inner content, i.e., question-answer which appears in the consciousness of the highest Lord...
Abhinavagupta, *Ibid.*, p. 48.

40. Abhinavagupta, offers an explanation of *khecarīsamatā*, *Ibid.*, p. 38.

41. Original quotation by Somananda in ***Śivadṛṣṭi***. III. 94.
quoted by Abhinavagupta, ***Paratriśika Vivaraṇa***. p. 40.

42. T.M.P. Mahadevan, ***The Hymns of Śaṅkara*** (Delhi: Motilal Banarsidass, 1986) p. 106.

43. Śrī Aurobindo, ***The Life Divine*** Volume 1. (Pondicherry: Śrī Aurobindo Ashram, 1977) p. 347.

44. Śrī Aurobindo, ***The Life Divine*** p. 356.

45. Śrī Aurobindo, ***The Mother*** (Volume 25) (Pondicherry: Śrī Aurobindo Birth Centenary Library, 1972) pp. 38 and 40.

Chapter 8

Aesthetics and Idealism

tadavaitam vande parama śivaśaktyātma nikhalam
Abhinavagupta. ***Īśvara Pratyabhījña Vimarsinī***. Maṅgalācaraṇa.

In investigating the nature of art experience, it is surely not enough to point out the superficial characteristics of the art object or merely to discuss the dynamics of the experience, but also to inquire whether or not such an experience has a philosophic underpinning. This becomes important as aesthetics does not form a formal part of the Indian philosophic tradition. If a philosophic foundation for art experience is indeed found, it not only confers upon art experience a legitimacy but gives it an exalted status as well, setting it apart from a superficial art sensation. In conducting this inquiry it may become necessary to adopt an eclectic approach and draw from the various philosophic schools and also be prepared to use Western idioms when necessary thereby extending the frame of inquiry. Radhakrishnan himself pointed out that "the most effective development (in Indian philosophy) is in the presentation of India's fundamental thought in the idiom of our age and its development in new directions."[1] He further reminds us that "Truth may be immutable but the form in which it is embodied consists of elements which admit of change."[2] Raju echoes the same sentiment when he says that "the principles of our traditional thought ... can be applied to other spheres of our experience".[3]

It is an accepted modern practice to group philosophic doctrines under broad rubrics such as Idealist and Realist, a practice that entails obvious advantages as well as problems. Such a classification, as long as it is not rigidly applied, helps in pointing out certain shared tenets and common directions and represents a certain catholicity of vision. Not to attempt such an ecumenical analysis could be considered parochial. The obvious drawback is that in providing a label for a system of thought, and putting it in a pigeon hole, one might blur the finer points of that thought system.

The sixth century BC is considered an axial period in the development of Indian thought. This, as Radhakrishnan says was, "the age of the Buddha (which) represents the great springtide of philosophic spirit in India ... it was a time when the critical side of philosophy became as important as the speculative."[4] During this time *anvikṣikī* or logic came to be formally accepted as a philosophic tool and on this basis schools were divided into orthodox or *āstika* and heterodox or *nāstika*. A parallel situation occurred in the West when the advent of science in the seventeenth century divided schools of philosophy into Idealist and Realist, and more recently in the early twentieth century, when Moore, Russell and others led a revolt against the traditional Hegelian Idealism which had dominated Western philosophy since the nineteenth century. It is interesting that although these two developments were separated by almost twenty centuries, the underlying ferment was similar, *anvikṣikī* in India and science in the West, a dissatisfaction with tradition and a need to explore the world of man with the tools of logic and reason, a desire to move outward rather than inward, to investigate the object rather than the subject.

In trying to find a home for aesthetic experience, it is important that we pay equal attention to the artist and the aesthete alike, to the art object and the experience it generates, to the object and the subject, equally. Any school which favours one over the other would alienate the art object from art experience and the artist from the aesthete and not be acceptable to an *advaitin* of art.

The problem of defining Idealism has landed Western philosophers in a quagmire with widespread disagreement even at the most fundamental level. One of the main reasons for this is the basis on which the definition is attempted. Western scholars tend to define Idealism on an ontological basis which brings in concepts of the Absolute and raises questions of value, whereas in the Indian tradition the issue is mainly epistemic. Raju points out that "the problem of reality cannot be detached from the problem of knowledge ... reality is what is known to be real and is an object of knowledge."[5]

Dasgupta discovers the foundation of Indian Idealism in the Upaniṣads and defines Idealism as a doctrine which considers reality spiritual rather than material.[6] Stated in epistemic terms, it implies that ultimate Reality cannot be cognised by the standard material modes of cognition such as *pratyakṣa* and *anumāna* alone, that neither a sense report nor intellectual inference, although both are provisionally valid, is enough to lead us to what is ultimately Real. Ultimate Reality for the Upaniṣadic *ṛṣis* is the reality behind the appearance, a reality that is super-sensual and intuitive, a state not just of mental construction or imagination but of discovery, a state of gnosis or *ānanda* that is "not so much produced as achieved",[7] which needs not just the mind but the other mind, a mind behind the mind, the *manaso manaḥ*.[8] This hierarchy of the mind, reminding one of the "two birds on the self same tree"[9] of the ***Śvetāśvatara Upaniṣad***, a lower, material or cognitive and a higher spiritual or non-cognitive, becomes the hallmark of Indian Upaniṣadic Idealism.

This mystical concept of Indian Idealism as set out in the Upaniṣads, although of seminal value, did not address itself in sufficient detail to problems which were the focus of attention of later philosophers in the tradition. These problems were: (i) what is the nature of the object of true cognition? (ii) is there a bridge between matter and mind or object and subject? and (iii) what is the epistemic status of *bhakti*? These were the issues that were to engage the attention and divide Indian philosophers of the Idealist mould as the tradition evolved. Śaṅkara's lucid exposition of the epistemology of Advaita Vedānta is attractive to an aesthetician on first encounter, particularly as it makes knowledge *vāstu tantra* or object-dependent and gives provisional credence to the objective world; but on closer examination, its stand on the nature of the object of true cognition, namely *nirguṇa brahman* would not allow the art object its bonafides, thereby making it unacceptable. At the end of the day, the material world is only provisionally real for Śaṅkara, it is *māyā* which must be negated in order to experience *brahman.* Further, Śaṅkara's *nirguṇa brahman* is passive, leaving no room for creativity in the process of acquiring knowledge, knowledge being merely removal of ignorance. The Vijñānavādin's brand of Idealism with its insistence of *śūnyatā* would be totally nihilistic from an artist's and aesthetician's viewpoint for it gives epistemic status neither to the artist, the art object nor the aesthete. The epistemology of the theistic schools of Vedānta and later *bhakti* aestheticians appear interesting to an aesthetician particularly as their practice relies heavily on art-centred temple rituals, but since they subsume the whole process under *bhakti,*[10] aesthetic experience would be denied its uniqueness, autonomy and secular status and removed from the realm of knowledge, a position once again unacceptable to aestheticians, for our basic question as aestheticians is, does art experience lead to knowledge? Another major problem with the *bhakti* schools is that for an experience to be valid it has to be sacred which implies that secular experiences cannot be accommodated in their orbit. In rejecting Śaṅkara's and Rāmānuja's Vedānta as unsuitable for a study of a truly *advaitic* aesthetic experience, we reserve the right to be eclectics and refer to portions of their ideas inasmuch as they are applicable to an understanding of the aesthetic experience. For aesthetics in the Indian tradition is non-sectarian. This leaves Tantra and in particular Kāśmīr Śaivism, among the *advaitic* schools, to provide a philosophic underpinning for aesthetic experience.

Kāśmir Śaivism seems to provide an almost perfect home for experience in general and aesthetic experience in particular, for rightly has it been called *anubhavavāda.* With its emphasis on *kriyā* as the basis of knowledge it provides an active role for the mind, recognising the creativity of the artist and demanding a similar recreativity on the part of the aesthete, making knowledge an active rather than a passive process, and emphasising that without *vimarśa*, or determinate cognition, Śiva would only be a *śava*, for Śiva is *prakāśa-vimarśamaya*, a *sāmarasya*, a perfect blend of *prakāśa* and *vimarśa*, the *aham* and the *idam*. The Kāśmir Śaivite concept of *vimarśa* being an integral part of knowledge not only gives validity to *pratyakṣa* and *anumāna*, as modes of cognition, but encourages an exultation rather than a negation of these *pramāṇas*. *Vimarśa* does not restrict our experience to the sacred but leaves the door wide open for secular experiences as well, a position most suited to aesthetic experience. If the concept of *vimarśa* lends credibility to the objective world as exemplified by the art object, the doctrine of *ābhāsa* ensures the transcendence and inwardness of the art experience, emphasising that, if the art experience is to be knowledge and not merely a superficial psychological art sensation, it must move inward and become part of the I-consciousness, become spiritual rather than remain merely sensual, non-cognitive rather than merely cognitive, in other words the experience has to become *āgama*, for without that there would not be perfect Śiva consciousness, which is *prakāśa-vimarśamaya*. *Āgama* is to be understood not merely as the scripture of Tantra but as intuitive spiritual consciousness, in which there is the coming together of the subject and object, and in which the particular becomes the universal. *Āgamic* consciousness then becomes the ground of all *pramāṇas*[11] not a content-free, but a concept-loaded consciousness, which incorporates knowledge generated by the *pramāṇas*. Here Kāśmīr Śaivism parts company with Saṅkara's Advaita Vedānta, but by the same token, makes itself vulnerable to a potential epistemic problem which it shares with Tantra in general. While *vimarśa* ensures that the art object does not forfeit its reality, a question that can be raised is whether there no limitation on what can become a fit object for cognition? While the left handed Tāntrics make themselves open to ambiguity in insisting on the "five Ms", the Kāśmīr Śaivites seem to prefer, though not insist, that an art object is the desired object of cognition and aesthetic experience is the favoured mode of experiencing reality. If this be the case, the onus is on the object in being a fit object of cognition.

A second epistemic problem with Kāśmir Śaivism is that it must ensure that *vimarśa* be allowed to rise to its spiritual height and not be stunted at a psychological level. This it does through its doctrine of *ābhāsa* and *pratyabhijña*, which makes it certain that the experience leads to higher knowledge rather than remain a superficial psychological experience, a type of knowledge that allows an identity in difference, yet without permitting any duality whatsoever. Thus, in this doctrine, the object of cognition and the cognising subject both share the responsibility in ensuring that cognition leads to a realisation of ultimate Reality. Kāśmīr Śaivism on the one hand fulfils the basic tenet of Idealism and at the same time allows the object to retain its identity, ensuring that the object is not merely instrumental but inherent in the experience, leading some scholars to call this doctrine neither strictly Idealist nor Realist, but a form of transcendent Realism. It is well to remember that although *prakāśa-vimarśamaya* is thc perfect blend of the two modes of cognition, the outward and the inward, the cognitive and the non-cognitive, it is the inward, restful, or the Śiva *tattva* that is dominant and in which the experience is finally grounded, and it is this that drives the experience to its ultimate height; thus, it is that though Kāśmīr Śaivism can be looked upon as a doctrine of transcendent Realism, in the ultimate analysis it is undeniably Idealistic.

A perfect model of the Kāśmīr Śavism epistemology is the image of *ardhanārīśvara*, which demonstrates *prakāśa-vimarśamaya* through the perfect harmony of Śiva and Pārvatī, the mirror held in the left hand of Pārvatī illustrating the all important concepts of *ābhāsa* and *pratyabhijña*. Śiva's first lustful cognition reveals the sensual Pārvatī, the second and subsequent recognition reveals the mirror which in turn reflects Śiva himself, demonstrating the process of *pratyabhijña* or *biṁba-pratibiṁba*. Pārvatī is the very embodiment of beauty and becomes a fit object of cognition, and interestingly none other than Śaṅkara composed the ***Saundaryalaharī*** extolling the beauty of Pārvatī. Śiva, *yogeśvara* himself, is the perfect cognising subject, illustrating once again the cardinal feature of Kāśmīr Śaivism that the epistemic onus is shared by both the object and the subject, Pārvatī and Śiva. It is worth pointing out that in the *ardhanārīśvara* image, Śiva is visually larger than Pārvatī, not merely in an anatomical sense but also in an epistemic sense, emphasising that it is Śiva, or the epistemic subject, that drives the experience, and is the ultimaate resting point of experience, fulfilling the basic tenet of Idealism. *Ardhanārīśvara* is a perfect visual depiction of *Āgama*, a plastic representation of the dialogue between Śiva and Pārvatī, an artistic model of Tāntric epistemology. Abhinavagupta demonstrates the concept of *ābhāsa* through the use of Sanskrit grammar. He states that in the sentence, "*sa ca tvam ca aham tiṣṭhāmaḥ*" ... the verb *tiṣṭhāmaḥ* is indicative of the fact that the third and the second person are absorbed in the first. Abhinavagupta states that just as the third person has to surrender itself to the second and the second to the first in order that they may be used together, so also the *prameya* (object) or *nara* has to surrender itself to *pramāṇa* (knowledge) or Śakti, to be known, and *pramāṇa* has to surrender itself to *pramātā* (knower) or Śiva for its final fulfilment.[12]

Having determined that Kāśmir Śaivism is a doctrine of *anubhavavāda* and is capable of providing the necessary philosophic undergirding of the Idealist variety, for any objective or material experience, our next step is to demonstrate that aesthetic experience shares the same foundational premises, and if this be the case, we can then declare with certainty that aesthetics and Idealism stand and fall together in the Indian tradition. Our task now is to show that the *ardhanārīśvara* is a model not only of Idealism of the Kāśmīr Śaivism variety but of aesthetic experience as well. There are two basic components of the Tāntric epistemology: the Śakti *tattva* or the apprehending consciousness which having cognised the object turns itself inwards, and the Śiva *tattva* which ensures that this consciousness rises to its ultimate height and becomes spiritual rather than remain psychological. In the case of art and aesthetic experience the Śiva *tattva* is none other than the *pratibhā* or the creative genius of the artist and the aesthete alike, about which the tradition is quite rightly silent. All that can be said about *pratibhā* is that it depends upon the *śikṣā* (training) and *saṃskāra* (latent psychic impressions) of the artist and the aesthete. *Pratibhā* cannot be analysed further, and any attempts to do so would be to degrade the creative aspects of art and aesthetic experience alike and to reduce it to a psychological level. However, the Śakti *tattva*, as applied to an aesthetic experience, can be further analysed to understand what it is about the art object that turns the experience inward to become as it were the mirror of Pārvatī, encouraging not just cognition but recognition or *pratyabhijña*. The onus of this aspect of aesthetic experience is entirely on the art object and the inquiry necessarily centres around those features of the art object that promotes a deep, introspective, deliberate art experience rather than a superficial art sensation. Since art, even within the classical Indian tradition, takes so many different forms, this inquiry can touch only on certain artistic principles rather than elaborate on artistic details. Of the many principles which underlie Indian art, three main ideas have been chosen in this chapter, ideas that are integral not only to art creation but also to art appreciation, namely *dhvani, pramāṇa* and *sādṛśya*. These three artistic principles have been discussed in the previous chapters but it is essential to refer to them once again to show how they ensure an Idealist position when it comes to an aesthetic experience in the Indian tradition.

Translated variously as 'reverberation' or 'vibration' *dhvani* has come to occupy a central place in Indian aesthetics. Attributed to Ānandavardhana the concept had its origins even earlier. It is usual to understand *dhvani* in tandem with *rasa* but we have extended the term to have a much wider application and it is also applied not only to *nāṭya* and *kāvya* but also to *rūpa*. Ānandavardhana simply defines *dhvani* as "*dhvanirnāma arthāntaram*"[13] or *dhvani* is another or extended meaning, and refers to the concept of *vyaṅgya* or the ability of art to suggest a meaning indirectly. We are told in no uncertain terms by the *dhvanivādins* that this suggested meaning is available only to the refined and the sensitive. Mammaṭa says that, "the expressed meaning produces a mere comprehension in one who knows the meaning of words, while the suggested meaning produces charm in men of taste alone".[14] There are a number of implications in the concept of *dhvani* but one that is of importance to us is, in our inquiry whether or not aesthetics can be considered Idealistic, is that the realisation of *dhvani* invloves the transformation of the primary meaning, not suddenly, as happens in the understanding of metaphor, but one that is gradual or *asamlakṣayakrama* like a "needle going through a pile of lotus leaves",[15] each layer yielding a deeper and more intense meaning, each more profound and satisfying than the one before it. This is what contributes to the inwardness of the art experience and ensures that the mind is not just a silent spectator in the aesthetic experience but has a creative role in letting the primary meaning expand through the process of *dhvani* to a stage of aesthetic rapture or *camatkāra*. Although the concept of *dhvani* was developed in the framework of *kāvya*, it is equally applicable to the visual and performing arts and as well to traditional architecture. Symbolism or *parokṣa* which is an integral part of *rūpa, citra, vāstu* and *nāṭya* in the Indian tradition, can be understood as a wider application of *dhvani*. The entire symbol system, as exemplified by the *mudrās* and *bādhras* of the *rūpa* demands that the aesthete dip into his inner spiritual resources to bring the art experience to fulfilment. Another example of the *parokṣa* nature of Indian art is the interrelationship between the mood of the *nāyikā* and the surrounding landscape as seen in the Tamil Sangam poetry and later in the miniature painting of the Punjab hills and especially in the paintings of the *bārāmāsa* genre, where the central artistic mood of the *nāyikā* is subtly suggested by the landscape and not overtly stated. A prime example of the suggestiveness of plastic art is the Buddha image that was developed in the Indian tradition; the fact that the Gāndhāra image of the Buddha was rejected in favour of the Mathurā image is the demonstration of the need for the Indian psyche to relate to *parokṣa* rather than to *pratyakṣa*. Whether in artistic emotion or form, suggestiveness is the ***sine qua non*** of classical Indian art, leading the aesthete to a state of inward resolution, contemplation and ultimate realisation.

If *dhvani* is the essence of poetry, *pramāṇa* and *sādṛśya* are the hallmark of Indian visual art. *Pramāṇa* refers to the harmonious proportions of the plastic form by which it achieves organic unity and becomes a reflection of the form of the cosmic *Puruṣa*. It is significant that the proportions prescribed in the *śāstras* are not based on the empirical study of natural forms and shapes but on idealised conceptions in the minds of the creators of aesthetic forms. *Pramāṇa* in the Indian visual tradition signifies not just linear measurements, but also rhythm and harmony. This combination and interrelationship of measurement (*māna*) and harmony (*tāla*) is brought out by the term *tāla-māna*. Modern interpreters of the Indian tradition have stressed the importance of *tāla-māna* and have emphasised that this measured inner rhythm of the *rūpa* bears witness to the correlation between the microcosm and the macrocosm. Coomaraswamy maintains that, according to the tradition, all rhythm in art corresponds "in the last analysis to cosmic rhythms."[16] Tagore has rightly said that "It is rhythm that churns up images from the vague and makes tangible what is elusive."[17] The inner rhythm of the *rūpa*, based on its proportions, creates the impression of movement, a movement ***in situ***. Niharranjan Ray says that the measured rhythm of the *rūpa* is to be correlated with the rhythm of the life-breath (*prāṇa*) of the universe. As he puts it, the *rūpa* is endowed with an "inner reality of rhythmic vitality and movement (or) *prāṇa* which is its essential form."[18] *Pramāṇa* is the *dharma* of the Indian visual form, a *dharma* that not only ensures conformity to the tradition on the part of the artist but leads the aesthete inwards to a deep and spiritual realisation rather than to an outer and superficial art encounter. In its understanding and implementation of *sādṛśya* or verisimilitude, the Indian visual artistic tradition has ensured that Indian images portray not a mere outer photographic reality but reach out to depict the inner essence of the subject.

The best example of *sādṛśya* in the Indian tradition is the acceptance of the Mathurā and eventually the Gupta, rather than the Gāndhāra image of the Buddha. As Śrī Aurobindo rightly points out "for the Indian mind form does not exist except as a creation of the spirit and draws all its meaning and value from the spirit."[19] Kramarisch lends support to this concept when she says that "the figures of Indian sculpture are based primarily on a reality which is not seen but felt."[20]

Thus both *pramāṇa* and *sādṛśya*, cardinal principles of art in the Indian tradition, confer on the art object a sanctity and a beauty and ensure an inwardness of the aesthetic experience, the aesthete not merely reacting to the superficial sensory aspects of the art object but rather to its artistically embedded signals, which propel the aesthetic experience to an inner, more dynamic, aesthetic rapture. *Dhvani* or suggestiveness as an artistic principle incorporates the various *gāthās* and the *kathās* or myths, symbols and allegory, that are an integral part of classical Indian art, which lead the aesthete away from the superficial to the deeper. Stated differently, these features ensure that there is not only a *sākṣātartha* a superficial, initial meaning, but a *parokṣārtha* or an ultimate, deeper, more contemplative meaning in artistic cognition. An analysis of aesthetic experience based on these two levels of *artha* seems to be in accord with the basic tenets of Indian Idealism and Kāśmir Śaivism in particular, and furthermore, it establishes the fact that aesthetic criticism in the Indian tradition is possible only on Idealist premises. It may be safely said that the art object possesses essential qualities which demand of the aesthete that he bring a certain kind of attention to it; to the sensitive and the refined aesthete, a *sahṛdaya*, who responds to the artistic signals from an art object, every initial art experience is only tentative and incomplete as it were, for it is not until he processes the artistic information inwardly and intuitively that the aesthetic experience comes to a fruition. As Śaṅkara has pointed out, the essence of knowledge is *brahman* and, where there is *brahman*, there is delight.[21] It is only a *brahman* seeking aesthete who can declare that "art is knowlewdge"[22] and proclaim, along with the Upaniṣadic seers, "*raso vai sah. rasam hyevāyam labdhvā ānandī bhavati*",[23] and so saying he is undeniably placing aesthetics in the Idealist stream.

NOTES

1. S. Radhakrishnan, ***The Indian Mind***. Charles Moore, editor (Honolulu: East-West Center Press, University of Hawaii, 1967) p. 175.
2. S. Radhakrishnan, ***Indian Philosophy***. (London: George, Allen & Unwin

Ltd., 1966.) p. 777.

3. P.T.Raju, ***Idealist Thought of India***. (London: George, Allen & Unwin Ltd., 1963) p. 26.
4. S. Radhakrishnan, ***Indian Philosophy***. p. 17.
5. P.T. Raju, ***The Indian Mind***. p. 55.
6. S. Dasgupta, ***Indian Idealism***. (Cambridge University Press, 1962) p. 27.
7. S. Radhakrishnan, ***An Idealist View of Life***. (Bombay: George Allen & Unwin Private Ltd., 1976) p. 142.
8. *manaso manaḥ.*
   The mind of the mind.
   Kenopaniṣad, 1.2
9. ***Svetāśvtara Upaniṣad*** 4.6.
10. Radhakrishnan summarises the problem why *bhakti* cannot serve as the basis of aesthetics when he says, "What Ramanuja calls the subject is not the subject truly conceived as subject, but is a subject which is itself objectified and reduced to one of the many finite objects contained in experience." S.Radhakrishnan, ***Indian Philosophy***. p. 717. In thus removing the *bonafides* of the subject *bhaktivāda* fails to satisfy the basic requirement of a *jñāna* experience, viz. that knowledge can transpire only between a subject and an object.
11. *pramāṇāni pramāveśe svabalakranakramāt, yasya vaktrāvalokini prameye tam numaḥ śivam.*
    Original quotation from Abhinavagupta's ***Īśvara Pratyabhijña Vimarśinī.*** 2.2.
    quoted by K. Mishra, ***Significance of the Tantric Tradition***. (Varanasi: Ardhanarisvara Publications, 1981) p. 106.
12. Abhinavagupta, ***Parātriśikā-Vivaraṇa*** (Delhi: Motilal Banarsidass, 1988) pp. 75-76.
13. *dhvanirnāma arthāntaram*
    Dhvani is just another meaning.
    Ānandavardhana, ***Dhvanyāloka.*** (Delhi: Motilal Banarsidass, 1982) K. Krishnamoorthy (editor) 1.13.
14. Mammaṭa, ***Kāvyaprakāśa***. (Delhi: Motilal Banarsidass, 1977) R.C. Dwivedi (editor) Vol. I 5.47cd gloss, p. 175.
15. *padma patra śata vyati bheda nayena.*
    This original quotation by Abhinavagupta has in turn been quoted by all commentators including Mammaṭa. See Mammaṭa, ***Kāvyaprakāśa***. Vol 1. p. 285.
16. A. Coomaraswamy, *The Transformation of Nature in Art*. (New York: Dover Publications, 1956) p. 179.
17. Rabindranath Tagore, ***On Art & Aesthetics***. (Bombay: Orient Longmans, 1961) p. 79.
18. Niharranjan Ray, ***An Approach to Indian Art***. (Chandigarh: Punjab University Bureau, 1974) p. 108.
19. Śrī Aurobindo. ***The Foundations of Indian Culture.*** Volume 14,

(Pondicherry: Śrī Aurobindo Birth Centenary Library, 1972) p. 229.

20. S. Kramarisch, ***Indian Sculpture in the Philadelphia Musuem of Art.*** (Philadelphia: University of Pennsylvania Press, 1966) p. 29.
21. *brahma ca jijñāsubhiḥ prītipurvakameva gṝhyate.* Śaṅkara's commentary on ***Taittirīya Upaniṣad*** 2.7.
22. "Art as the disclosure of the deeper reality of things is a form of knowledge." S. Radhakrishnan, ***An Idealist View of Life***. p. 152.
23. ***Taittirīya Upaniṣad*** 2.7.

Epilogue

Vimalakalasrayabhinavasrsimaha janani
Bharitatanusca pancamukhaguptarucirjanakah
Tadubhayayamalasphuritabhavavisargamayam
Hṛdayam annutaramrtakulam mama samsphuratat.
Abhinavagupta. ***Parātriśikā Vivaraṇa,*** 1

If the turn of the present century was an axial period for Indian aestheticians, who led a renaissance in the visual and performing arts, the present period for Indian art, marked as it is by art festivals and glossy art books, seems to be characterised by a certain superficiality and a drifting away from its roots. What was once the preserve of the cave temples is now displayed in exhibitions, what was once in the hands of *ṛṣis* and *kavis* seems to have been taken over by art historians. Increased awareness of Indian art seems to have been at the cost of a proper understanding of its methods and meanings. Art appreciation seems to have replaced art experience. It is important to state this to provide a concluding scenario for the present inquiry, which endeavours to put classical Indian art and aesthetics in its proper perspective. The inquiry has shown that an art object is not a mere inert object but so rich with meaning and that it is capabale of evoking manifold emotions and thereby transforming the prepared aesthete, and in this sense the art object is not only a noun but a verb. Towards this end, this inquiry is a small but original contribution.

The inquiry has been an undertaking to demonstrate that aesthetic experience in the classical Indian tradition, on its own merit, without being subordinated to rituals and practices commonly held under the rubric of religion as narrowly defined, is capable of providing a transcendent and *advaitic* experience to a prepared aesthete. Two major art experiences, in the *mārgī* tradition have been chosen, and it has been demonstrated by presenting their dynamics, that each leads the aesthete to a higher experience. From the perspective of its dynamics, it has been shown, that *dhvani* understood in its wider sense as the transformation of meaning, is the central artistic device of classical Indian art. It has been further demonstrated, that from amongst the schools of Indian thought, Kāśmīr Śaivism provides the legitimacy to aesthetic experience, and within its *advaitic* framework, art experience can be understood as a form of yoga. Ontologically, Kāśmīr Śaivism affords a reality to art objects and art experience alike. Epistemologically, Kāśmīr Śaivism, points to the twin concepts of *bhoga* and *viśrānti*, as essential for a *yoga* of art. It is important to point out that in opting for Kāśmīr Śaivism as a school of thought, within which to understand art experience, one is not committed to the rituals and practices of either Kāśmir Śaivism in particular or Tāntrism in general. In positing *brahmānanda*, albeit of the *sahodara* variety, as the end point of a sustained aesthetic experience, the Indian tradition has not only recognised the value of aesthetic experience but set-up a parallel, secular, autonomous, non-sectarian avenue, parallel to the commonly understood religious practices, for transcendent realisation. This is important, as it not only confirms a certain epistemic bonafides to art, but clearly suggests that religion, as narrowly defined and understood, need not be the only recourse for those who seek *ānanda.* It asserts that the joyous realisation of art is not only an integral part of life but can be made a deeply meaningful and chastening experience, that *jñāna* need not be confined to what is sacred, and that there is a certain sanctity about the creative process within man. For creativity, both for the artist and the aesthete, is the essence of art and art experience, and in recognising art as a yoga we are equating *jñāna* with creativity.

The creation and realisation of art, has been, and will remain, in the Indian tradition, an exalted experience, consorting with every aspect of Indian life, but yet at the same time retaining its freedom, for itself and its followers.

Bibliography

Abhinavagupta. ***Abhinavabhāratī.*** (commentary on Bharata's Nāṭyaśāstra) see Bharata.

Abhinavagupta. ***Īśvara-Pratyabhijña Vimarśinī.*** K.A. Subramania Iyer and K.C.Pandey (editors) Delhi: Motilal Banarsidass, 1986.

Abhinavagupta. ***Locana.*** (commentary on Ānadavardhana's *Dhvanyāloka)* see Ānadavardhana.

Abhinavagupta. ***Parātriśikā Vivaraṇa.*** Jaideva Singh (translator), Bettina Baumer (editor). Delhi: Motilal Banarsidass, 1988.

Abhinavagupta. ***Pratyabhijñāhṛdayam.*** Jaideva Singh (editor) Delhi: Motilal Banarsidass, 1987.

Anand, Mulk Raj. ***The Hindu View of Art.*** Bombay: Asia Publishing House, 1957.

Anand, Mulk Raj. ***Madhubani Painting.*** Delhi: Publication Division, Ministry of Information and Broadcasting, Government of India, 1984.

Ānandavardhana. ***Dhvanyāloka.*** (ed.) K. Krishnamoorthy. Delhi: Motilal Banarsidass, 1982.

Ānandavardhana. ***Dhvanyāloka*** (with Locana). Bombay: Nirnaysagar Press, 1935; rpt. New Delhi: Munshiram Manoharlal, 1983, Kavyamala Edition.

Archer, A.G. ***Loves of Krishna.*** London: George Allen & Unwin, 1957.

Aurobindo, Śrī. ***The Mother.*** (Volume 25) Pondicherry: Sri Aurobindo Birth Centenary Library, 1972.

Aurobindo, Śrī. ***The Foundations of Indian Culture.*** Volume 14, Sri Aurobindo Birth Centenary Library, Pondicherry: Sri

Aurobindo Ashram Trust, 1971.

Aurobindo, Śrī. ***The Hour of God***. Volume 17, Sri Aurobindo Birth Centenary Library, Pondicherry: Sri Aurobindo Ashram Trust, 1971.

Aurobindo, Śrī. ***The Human Cycle***. Pondicherry: Sri Aurobindo Ashram, 1971.

Aurobindo, Śrī. ***Life Divine***. Pondicherry: Sri Aurobindo Ashram, 1977.

Aurobindo, Śrī. ***The Synthesis of Yoga.*** Pondicherry: Sri Aurobindo Ashram, 1955.

Aurobindo, Śrī. ***The Upanishads.*** Pondicherry: Sri Aurobindo Ashram, 1972.

Banerjea, Jitendra Nath. ***The Development of Hindu Iconography.*** Calcutta: University of Calcutta, 1956.

Barrett, D. and Gray, B. ***Indian Painting***. New York: Skira-Rizzoli, 1978.

Bernard, Theos. ***Hindu Philosophy***. New York: Greenwood Press Publishers, 1968.

Bharata. ***Nāṭyaśāstra***. (ed.) Madhusudan Sastri. Varanasi: Benaras Hindu University, 1972.

Bose, A.C. ***The Call of The Vedas.*** Bombay: Bharatiya Vidya Bhavan, 1970.

Canady, J. ***What is Art?***. New York: Alfred A. Knopf, 1980.

Chinmayananda, Swami. ***Discourses on the Chandogya Upanishad.*** Madras: Chinmaya Publication Trust, (date not given).

Chattopadhyay, Kamaladevi. ***India's Craft Tradition***. New Delhi: Publications Division, Government of India, 1980.

Coomaraswamy, A.K. ***The Dance of Shiva on Indian Art and Culture***. New Delhi: Sagar Publications, 1976.

Coomaraswamy, A.K. ***The Transformation of Nature in Art.*** New York: Dover Publications, 1934.

Coomaraswamy, A.K., Lipsey, Roger (ed).***Selected Papers***. Volume One: Traditional Art and Symbolism. Princeton: Princeton Univeristy Press, 1977.

Coward, Harold. (ed.) ***Studies in Indian Thought***. The Collected Papers of Prof. T.R.V. Murti, Delhi: Motilal Banarsidass,

1983.

Coward, Harold. ***The Sphota Theory of Language***. A Philosophical Analysis. Delhi: Motilal Banarsidass, 1986.

Coward, Harold and Sivaraman, Krishna (editors). ***Revelation in Indian Thought.*** Emeryville California: Dharma Publishing, 1977.

Dimock, Edward C. Jr. ***The Place of the Hidden Moon***. Chicago: The University of Chicago Press, 1966.

Eliade, Mircea. ***Symbolism, the Sacred and Arts***. New York: Corssroads, 1986.

Eliade, Mircea. ***The Myth of the Eternal Return.*** Bollingen Series XLVI, Princeton: Princeton University Press 1954.

Eliade, Mircea. ***Yoga Immortality and Freedom***. Bollingen Series LVI, Princeton: Princeton Univeristy Press, 1969.

Gonda, J. ***The Vision of the Vedic Poets***. The Hague: Mouton & Co., 1963.

Goswamy, B.N. and Dallapiccola, A.L. (editors). ***Krishna The Divine Lover***. Myth and Legend through Indian Art. Bombay: B.I. Publications, 1982.

Gnoli, Raniero and Patwardhan M.V. ***Śāntarasa and Abhinavagupta's Philosophy of Aesthetics***. Poona: Bhandarkar Oriental Research Institute, 1969.

Gnoli, Raniero. ***The Aesthetic Experience According to Abhinavagupta.*** Chowkhamba Sanskrit Studies, Vol. LXII. Varanasi:Chowkhamba Sanskrit Series Office, 1968.

Gupta, S.P. ***Roots of Indian Art***. Delhi: B.R. Publishing Corporation, 1980.

Havell, E.B. ***The Art Heritage of India***. Bombay: D.B.Taraporevala Sons, 1964.

Hawley, John Stratton and Wulff, Donna Marie (editors). ***The Divine Consort.*** Radha and the Goddesses of India. Boston: Beacon Press, 1982.

Heimann, Betty. ***Facets of Indian Thought***. London: George Allen & Unwin Ltd., 1963.

Hiriyanna, M. ***Art Experience.*** Mysore: Kavyalaya Publishers, 1954.

Hiriyanna, M. ***Indian Conception of Values***. Mysore: Kavyalaya

Publishers, 1975.

Hiriyanna, M. ***Outlines of Indian Philosophy***.London: George Allen & Unwin Ltd., 1932.

Kocmarek Ivan (editor), ***Language and Release***. Sarvajnatman's Pancaprakriya. Delhi: Motilal Banarsidass, 1985.

Khanna, M. ***Yantra***. The Tantric Symbol of Cosmic Unity. London: Thomas and Hudson, 1979.

Kramrisch, Stella. ***Indian Sculpture***. Delhi: Motilal Banarsidass, 1981.

Kramrisch, Stella. ***Exploring India's Sacred Art.*** Philadelphia: University of Pensylvannia Press, 1983.

Kramrisch, Stella. ***The Hindu Temple***. Delhi: Motilal Banarsidass, 1976.

Kramrisch, Stella. ***The Presence of Śiva.*** Princeton: Princeton University Press, 1981.

Krishnamoorthy, K. ***The Dhvanyāloka and its Critics***. Mysore: Kavyalaya Publishers, 1968.

Lannoy, Richard. ***The Speaking Tree***. London: Oxford University Press, 1971.

Mahadevan, T.M.P. ***Invitation to Indian Philosophy.*** New Delhi: Arnold Heinemann Publishers, 1974.

Mahadevan, T.M.P. ***The Hymns of Śaṅkara***. Delhi: Motilal Banarsidass, 1986.

Mammaṭa, R.C. Dwivedi (editor). ***Kāvyaprakāśa***. New Delhi: Motilal Banarsidass, 1977.

Masson, J.L. and Patwardhan, M.V. ***Aesthetic Rapture.*** Poona: Deccan College Postgraduate and Research Institute, 1970.

Miller, Barbara Stoller (editor and translator). ***Gītagovinda of Jayadeva, Love Song of the Dark Lord.*** Delhi: Motilal Banarsidass, 1984.

Miller, J. ***The Vedas***. London: Rider & Company, 1974.

Mishra, Kamlakar. ***Significance of the Tantric Tradition.*** Varanasi: Ardhanarisvara Publications, 1981.

Mukerjee, Radhakamal. ***The Culture and Art of India.*** London: George Allen & Unwin Ltd., 1959.

Pandey, K.C. ***Abhinavagupta An Historical and Philosophical Study.*** Varanasi: Chowkhamba Sanskrit Series Office, 1963.

Pandey, K.C. ***Indian Aesthetics***. Varanasi: Chowkhamba Sanskrit Series Office, 1959.

Pandeya, R.C. ***The Problem of Meaning.*** Delhi: Motilal Banarsidass, 1963.

Pandit, B.N. ***Aspects of Kashmir Śaivism***. Srinagar: Utpal Publications, 1977.

Pandit, Sneh. ***An Approach to the Indian Theory of Art and Aesthetics***. New Delhi: Sterling Publishers, 1980.

Pathak, Rangnath. ***Sphoṭadarśan***. Patna: Bihar Rashtrabasha Parishad, 1967.

Pillai, Raghavan K. ***The Vākyapadīya***. Delhi: Motilal Banarsidass, 1971.

Radhakrishnan, S. ***An Idealist View of Life.*** Bombay: George Allen & Unwin (India) Pvt. Ltd., 1976.

Radhakrishnan, S. (editor). ***The Cultural Heritage of India***. Calcutta: Ramakrishna Institute of Culture, 1937.

Raghavan, V. ***Studies on Some Concepts of the Alamkara Sastra***. Madras: The Adyar Library and Research Centre, 1973.

Raghavan, V. ***The Number of Rasas***. Madras: The Adyar Library, 1940.

Raja, Kunjunni, K. ***Indian Theories of Meaning.*** Madras: The Adyar Library Series, Vol. 91, 1963.

Raju, P.T. ***Idealist Thought of India***. London: George Allen & Unwin Ltd., 1966.

Ray, Niharranjan. ***An Approach to Indian Art.*** Chandigarh: Punjab University Publication Bureau, 1974.

Ray, Niharranjan. ***Idea and Image in Indian Art.*** Delhi: Munshiram Manoharlal Publishers Pvt. Ltd., 1973.

Redington, James D. ***Vallabhācārya on the Love Games of Kṛṣna***. Delhi: Motilal Banarsidass, 1983.

Sastri Kuppuswami, S. (editor). ***A Primer of Indian Logic.*** incorporating Annambhaṭṭa's ***Tarkasangraha***. Madras: Kuppuswami Research Institute, 1961.

Shah, Priyabala. (editor). ***Viṣṇudharmottara Purāṇa***. Third Khaṇḍa, Vols. I and II. Baroda: Oriental Institute, 1961.

Sharma, L.N. ***Kāśmīr Śaivism***. Varanasi: Bhartiya Vidya Prakashan. 1972.

Sinha, Jadunath. ***Indian Psychology.*** Calcutta: Sinha Publishing House, 1961.

Singer, Milton (editor) ***Krishna: Myths, Rites and Attitudes.*** Honolulu: East-West Center Press, 1966.

Sivaramamurti, C. ***Citrasūtra of the Viṣṇudharmottara.*** New Delhi: Kanak Publications, 1978.

Tagore, Rabindranath. ***On Art and Aesthetics.*** Calcutta: Orient Longmans, 1961.

Tagore, Rabindranath. ***Personality***. London: Macmillan and Co., 1959.

Tagore, Rabindranath. ***The Religion of Man***. London: Unwin Books, 1931.

Tagore, Rabindranath. ***Sādhanā, The Realization of Life.*** Tuscon: Omen Communications Inc., 1972.

Vatsyayan, Kapila. ***The Square and the Circle of the Indian Arts***. Delhi: Roli Books International, 1983.

Viśvanātha, Satyavrat Singh, (editor). ***Sāhityadarpaṇa.*** Hindi Edition. Varanasi: Chowkhamba Sanskrit Series, 1976.

Woodroffe, John. (Arthur Avalon, pseudonym). ***Principles of Tantra.*** Madras: Ganesh & Co., 1969.

Woodroffe, John. ***Śakti and Śākta.*** Madras: Ganesh & Co., 1965.

Woodroffe, John. ***The Great Liberation: (Mahānirvāṇa Tantra)***. Madras: Ganesh & Co., 1963.

Zimmer, Heinrich. ***Artistic Form and Yoga in the Sacred Images of India***. Princeton: Princeton University Press, 1984.

Zimmer, Heinrich. ***Myths and Symbols in Indian Art and Civilisation.*** New York: Harper Torch Books, The Bollingen Foundation, 1946.

Index

AUTHORS

Abhinavagupta 3, 40, 52, 54, 56, 58-59, 123, 126, 128, 134, 137, 140, 142, 160, 161, 175
Anand, Mulk Raj 74, 76
Ānandavardhana 29, 37, 40, 83, 90, 91, 176
Apte, V.S. 15
Aśvaghoṣa 22
Aurobindo, Śrī 3, 4, 16, 17, 53, 69, 99, 100, 109, 122, 143, 144, 165, 178

Barett, D. 9, 12
Bharata 7, 39, 40, 48, 50, 54
Bhartṛhari 24, 27, 28, 29, 30, 32, 33, 34, 35
Bhaṭṭa Nāyaka 50, 51

Chattopadhyay, K. 6
Chari, V.K. 24
Coomaraswamy, A.K. 1, 2, 7, 10, 16, 17, 47, 54, 78, 86, 108, 109, 110

Dasgupta, S. 5, 171
Desai, D. 9
Dimock, E.C. 156

Eliade, M. 100

Gonda, J. 46

Havell, E. 3
Hiriyanna, M. 8, 17, 52, 122, 131

Jaimini 22, 24, 25
Jayadeva 156, 158

Kālidāsa 8, 32, 33
Kramrisch, S. 13, 111, 124
Kumārila. 24, 26

Mammaṭa 7, 91, 176
Matilal, B.K. 5, 33, 37, 88, 95
Miller, J. 3

Pandey, K.C. 58
Pandeya, R.C. 34
Pandit, S. 11, 57
Panikkar, R. 110
Pāṇinī 22
Patañjali 21, 134, 140
Prabhākara 24

Radhakrishnan, S. 123, 160, 170
Raghavan, V. 55
Raja, K.K. 27, 30
Raju, P.T. 169, 171
Ramakantha 40
Ray, N. 11, 17, 56, 77

Śabara 22, 24, 28
Sarvajñātman 28, 29
Sastri, K.S. 36
Subramanian, V. 7, 8

Tagore, R. 5, 13, 16, 47, 54, 65, 71, 72, 76, 77, 83, 92, 93, 128, 143, 144

Vatsyayan, K. 103, 107
Viśvanātha 57

Woodroffe, J. 101

Yāska 22

Zimmer, H. 74, 75, 98, 104

SANSKRIT TERMS

abhidā 88
ābhāsa 126, 127, 128, 129, 174
ādi śilpī 5
adbhuta 53
advaita 2, 6, 12, 13, 15, 16, 29, 30, 35, 36, 49, 50, 51, 55, 67, 80, 84, 86, 91, 92, 109, 110, 125, 127, 132, 133, 139, 142, 145, 162, 165, 170, 172, 184
āgama 3, 173, 175
ākāṅkṣā 27, 89, 90, 93
akhaṇḍavāda 32
alaṃkāra 11, 21, 84, 88
alaukika 50, 56, 58
āliṅgan 98, 162
anuttara 162
anubhava 20
anumāna 19
apoha 31
apūrṇakhyāti 138, 139
apauruṣeyatva 2
ardhanārīśvara 60, 159, 161, 162, 164, 175
artha 9, 10, 20, 22, 23, 24, 25, 26, 27, 28, 30, 31, 32, 33, 34, 35, 36, 37, 38, 45, 83, 84, 87, 88, 89, 92, 113, 122, 184
asat 33
ātman 49

bhakta 6, 7, 66, 74, 110, 156
bhakti 7, 14, 16, 29, 124, 142, 155, 162, 172
bhairavamudrā 135
bhāvanā 28
bhoga 56, 133, 134, 135, 140, 141, 142, 143, 144
bimba-pratibimba 162, 163
bindu 105, 106
brahmajijñāsu 6
brahman 6, 29, 30, 36, 55, 59, 65, 105, 113, 125, 142, 172, 179

camatkāra 54, 57, 58
citra 12
cittavṛtti 37
codanalakṣaṇo 24

deś 8, 65, 78
dharma 25, 77, 110
dharmajijñāsā 24
dhīya 46, 49, 57
dhvani 29, 32, 37, 51, 83, 84, 89, 90, 91, 92, 100, 131, 176, 179, 184
dhyāna 73, 74, 75, 76

ghaṭapradīpanāaya 91
guheśu vrateśu 3

hṛd 46, 52, 53, 57

jñāna 16, 184

kāma 11
karma 4
kavi 6, 34, 40, 49, 53
kāvya 7, 8, 22, 30, 38, 39, 48, 50, 60, 84, 121, 124, 157, 177
krīḍā 49
kriyā 4

laukika 50, 56, 58

manas 35
mārgī 8, 9, 10, 12, 66, 67, 69, 71, 72, 74, 75, 77, 78, 121, 122, 140
māyā 77, 126, 129, 130
mīmāṁsā 24, 25, 26, 27, 28, 30, 31, 36, 38, 87
mithyā 38
mukhyārthabādha 90, 93, 96
mukhyāvṛtti 28

nāda 14, 32, 33, 34, 35, 38
nāgarika 6
narasiṁha 32
nāṭya 12, 75, 108, 109, 124
niṣpatti 51
nitya 25
nityatva 25, 26

parakīya 155
parokṣa 9, 25, 37, 45, 46, 51, 66, 83, 84, 85, 86, 87, 88, 90, 91, 92, 93, 94, 95, 96, 97, 100, 101, 106, 108, 109, 110, 111, 112, 113, 131, 133, 138, 164, 177, 179
prajāpati 4, 6, 50
prakāśa 129, 130, 132, 133, 135, 136, 164, 173
prākṛt 9
pramāṇa 19, 20, 22, 39, 46, 76, 77, 78, 83, 84, 86, 87, 88, 92, 131,137, 138, 163, 173, 176, 177, 178
pratibhā 4, 6, 49
*pratyabhijña*137, 159, 160, 161, 164, 176
pratyakṣa 19, 20, 46, 95, 96, 98, 131, 171, 177
prītiḥ 24
puruṣa 12, 13, 67, 68, 69, 70, 71, 72, 73, 76, 78, 79, 102, 107
puruṣārtha 11, 24

rājopacāra 8
rasa 10, 11, 12, 13, 14, 16, 45, 47, 48, 49, 50, 51, 52, 53, 54, 55, 56, 57, 60, 66, 85, 90, 98, 121, 131, 136, 154, 157, 158, 176
rasika 6, 7, 8, 12, 34, 59, 66, 85
rekhā 104, 105
ṛṣi 5, 14, 20, 21, 46, 49, 73, 183
rūpa 10, 12, 13, 16, 45, 66, 67, 69, 70, 72, 73, 74, 75, 76, 77, 79, 80, 85, 101, 102, 103, 104, 105, 106, 108, 111, 112, 113, 121, 131, 136, 178
rūpaprajña 8

śabda 19, 20, 21, 22, 23, 24, 25, 26, 27, 28, 29, 30, 31, 32, 33, 36, 37, 38, 39, 40, 86, 89, 95, 132
śabdabrahman 29, 30, 32, 36, 38
śabdatattva 35
śabdajñānam 28
sādhāraṇīkṛt 52, 55
sādṛśya 76, 78, 79, 178
sahṛdaya 8, 51, 52, 179
sākṣāt 19, 37, 45, 46, 51, 66, 79, 84, 85, 86, 90, 93, 108, 109, 112, 138, 179
samādhi 136
saṃskāra 37, 50
saṃvega 54
saṅketa 38, 39
Sanskrit 9, 22
śāstra 5, 9, 12, 54, 74, 77, 141, 178
satya 32
sattārka 140
śikṣā 37
śleṣa 100
spanda 4, 129
sphoṭa 30, 31, 32, 33, 35, 36, 37, 38, 39, 111
sphoṭavāda 36, 39, 83
śramaṇa 21, 25
suparṇa 5
svarūpa 34, 38

tāla 14, 76, 178
tanmayībhāva 52, 53, 59, 60
tantra/Tāntric 33, 70, 127, 128, 133, 134, 138, 139, 140, 141, 173

upacārasatta 34

vācaka 32
vācya 32
Vāk 21
vākya 36, 94
vākyārtha 28
vikāsa 58
vimarśa 58, 129, 130, 132, 133, 135, 136, 164, 173, 174
viraha 156

viśrānti 58, 60, 132, 134, 135, 136, 143
vistāra 58
vyavahāradarśanam 25

yajña 21, 22, 24, 30, 31, 68, 102, 106, 112
yantra 74, 101, 102, 103, 104, 105, 106, 107, 108
yoga 2, 12, 15, 16, 133, 184
yogī 53